13th Edition

BABY BARGAINS

Your Baby Registry Cheat Sheet

Denise & Alan Fields

Copyright Page and Free Range Production Credits

The reviews in this book are made from scratch
The ink used to print this book contains no GMO's
The paper used in this book is locally sourced and gluten-free
The cover/interior design by Epicenter Creative is hormone-free
The index in this book was wild caught and contains no preservatives
The back cover photograph by Moses Street utilizes all-natural light
Computers used to produce this book were powered by fair trade electrons

To order this book, go to BabyBargains.com or call 1-800-888-0385. Baby Bargains is published by Windsor Peak Press, 436 Pine Street, Boulder, CO 80302.
Questions or comments? E-mail the authors at authors@babybargains.com. Call us at (303) 442-8792.

Learn more about this book online at BabyBargains.com

Distributed to the book trade by Ingram Publisher Services, 866-400-5351.

Library Cataloging in Publication Data

Fields, Denise
Fields, Alan
    Baby Bargains: Secrets to saving 20% to 50% on baby cribs, car seats, strollers, high chairs and much, much more/ Denise & Alan Fields
    286 pages.
    Includes index.
    ISBN 978-1-889392-63-9
1. Child Care—Handbooks, manuals, etc. 2. Infants' supplies—Purchasing—United States, Canada, Directories. 3. Children's paraphernalia—Purchasing—Handbooks, manuals. 4. Product Safety—Handbooks, manuals. 5. Consumer education.
    649′.122′0296—dc20. 2021.

Version 14.0

CONTENTS

Chapter 1

"IT'S GOING TO CHANGE YOUR LIFE"

Chapter 2

NURSERY NECESSITIES: CRIBS, DRESSERS & MORE

Chapter 3

BABY BEDDING & DECOR

Chapter 4

DIAPER PAILS, POTTY SEATS, BATH & SKIN CARE

Chapter 5

BABY CLOTHES DIAPERS AND WIPES

Chapter 6

FEEDING BABY: BREASTFEEDING, BOTTLES, HIGH CHAIRS

Chapter 7

AROUND THE HOUSE: PLAY YARDS, MONITORS, BOUNCERS & SAFETY

Chapter 8

CAR SEATS

Chapter 9

STROLLERS, DIAPER BAGS AND OTHER TO GO GEAR

Chapter 10

CARRIERS

Chapter 11

ODDS & ENDS

Chapter 12

PREGNANCY GEAR

Chapter 13

CONCLUSION: WHAT DOES IT ALL MEAN?

CHAPTER 1

"It's Going to Change Your Life!"

Inside this chapter

That had to be the silliest comment we heard while we were pregnant with our first baby. Believe it or not, we even heard this refrain more often than "Are you having a boy or a girl?" and "I'm sorry. Your insurance doesn't cover that." For the friends and relatives of first-time parents out there, we'd like to point out that this is a pretty silly thing to say. Of course, we knew that a baby was going to change our lives. What we didn't realize was how much a baby was going to change our pocketbook.

Oh sure, we knew that we'd have to buy triple our weight in diapers. What we didn't expect was the endless pitches for cribs, gear, toys, clothing and other items parents are required to purchase by FEDERAL BABY LAW.

We quickly learned that having a baby is like popping on the Juvenile Amusement Park Ride from Consumer Hell. Once that egg is fertilized, you're whisked off to the Pirates of the Crib ride. Then it's on to marvel at the little elves in StrollerLand, imploring you to buy brands with names you can't pronounce. Finally, you take a trip to Magic Car Seat Mountain, where the confusion is so real, it's scary.

Consider us your tour guides—the Lilo to our Stitch, the Phineas to your Ferb, the . . . well, you get the idea. Before we enter BabyLand, let's take a look at the Four Truths That No One Tells You About Buying Stuff For Baby.

The Four Truths That No One Tells You About Buying Stuff for Baby

1 BABIES DON'T CARE IF THEY'RE WEARING DESIGNER CLOTHES. Babies just want to be comfortable. They can't even distinguish between the liberals and conservatives on "Meet the Press," so how would they ever be able to tell the difference between Baby Gucci crib bedding and another less famous brand that's just as comfortable, but 70% less expensive? Our focus is on making your baby happy—at a price that won't break the bank.

2 MOST BABY GEAR ISN'T TESTED FOR SAFETY. One of the biggest myths about baby gear is that every product you see on the shelf at a baby superstore is safety tested before it hits the market. Sadly, that isn't true.

Here are the scary facts: 60,600 children under age five were injured (requiring emergency room visits) by nursery products in 2019 (the latest year figures are available). During a recent three-year period, those same baby products caused 119 deaths per year. (Source: 2020 Consumer Product Safety Commission report based on 2019 data).

Yes, there are safety regulations for a couple of baby gear categories (cribs and car seats). But most other categories only have **voluntary** safety rules and standards. You read that right—anyone can sell a baby gizmo that doesn't meet safety guidelines. (Maybe federal regulators will catch it before it injures children—or maybe not).

So it is up to you as a parent to understand the basic safety guidelines for baby gear. Each chapter of this book will go over safety basics to arm you with in-depth advice on keeping your baby out of trouble. We'll tell you which products we think are dangerous and how to safely use other potentially hazardous products.

3 **MURPHY'S LAW OF BABY TOYS SAYS YOUR BABY'S HAPPINESS WITH A TOY IS INVERSELY RELATED TO THE TOY'S PRICE.** Buy a $200 shiny new wagon with anti-lock brakes, and odds are baby just wants to play with the box it came in. As we survey baby gear, we will point out the wastes of money (spoiler alert: smart baby monitors—not worth your money).

4 **IT'S GOING TO COST MORE THAN YOU THINK.** Whatever amount of money you budget for your baby, get ready to spend more. Here's a breakdown of the average costs of bringing a baby into the world today:

The Average Cost of Having a Baby
(based on industry estimates for a child from birth to age one)

Crib, mattress, dresser, rocker	$1680
Bedding / Decor	$350
Baby Clothes	$665
Disposable Diapers	$910
Maternity / Nursing Clothes	$1420
Nursery items, high chair, toys	$575
Baby Food / Formula	$1160
Stroller, Car Seats, Carrier	$800
Miscellaneous	$570
TOTAL	**$8130**

The above figures are based on a survey of 1000 readers, buying name brand products at regular retail prices.

Bedding/Decor includes not only bedding items but also lamps, wallpaper, and so on for your baby's nursery. Baby Food/Formula assumes mom breastfeeds for the first six months and then feeds baby jarred baby food and formula until age one. If you plan to bottle-feed instead of breastfeed, add another $730 on to that figure. (Of course, the goal is to breastfeed your baby as long as possible—one year is a good target.)

Sure, you do get a tax credit for that bundle of joy, but that only amounts to (roughly) $2000 this year (depending on the tax bracket). Plus, there is a child care tax credit for up to

$3000 depending on your income. But those tax goodies won't nearly offset the actual cost of raising a child. And as you probably realize, our cost chart is missing some expensive "extras" . . . like medical bills, childcare, saving for college, etc. Here's an overview of those extras.

Scary Number: The Cost of Raising Baby to 18

$284,570. That's what the federal government says it costs to raise a child born in 2021 to age 18. Those costs include food, transportation, housing, clothes and child care.

But let's talk about child care. Critics say the federal government grossly underestimates this cost (the feds say parents spend $2,870 to $5,170 on child care each year for the first two years).

So what does child care really cost? According to the National Association of Child Care Resource and Referral Agencies, the average annual bill for an infant in full-time childcare is $9991.

College is another expense the government leaves out of their figures. The College Board estimates that four years at a public college averages $77,960 (tuition, fees, room and board). At a private college, that same figure is $132,800. Given current rates of return, you have to put away $300 per month every year for 18 years to afford that public school.

The take-home message: raising a baby ain't cheap.

Reality Check: Does it Really Cost That Much to Have a Baby?

Now that we've thoroughly scared you enough to inquire whether the stork accepts returns, we should point out that children do NOT have to cost that much. Even if we focus just on the first year, you don't have to spend $8130 on baby gear. And that's what this book is all about: how to save money and still buy the best. Follow all the tips in this book, and we estimate the first year will cost you $4470. Yes, that's a savings of over $3600!

Now, at this point, you might be saying "That's impossible! I suppose you'll recommend shopping garage sales and dollar stores." On the contrary, we'll show you how to get *quality* name brands and safe products at discount prices. Most importantly, you will learn how not to WASTE your money on dubious gear. And much more. Yes, we've got the maximum number of bargains allowed by federal law.

A word on bargain shopping: when interviewing hundreds of parents for this book, we realized bargain seekers fall into two frugal camps. There's the "do-it-yourself" crowd and the "quality at a discount" group. As the name implies, "do-it-yourselfers" are resourceful folks who like to take second-hand products and refurbish them. Others use creative tricks to make homemade versions of baby care items like baby wipes and diaper rash cream.

While that's all well and good, we fall more into the second camp of bargain hunters, the "quality at a discount" group. We love discovering a name brand stroller for 75% off on Craigslist. Or the discount version of an expensive designer furniture brand, sold at a 20% discount. We also realize savvy parents save money by not *wasting* it on inferior goods or useless items.

While we hope that *Baby Bargains* pleases both groups of bargain hunters, the main focus of this book is not on do-it-yourself projects (exception: IKEA furniture assembly). Our emphasis is on identifying best buys for the dollar and not wasting your money, as well as on the best discount online sources.

What? No One Paid You to Recommend Their Product?

Yes, it's true. We don't get paid by the brands we review.

We also do NOT accept samples or other freebies from companies we review—if we are doing a first-hand inspection of a product, we purchase it on our own at regular retail prices. When we visit factories or other company facilities, we pay all our travel expenses. We don't accept gifts from companies we review.

Why? We believe that when you take a freebie, there is an obvious quid pro quo—a baby gear company isn't going to give you a $500 stroller and not expect anything less than a nice review in return. To remain objective, you can't accept free samples, gift baskets, etc.

Here's how we make a living: we sell the book you are reading. We also have affiliate links on our free web site (BabyBargains.com). When you read our review of a car seat and you click through on a link to purchase it, we may make a small commission from the site selling the product. If you hate the car seat and return it, we don't make any commission. FYI: Affiliate links do not affect the price you pay.

We also use software to affiliate links posted by users of our message boards, which are

The 7 Commandments of Baby Bargains

Yes, we've come down from the mountain to share with you our SEVEN commandments of *Baby Bargains*—the keys to saving every parent should know. Let's review:

1 **SAFETY IS JOB ONE.** As a parent, your baby's safety is paramount. We never compromise safety for a bargain—that's why we don't recommend hand-me-down cribs or used car seats, no matter how cheap they are. Good news: follow our social media channels (Facebook, Twitter) to get alerts on major recalls. See the back of this book for our social media handles.

2 **FOCUS ON THE BASICS.** Big box baby stores are so overwhelming, with a blizzard of baby products. Key on the basics: setting up a safe place for baby to sleep (the nursery) and safe transport (car seats). Many items like high chairs, toys, and so on are not needed immediately.

3 **WEED OUT THE FLUFF.** Our advice: take an experienced mom with you when you register. A mom with one or two kids can help you separate out needed items from the rest.

free. There are ads on our message boards (visible only to unregistered users) and other parts of our web site. These revenue sources are used to pay for bandwidth and server maintenance.

Of course, given the sheer volume of baby stuff, there's no way we can personally test everything. To solve that dilemma, we rely on reader feedback to help us figure out which are the best products to recommend. We receive over 200 emails a day from parents; this helps us spot overall trends on which brands/products parents love. And which ones they want to destroy with a rocket launcher.

Of course, one bad review from one parent doesn't mean we won't recommend a product—we combine multiple review sources to come up with an overall picture as to which brands are best.

The prices you see in our book were accurate as of press time. We aim to print actual selling prices (versus suggested retail prices) in our book—we do this by surveying stores and web sites. While the publisher makes every effort to ensure their accuracy, errors and omissions may exist. That's why we update this book with every new printing—make sure you are using the most recent version (go to BabyBargains.com and click on Book and then Which Version?).

Our door is always open—we want to hear your opinions. Message us on Facebook at Facebook.com/BabyBargains. Email us at authors@BabyBargains.com to ask a question, report a mistake, or just give us your thoughts.

So, Who Are You Guys Anyway?

Why do a book on saving money on baby products? Don't new parents throw caution to

4 **TWO WORDS: FREE MONEY.** As a parent, you NEVER pass up free money! From tax deductions to tax credits, being a parent means freebies. And don't overlook your employer: take advantage of benefits like dependent care accounts—using PRE-TAX dollars to pay for child care will save you HUNDREDS if not THOUSANDS of dollars.

5 **MORE FREEBIES.** Many companies throw swag at new parents, hoping they will become future customers. We keep an updated freebie list on our web site—get free diapers, bottles, and more. Go to BabyBargains.com/freebies for the latest update!

6 **SHOP AT STORES THAT DO NOT HAVE "BABY" IN THEIR NAME.** Costco for diapers? Pet web sites for safety gates? IKEA for high chairs? Yes! Yes! Yes! You can save 30% or more by not buying items at baby stores.

7 **ONLINE SHOPPING SAVVY.** Let's face it: as a new mom and dad, you probably won't have much time to hit the mall. The web is a savior—but how do you master the deals? One smart tip: ALWAYS use coupon codes for discounts or FREE shipping. Our readers post codes/sales daily to the Bargain Alert Forum on our free message boards (BabyBargains.com).

the wind when buying for their baby, spending whatever it takes to ensure their baby's safety and comfort?

Ha! When our first child was born, we quickly realized how darn expensive this guy was. Sure, as a new parent, you know you've got to buy a car seat, crib, clothes and diapers . . . but have you walked into one of those baby "superstores" lately? It's a blizzard of baby stuff piled to the ceiling, with a bewildering array of "must have" gear, gadgets and gizmos, all claiming to be the best thing for parents since sliced bread.

Becoming a parent in this day and age is both a blessing and curse. The good news: parents today have many more choices for baby products than past generations. The *bad* news: parents today have many more choices for baby products than past generations.

Our mission: make sense of this stuff, with an eye on cutting costs. As consumer advocates, we've been down this road before. We re-

What you need, when

Yes, buying for baby can seem overwhelming, but there is a silver lining: you don't need ALL this stuff immediately when baby is born. Let's look at what items you need quickly and what you can wait on. This chart indicates usage of certain items for the first 12 months of baby's life:

Item	Birth	3	6	9	12+
Nursery Necessities					
Cradle/bassinet	▓				
Crib/Mattress	▓	▓	▓	▓	▓
Dresser	▓	▓	▓	▓	▓
Glider Rocker	▓	▓	▓	▓	▓
Bedding: Cradle	▓				
Bedding: Crib	▓	▓	▓	▓	▓
Clothing					
Caps/Hats	▓	▓	▓	▓	▓
Blanket Sleepers	▓	▓	▓	▓	▓
Layette Gowns	▓	▓			
Booties	▓	▓			
All other layette	▓	▓	▓		
Around the House					
Baby Monitor	▓	▓	▓	▓	▓
Baby Food (solid)			▓	▓	▓
High Chairs			▓	▓	▓
Places to Go					
Infant Car Seat	▓	▓	▓		
Convertible Car Seat*			▓	▓	▓
Full-size Stroller/Stroller Frame	▓	▓	▓	▓	▓
Umbrella Stroller			▓	▓	▓
Front Carrier	▓	▓	▓		
Backpack Carrier			▓	▓	▓
Safety items			▓	▓	▓

Months of Use column headers: Birth, 3, 6, 9, 12+

You can use a convertible car seat from birth (instead of an infant car seat) if you prefer.

searched bargains and uncovered scams in the wedding business when we wrote *Bridal Bargains*. Then we penned an exposé on new homebuilders in *Your New House*.

Yet, we found the baby business to be perplexing in different ways—instead of outright fraud or scams, we've discovered some highly questionable products that don't live up to their hype—and others that are outright dangerous. We learned that most juvenile items face little (or no) government scrutiny when it comes to safety, leaving parents to sort out true usefulness and safety from sales hype.

So, we've gone on a quest to find the best baby products, at prices that won't send you to the poor house. Sure, we've sampled many of these items first hand. But this book is much more than our experiences—we interviewed over 17,000 new parents to learn their experiences with products. Our message boards have over 48,000 members, buzzing with all sorts of product feedback and advice. We also attend juvenile product trade shows to visit with manufacturers and retailers to discover what's new. The insights from retailers are especially helpful, since these folks are on the front lines, seeing which items unhappy parents return.

Our focus is on safety and durability: which items stand up to real world conditions and which don't. Interestingly, we found many products for baby are sold strictly on price . . . and sometimes a great "bargain" broke, fell apart or shrunk after a few uses. Hence, you'll note some of our top recommendations aren't always the lowest in price. To be sensitive to those on really tight budgets, we also identify "budget-friendly" picks in our recommendations.

We get questions: Top 6 Questions & Answers

From the home office here in Boulder, CO, here are the top six questions we get asked here at *Baby Bargains*:

1 **HOW DO I KNOW IF I HAVE THE CURRENT EDITION?** We strive to keep *Baby Bargains* as up-to-date as possible. As such, we update it periodically with new editions. But if you just borrowed this book from a friend, how do you know how old it is? First, look at the copyright page. There at the bottom you will see a version number (such as 14.1). The first number (the 14 in this case) means you have the 14th edition. The second number indicates the printing—every time we reprint the book, we make minor corrections, additions and changes. Version 14.1 is the first reprint of the 14th edition and so on.

So, how can you tell if your book is current or woefully out-of-date? Go to our web page at BabyBargains.com and click on Book and then "Which version?"—this shows the most current version. (One clue: look at the book's cover. We note the edition number on each cover. And we change the color of the cover with each edition.) We update this book every two years (roughly). About 30% to 40% of the content will change with each edition. Bottom line: if you pick up a copy of this book that is one or two editions old, you will notice a significant number of changes.

2 **I AM LOOKING FOR A SPECIFIC PRODUCT BUT I DON'T KNOW WHERE TO START! HELP!** Let's say you are in a store and are wondering which infant car seat to purchase. Flip to our car seats chapter and you'll discover our recommendations, from best infant car seat (overall) to best budget-friendly pick, best pick for urban parents and so on.

3 **WHAT IS ONLINE THAT ISN'T IN THIS BOOK?** We have dozens of additional articles on our web site for toddlers and older kids, from crafting to outdoor fun, home comfort to health and safety.

Check out our popular message board where you can discuss gear, parenting and more with other parents to be.

Looking for breaking news items about safety recalls and other baby gear news? Check our social media: Facebook (facebook.com/babybargains) or Twitter feed (@babybargainbook).

4 **CAN I ASK A QUESTION?** Sure, our door is always open—email us at authors@babybargains.com. We value your feedback, so feel free to tell us how to make our book or web site better.

5 **WHY DO YOU SOMETIMES RECOMMEND A MORE EXPENSIVE PRODUCT THAN A CHEAPER OPTION?** Yes, this is a book about bargains, but sometimes we will pick a slightly more expensive item in a category if we believe it is superior in quality or safety. In some cases, it makes sense to invest in better-quality products that will last through more than one child. And don't forget about the hassle of replacing a cheap product that breaks in six months.

To be sure, however, we recognize that many folks are on tight budgets. To help, we offer budget-friendly recommendations as well.

Another note: remember that our brand reviews online cover many options in a category, not just the cheapest. Don't be dismayed if we give an expensive brand an "A" rating—our ratings are based on quality, construction, innovation and more. Yes, we will try to identify the best values in a category as well.

6 **WHAT OTHER PARENTING BOOKS DO YOU PUBLISH?** We have three other best-selling books: *Expecting 411, Baby 411* and *Toddler 411*. Co-authored by an award-winning pediatrician, these books answer your questions about pregnancy, your baby's sleep, nutrition and more. See the back of this book for details.

What's New in This Edition?

Welcome to the 14th edition—this year marks our 28th year of covering the baby biz. Yes, we started writing this book way back in 1993. Before Amazon shipped its very first book. Before Google. When dinosaurs roamed the Earth.

We've streamlined Baby Bargains in this new edition, focusing more on specific recommendations for different parenting lifestyles (cribs for urban parents with little space, etc). And let's not forget our grandparent readers—we've got specific ideas for you on cribs, high chairs and more.

New in this edition, we added more than a dozen new review areas that focus on subjects like sippy cups, toddler pajamas and even baby sunglasses.

We've expanded our eco-friendly recommendations this year, calling out specific ideas for furniture, diapers, organic baby food and more.

Of course, we've kept the features you love about *Baby Bargains*, such as our ever-popular baby registry at-a-glance (Appendix A).

Ebooks

Prefer to read this book as an ebook? We've got you covered with ebook versions of this book available for your Kindle, iPad/iPhone, Android device and other e-readers.

Let's Go Shopping!

Now that all the formal introductions are done, let's move on to the good stuff. As your tour guides to BabyLand, we'd like to remind you of one key rule: the Baby Biz is just that—business.

The juvenile products and baby care (food, diapers) industry is a $23 BILLION DOLLAR business in the U.S. Yes, stores and brands are out there to "help" you care for your baby—but their job is also to *sell* baby gear.

But that's not *our* job! We want to help you prepare for baby and keep her safe without breaking the bank. So let's get going . . .

CHAPTER 2

Nursery Necessities: Cribs, Dressers & More

Inside this chapter

What's the best crib on the market today? For space-challenged parents? For design enthusiasts? This chapter covers cribs, crib mattresses, dressers, rocker gliders, bassinets and more.

We've got a bit of ground to cover in outfitting your nursery—so let's begin at the beginning: your baby's crib.

The Best Baby Crib

Yes, job #1 for any new parent is to set up a safe sleep space for your new baby. And buying a crib should be straight forward, right?

Yet step into a baby megastore and you'll quickly note they have 20+ different nursery "vignettes"—cleverly put-together looks that match a crib, dresser and a zillion accessories.

Ditto for typing "crib" into Amazon's search box—out pops 69 *pages* of results. That's when you feel your head start to spin . . . and now you've got crib overload.

Deep breath! Let's cut through the clutter and go over some basics.

7 Things No One Tells You About Buying A Crib!

1 WHETHER THEY COST $70 OR $700, ALL CRIBS SOLD IN THE **U.S.** AND **CANADA** MEET MANDATORY SAFETY RULES. Yes, you read that right—that crib at IKEA for under $100 is just as safe as the European designer model from a fancy boutique that runs $2000.

Do cheap cribs have dangerous designs? No. Long gone are the days when you had to measure slats to make sure they were the correct distance. If a crib is sold in a major store or reputable online site, you can rest assured it meets current safety standards. Unlike other baby gear, safety standards for cribs are *mandatory* in the U.S. and Canada.

That said, we would suggest buying from an *established* brand name. Yes, some web sites sell cribs from obscure brands with little or no history in the U.S. The concern here is whether you'd be able to contact them to buy replacement parts. Or how would they handle a safety re-call?

2 **ALMOST ALL CRIBS SOLD TODAY ARE IMPORTED FROM ASIA. YES, EVEN THOSE WITH ITALIAN-SOUNDING NAMES.** China and Vietnam are the two biggest exporters of cribs to North America. In fact, we'd estimate that 97% of the cribs sold in the U.S. are imported from Asia. The rest are imported from Eastern Europe (Latvia, Romania) with a smattering from Italy and Canada. And yes, there is a company or two left in the U.S. that makes cribs domestically (El Greco, for example).

We realize some readers are concerned about products from China, which has been through various product safety scandals over the years. For those folks, we recommend a crib or two made in North America (later in this chapter). Fair warning: this will cost you much more than an imported crib.

3 **CRIBS ARE SOLD A LA CARTE. AND REQUIRE ASSEMBLY.** When you shop for cribs, you often will find pictures like this:

But when you *buy* a crib, what you get is actually this:

Yep, that is it. Crib mattress? Extra. Sheets? Extra. Fancy wall decor? Extra. You get the picture.

Obviously, some of these items are required (mattress) and most are optional (besides sheets, just about everything else). And those extras (crib mattresses) can sometimes cost more than the crib itself. Just a heads up as you plan that nursery room budget!

4 **SIZE MATTERS.** Not the size of the crib, but the size of your baby's bedroom. Full-size cribs are all the same size: about 29" wide and 53" long. That's the *interior* dimensions. Cribs with fancy headboards or curved sides can be several inches wider/longer.

Fitting a full-size crib into a tiny secondary bedroom (or urban condo) can sometimes be a challenge. We recommend some options for those who are space-challenged later in this chapter.

And remember that the crib is just the start of your nursery furniture saga—most nurseries also have a dresser to store clothes. And perhaps a place to sit and nurse baby. Later you might want a desk and chair. Plan out space considerations before shopping.

Where the baby's crib should go in a nursery is another factor. The safest place for a crib is away from any heat or cooling source (ducts, radiators, etc). And you'll want to keep baby's crib away from windows and window coverings/blinds (cords are a strangulation hazard). Got a baby monitor as a gift? Keep the cord at least three feet from the crib.

We should note not all cribs are your standard rectangle. There are some funky cribs out there like round cribs (see right).

But remember this equation: more funky = more money. A round crib needs a special round mattress, round bedding, and so on . . . at prices typically much more than standard size crib accessories.

5 **TO CONVERT? OR NOT TO CONVERT?** Full-size cribs today come in two basic flavors: convertible, or not convertible.

Non-convertible cribs (we call them basic cribs) are just, well, cribs. They don't morph into other piece of furniture. As such, they are typically less expensive than convertible cribs.

As the name implies, convertible cribs . . . well, convert into several different stages as your child grows. Many "4-in-1" cribs are first cribs, then toddler beds (with a toddler rail replacing one side), "day beds" (no toddler rail) and then full-size beds. The different configurations look like this:

Crib
Toddler Bed
Daybed
Full Size Bed

The four different configurations of a convertible crib: crib, toddler bed with rail, day bed (no rail for older toddlers) and then finally full-size bed.

In order to do all this presto-change, you need (wait for it) an extra "conversion kit" which includes bed rails to make a full-size bed, connecting the headboard and footboard. These kits range from $100 to $200—that's on top of the crib price. And convertible cribs are more pricey than basic cribs—convertibles *start* around $250 and can easily soar into the $500's.

You could argue that even with this extra expense, you would save money in the long run because you are not buying a separate bed when a child outgrows a crib. But basic (non-convertible) cribs start around $100 and you can buy a twin bed for as little as $139. Like this one:

Homelegance twin platform bed with headboard. $139 on Amazon.

The take home message: convertible cribs aren't really money savers, but more of a choice in aesthetics.

Confusingly, there are several variations on convertible cribs. Some manufactures say they are "convertible" when all they mean is you can take the side rail off and then have a toddler bed. Doh! That doesn't count as convertible in our book. On the other hand, some crib makers include a toddler rail for free (the rail keeps a toddler from rolling out of the crib once the side rail is removed).

There is no right or wrong answer when it comes to whether to buy a basic or convertible crib. Some considerations: if space is tight, remember that using a standard crib and then buying a twin size bed may make much more sense than a convertible that morphs into a full size bed (full size beds are 15" wider than a twin).

Think about how the crib will look when converted. Is the headboard higher than the footboard? Some folks think that looks better than converted cribs where the headboard and footboard are similar in height, which is more common in lower price convertible cribs. Your choice, of course!

Some convertible cribs (like the affordable and popular Fisher-Price models) don't require special conversion kits or rails—you can use standard bed frames like the one below.

These rails run about $40. If you plan to have more than one child, it might make sense to buy an affordable basic crib you can re-use from child to child. Then as each one outgrows the crib, you can move them into a twin bed (headboard or footboard optional, of course).

This bed frame can morph from a twin bed to full-size, queen or king. $40 on Amazon.

6 **IT MAY TAKE 14 WEEKS TO SPECIAL ORDER THAT FANCY CRIB. YES, WE SAID 14 WEEKS. NOT DAYS. WEEKS.** There are three basic places to buy a crib: online, chain stores and specialty boutiques. Most online sites deliver in about a week.

Chain stores stock many cribs, while some styles require two to four week lead times (to ship in from a distribution center).

Specialty boutiques, however, are a mixed bag. Some do stock cribs for immediate purchase. Most, however, require you to special order. And that is where the 14 week wait can come in, which usually is an unpleasant surprise.

Most specialty stores carry upper-end crib brands that cost $500 to $2000. Some of these brands require a wait of 8-12 weeks for delivery, with a few up to 14 weeks. And sometimes deliveries can be delayed (port strike? earthquake? Chinese new year?), causing your furniture to go on back order for, say, 20 weeks. Plan accordingly!

7 **SAY NO TO . . .** used or hand-me-down cribs. Buy a brand-new crib to make sure it meets current standards.

Crib safety standards have changed over the years—not more than a few years ago, cribs had drop-sides that were implicated in safety issues (sides detached, resulting in injuries and in some cases, deaths). These cribs were outlawed in 2011.

We know well-meaning family members want to help by dusting off that family heirloom your grandfather used in the "old days." Or a friend has a crib in the attic from 1998 they are dying to ~~pawn off on you~~ graciously give you.

Here (right) is an antique iron baby crib, like many cribs lurking in relative's basements and attics. Does it meet current safety standards? That would be a big fat NO!

Remember that even a late-model crib can be dangerous if it is missing hardware or instructions. Buying new ensures your crib meets current safety standards and has all its parts and hardware.

The Best Baby Cribs

Enough with the safety advice! Let's get down to the recommendations! Here's what we are going to cover in this section:

- ◆ Best Crib Overall
- ◆ Best Budget-Friendly Crib (Basic)
- ◆ Best Crib for City Dwellers (and those with little space)
- ◆ Best Eco Baby Crib
- ◆ Best Crib Made In the USA.
- ◆ Best High Style Crib
- ◆ Best Travel/Portable Crib
- ◆ Best Crib for Short Parents
- ◆ Best Crib For Grandma's House

NURSERY NECESSITIES

The Best Baby Crib (Overall)

The **Union 3-in-1 convertible crib** is sold online (Amazon, Walmart) and made by DaVinci (part of the Million Dollar Baby empire). The basic crib ($119) is made of New Zealand pine and style-wise echoes the simple IKEA Gulliver crib.

Fans of this crib love the easy assembly and metal spring mattress support. The value, of course, goes without saying—especially with most other cribs running $200 to $300 or more.

As for drawbacks, the claim here is that this crib has four uses—crib, toddler bed, day bed and full-size bed. The caveat: the toddler bed and full-size bed require the separate purchase of a toddler rail ($70) and a full/twin size bed rail ($89); it's actually a DaVinci full size conversion rail kit.

And when converted to a twin or full bed, we'd bet the Union crib will look rather funky—that's because the headboard and footboard are the same size. If you really want a convertible crib, the **DaVinci Kalani** ($189) might be a better bet as it has a headboard that is higher than the footboard. (Perhaps in recognition of this limitation, Amazon now refers to the Union as a 3-in-1 convertible crib; they recently added a new Union 4-in-1 to the collection bundled with a DaVinci mattress).

Also: this crib has exposed screws and screw holes. That doesn't compromise safety; it's just an aesthetic issue. More expensive cribs hide this hardware, but that is the trade-off to get the price so low.

A final drawback: this crib is made from New Zealand pine, which is soft and can easily scratch. Hence, take great care when unpacking and assembling this crib. Even rubbing a buckle against the crib rail will scratch it (when you lean into the crib to pick up baby, for example).

Also: if your teething baby decides to munch on the crib rail, the finish will most likely come off. It isn't a health hazard (the paint is non-toxic), but this has alarmed more than a few parents. (If teething is an issue, you can use a cloth rail cover (about $20).

We realize a chewed-on crib doesn't look perfect, but having a baby in your house means everything will now be scratched, scuffed and chewed on—your crib will simply match the rest of your furniture. ("You can either have children or nice stuff!"—Dennis Miller).

FYI: The Union crib comes in five finishes, including blue and a natural finish, which is unusual at this price point. Typically, affordable cribs are offered in only one or two colors. The caveat to this is that we've noticed that Amazon has occasionally run out of some of the finishes. So if you have your heart set on a particular finish and see it in stock, we wouldn't wait to order it.

Also Great: Graco Benton

The **Graco Benton** is a simple $160 crib that is easy to put together and can morph into a full-size bed (when you use the curved side as a headboard and separately purchase bed rails).

Quality is good; we like the metal spring mattress platform—some low-end cribs come with flat wood boards as a mattress base, which we don't recommend. It takes about 45 minutes to assemble and we found it easier overall than most other cribs.

The curved headboard of the Benton gives this crib just a bit more style than the Union crib, which probably explains the small price difference.

Graco cribs are made by Stork Craft, which is unfortunate since we don't think much of this company's more pricey cribs and nursery dressers. But this basic crib is no frills and does what it needs to do—a safe, simple space for baby to sleep with a spring mattress platform.

Stork Craft was wise to license the Graco name for this crib. Folks trust the Graco name . . . while we'd guess Stork Craft doesn't ring a bell for most parents.

Like most sub-$200 cribs, the Graco Benton is made of soft pine, which will scratch easily. Take care with the assembly or moving the crib around. A simple belt buckle can leave a scratch when accidently rubbed against a crib rail.

To its credit, the Graco Benton comes in four different colors, including the ever-popular Pebble Grey. Many low-end cribs only come in white or brown.

We saw a few dissenting views among our readers and online reviewers. The crib's paint, which of course is non-toxic, chipped on a few Graco Benton cribs, according some online reviewers. It's hard to know if this because of poor finish quality on a few cribs or the way the crib was stored or handled by the consumer. Stork Craft's quality control can be iffy.

One parent said her Graco Benton crib was broken by a two year-old toddler who liked to jump around in his crib. The wood frame broke and the metal mattress support buckled.

Let's be honest: the Graco Benton is not a built-like-a-tank crib from American Baby Company Barn. Of course, those cribs run two to four times these cribs. The take-home message: if you plan to have multiple kids, you'd be better off buying something more substantial. For everyone else, the Graco Benton is a good choice at an affordable price.

Best Budget-Friendly Crib (Basic)

Another affordable simple crib is **IKEA's Gulliver** at $99. No, that's not a typo! A basic, modern crib for $99. The crib is just a crib—it doesn't convert to a full-size bed, etc. Also: the Gulliver only has two mattress positions. Very simple, but well made.

You can have any color for the Gilliver as long as it is white. FYI: IKEA has a few other crib styles (Sniglar, Solgul) that run $99 to $199 in colors other than white. We recommend these as well.

If you are into minimalist style, any of these cribs will fit the bill. Note that even though IKEA cribs are basic, they meet all U.S. safety standards. We've recommended this brand for years and readers agree—these are safe, good quality cribs.

Best Crib For City Dwellers
(and those with little space for a nursery)

If you live in the city, space may be at a premium. We have two solutions here, although both have drawbacks.

Our best pick for cribs for city dwellers is the **Stokke Sleepi**. Norwegian juvenile gear maker Stokke (pronounced stow-kuh) pitches its oval crib as a "system" that grows with your child: the Sleepi morphs from a bassinet to a crib, then a toddler bed and finally two chairs . . . all for a mere $900. You can buy just the crib for $700 (without the toddler bed conversion kit).

The Sleepi's oval shape and wheels makes it easier to move through narrow doors. The Sleepi is 29" wide; standard full-size cribs are 30" and more. That may not sound like much, but it can make the difference between fitting in a doorway or not. Plus few cribs come with wheels these days, as the Stokke does.

Also: you can use the Sleepi in bassinet mode for up to six months. The bassinet mode takes up just 26" in width. And the bassinet's simple style wins fans for its minimalist aesthetic.

So what's not to like about Sleepi, excluding its steep price? Well, an oval crib requires a special oval crib mattress ($200); and oval crib bedding ($29 for a sheet). As you might guess, choices are limited.

We also noted that Stokke has struggled with quality control issues in recent years, as expressed by our readers as well as customer reviews posted to Amazon. As a result, we gave them an overall grade of B-.

If the price and concerns about the Stokke Sleepi have you wishing for another alternative, consider plan B: a portable crib.

About 10% of all cribs sold in North America are these cribs, sometimes called portable cribs, mini cribs, folding cribs and so on.

As you can guess from the name, these cribs are narrower in both width (25" width versus 30" or more for full-size cribs) and length (about 39" vs 52").

Our top pick for portable crib is the **Babyletto's Origami Mini Crib** ($269). This simple crib folds away when not in use and comes with wheels to move it about a small apartment or condo. (Using the wheels is optional). Overall, we found the construction quality to be above average for this crib.

The downside to the Babyletto Origami Mini Crib? Well, it does take a while to assemble (a few users complained it was over an hour). And the crib only comes with a one-inch pad; you should probably replace this with a mattress that snugly fits it (37 x 23.875 mattress), such as the BabyLetto mattress ($120).

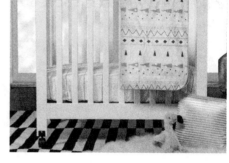

Here's the biggest drawback to the Origami mini crib—and it's the same drawback that affects nearly ALL mini crib: babies often outgrow them before they are old enough to go into a toddler or big kid bed.

Babyletto says the Origami crib can't be used "when a child begins to climb." Well, a typical child will hit that milestone around six to ten months when they can pull themselves up to a standing position. Some mini cribs (but not all) have lower rails than a standard size crib—and that makes climbing out easy for infants under a year old.

Hence, mini cribs are more like bassinet replacements. Keep in mind that most babies will use a crib for two or three years (and sometimes up to age four). And a crib is the safest place for babies to sleep.

Yes, there are stories floating around out there that a small baby can make it in a mini crib to age 3, but that is the exception.

So what happens when your baby outgrows a mini crib before their first birthday? Well, then you have to move to a full-size crib. Hence, you can use a mini crib as a bridge until you have more room in your apartment or condo . . . or you find living accommodations with more space!

Bottom line: a mini crib can make do for a while, but you'll be finding yourself purchasing a full-size crib as your baby nears one year of age.

Best Eco-Friendly Baby Crib

Babyletto's Lolly crib ($399) is our pick for top eco friendly crib. This crib is made by an established nursery furniture company with a good quality track record.

Babyletto is part of the Million Dollar Baby family of nursery furniture brands. The company has committed to making sure all its cribs are safe for your baby and the environment. Their cribs are made of New Zealand pine and are GreenGuard Gold certified.

What's that? GreenGuard Gold is an independent third-party certification that the nursery furniture item is low-emission—that is, emission of volatile compounds (VOC's) which can contribute to bad indoor air quality.

For the price, you also get a toddler rail included. The downside, this crib only converts to a toddler bed—no double bed for you. Another disappointment, the Lolly only has one matching storage option: a three-drawer dresser with removable changing tray.

Despite these drawbacks, we think the Babyletto Lolly is the best eco-friendly crib option out there today!

Best Crib Made in the USA

El Greco's Nest crib ($700 at RoomAndBoard.com) is our pick for the best made-in-the-USA crib. (FYI: 97% of all cribs sold in the U.S. are made in Asia, mostly China and Vietnam).

Based in Jamestown, New York, El Greco has been making furniture since 1975 but largely flies under the radar of the industry. Why? Because El Greco only makes a small number of cribs each year that are sold exclusively at Room & Board.

Quality is excellent—the Nest crib is made of solid maple, which is rare to find in nursery furniture these days. El Greco has never had a safety recall in 45+ years of business and their finishes are GREENGUARD-certified. El Greco posts detailed info on their manufacturing process on their web site.

The Nest crib comes in ten finishes/colors.

So what are the drawbacks? Well, the Nest is a basic crib that doesn't convert into a full-size bed like many other cribs in this price range. That makes the investment here steep. But if you plan to use this crib for more than one baby, you could justify the expense.

FYI: If you like El Greco but don't like the simple style of the Nest, the company sells a handful of other cribs at Room & Board, a 20-store chain of modern furniture stores. If you don't have one of those stores nearby, you can order El Greco cribs online at Room & Board's web site.

What if you don't have that much money but still want an American-made crib? Unfortunately, there isn't much beyond El Greco.

Yes, there are a handful of modern furniture companies like DucDuc that make cribs in the U.S., but most of these run $1000+. And we found El Greco's quality superior to these alternatives.

Best High-Style Crib

The **Ubabub Pod** crib is a futuristic show stopper—yes, it is insanely expensive ($3200) but wins our pick for best high style crib with its curved wood panels and acrylic sides with funky cut-outs. The detail and craftsmanship on this crib is something to behold.

The Pod comes with a custom-fitted mattress and the conversion kit to turn into a toddler

Not made in China

From lead paint in toys to tainted baby formula, China has had its share of, uh, quality control issues in the last 20 years. And some of our readers have asked us, not surprisingly, how to furnish a nursery with products NOT made in China. While that sounds simple, it isn't: 97% or more of baby furniture sold in the U.S. is made in China—so avoiding Chinese-made items takes some effort.

But there is good news: there ARE a handful of companies that make their furniture somewhere other than China. And yes, there are still firms that make furniture in the U.S.: ducduc, Capretti, El Greco, and Newport Cottages. Oak Designs (oakdesigns.com) makes dressers and twin beds domestically.

Other furniture makers import goods from countries other than China: Romina makes furniture in Romania; Bratt Décor and Bivona's Dolce Babi and Tiamo have factories in Vietnam. Oeuf imports its furniture from Latvia. Natart is made in Canada and Denmark.

A few caveats to this advice: first, production often shifts, so before you order, reconfirm with the manufacturer or retailer where the furniture is being made. Second, manufacturers that split production between China and other countries often don't publicize which furniture is made where. You have to ask.

bed that looks like something out of a movie set in 2093.

Distributed in the U.S. by the Million Dollar Baby family of nursery brands, Ubabub (pronounced "uber-bub") is actually based in Australia and sells its goods in both Oz and New Zealand. Ubabub has a good reputation for quality and a solid track record for safety.

Best Travel/Portable Baby Crib

After evaluating and testing 17 portable baby cribs, we pick the **BabyBjorn Travel Crib Light** ($300) as the best travel/portable baby crib. While not the cheapest option out there, we judged this ultra-light play yard (which folds up like an umbrella and fits in a small carry case) to be worth the investment.

Parent feedback has been universally positive. At 11 pounds, it is half the weight of a standard Graco Pack N Play.

The Travel Crib Light (13 lbs.) has breathable mesh sides with exterior metal poles and comes with an organic fitted sheet and mattress. The top edge includes a padded cover and it folds into a 19" x 23.5" x 5.5" bag. You'll note that the shape is rather different from a traditional play yard and it uses poles like you'd see on a camping tent.

Overall, readers like the Travel Crib Light. Fans love the easy set up and break down, and note that the fabric is nicer than other similar travel cribs. The mattress is pretty thick for a travel crib and the light weight makes it easy to lug around.

The only complaints: short parents may have a tougher time lowering baby into the crib and the exterior poles jut out at an angle, creating a tripping hazard. Yes, it is pricey, but if you plan to travel frequently with your baby it may be worth the expense.

Best Crib for Short Parents

If you are under 5'5", you may find reaching into a standard-size stationary crib challenging. Since most cribs sit a foot or two off the floor and drop-side cribs were phased out in 2011, shorter parents may find it difficult putting baby in a standard crib when the mattress is in its lowest position.

For those parents, a lower-profile crib may be just the ticket. A good, affordable bet: **Babyletto's Modo 3-in-1** crib (pictured) is made from New Zealand pine and is relatively affordable at $289. At only 34" tall, the Modo sits low to the ground making it much easier to put baby in and out of the crib.

The Modo is available in six color combinations including two-tone options (white top with brown or grey base) that gives it a modern spin.

We like that Modo is GREENGUARD Gold certified, plus it has four mattress levels.

While Babyletto touts the Modo's "3-in-1" conversion feature, the Modo only coverts into a toddler bed (the toddler rail is included, which is a nice touch). Hence, the Modo doesn't convert into a full-size bed for older kids.

Best Crib for Grandma's House

The best crib for the grandparents must be easy to set up and take down.

We suggest one of two options here: a portable crib like the **Dream On Me 2 in 1 Portable**

Folding Stationary Side Crib ($110) hits all the right notes—easy to assemble, folds away for storage and is affordable.

The biggest drawback: the Dream on Me crib is actually a mini crib that is only 38" long (versus 52" for a full-size crib). That means babies older than one year of age or larger infants may outgrow this crib before they are old enough to sleep in a toddler bed. One solution: go for our travel crib pick (see earlier in this section).

(FYI: Babies typically stay in a crib to age three or later. Once a child regularly climbs out of a crib, it is time for a big kid bed.)

Hence the key issue with any mini crib is safety—older babies (younger toddlers) can easily escape a mini crib. Full-size cribs? Not as much.

Therefore, our second option here is a full-size crib that is easily to assemble. Yes, such cribs do exist. Our pick for this would be the ***Delta Canton*** crib ($200)—Delta includes all the tools (basically, one allen wrench) and that makes the assembly easy-peasy, say our readers.

Next up: let's look at the best crib mattress for that new crib.

The Best Baby Crib Mattress

Odds are, you've already bought a mattress for yourself before and have a working knowledge of mattress lingo (box spring, memory foam). But the baby version of mattress shopping is more a bit more complex. And confusing.

One big difference: babies need to sleep on a *firm* mattress for safety reasons, much firmer than an adult would prefer. And because diapers leak, a waterproof pad to protect that mattress may be necessary.

A simple crib mattress typically runs $100 to $200, with some models starting at $70. What about pricey $300+ mattresses hand-made by Swiss monks from organic unicorn horn shavings? Are they really three times healthier or safer than the $100 choice? Let's discuss!

7 Things No One Tells You About Buying A Crib Mattress!

1 FORGET ALL THE FANCY CLAIMS: ALL YOU NEED IS A FIRM MATTRESS WITH A WATERPROOF COVER. What's inside the mattress (foam, coil, latex, mohair, etc) is a matter of personal preference. After reviewing dozens of studies on crib mattress safety, we found no evidence that one material is healthier than another . . . despite what crib mattress makers claim online.

As mentioned earlier, a simple crib mattress starts around $70. It should snuggly fit your crib with no gaps more than two fingers length between the mattress and the crib (see graphic at right).

And while you'd think it would be no-brainer, there are some crib mattresses sold with NON-waterproof covers, so buyer beware.

2 **THAT CRIB MATTRESS COULD COST MORE THAN YOUR CRIB.** Especially if you opt for an eco-friendly mattress or another specialty mattress. Many of these mattresses top $300 and even $400.

3 **THERE'S NO SUCH THING AS A "BREATHABLE MATTRESS."** Many parents are understandably concerned about SIDS (Sudden Infant Death Syndrome). Unfortunately, some crib mattress makers play on this fear by claiming their expensive mattress is made from special "breathable" material—and therefore has a lower suffocation risk than regular mattresses. Quick fact check: that's FALSE.

These magical claims may lead some parents to think it is ok to put baby to sleep on their stomach. Please don't—the safest way for baby to sleep in a crib is on their back . . . on a firm mattress. (We have a full discussion of SIDS and how to prevent it in our other book *Baby 411*, co-authored by a pediatrician who is a spokesperson for the American Academy of Pediatrics).

4 **KEY QUALITY FEATURE TO LOOK FOR: TRIPLE LAMINATED/REINFORCED VINYL COVERS.** These covers are more durable and less likely to tear (when you move the mattress around to change the sheets). Lower quality mattresses just have a single or double layer of vinyl.

5 **SAY NO TO THAT HAND-ME-DOWN.** Your friend's cousin has a crib mattress sitting in her attic that she'd love give you. Politely refuse. Why? Bacteria and mold can grow in an old mattress, even if it has a waterproof cover—and especially if it has been stored in a dank basement or unventilated attic. Plan to have more than one kid? We also suggest a new mattress with each baby.

6 **LIGHTER = BETTER.** Babies do all sorts of things in cribs other than occasionally sleep. When it is time to change the sheets, you have to wrestle with that crib mattress. And here, lighter mattresses (usually foam) are much easier to handle than heavier options (most likely coil mattresses). Another option: go for quick-change sheets that don't require you to wrestle with the mattress.

The added weight of coil mattresses doesn't add any benefits for baby or parent, so our rule stands: lighter = better.

7 **CONVENTIONAL CRIB MATTRESSES ARE NOT DANGEROUS.** Many expensive, eco-friendly crib mattresses are marketed with dark hints that conventional crib mattresses (made of petro-chemical foam or coils) are somehow dangerous. The online world is full of such claims:

"Common materials in crib, bassinet, cradle and porta-crib mattresses may be harmful and even potentially life threatening to your baby. The majority of mattress manufacturers use toxic, unsafe materials." —web site of an expensive eco-baby crib mattress.

So let's state it for the record: there is NO scientific evidence that sleeping on a conventional crib mattresses is harmful to your baby. Zip. Zero.

What about mattress materials giving off chemical odors? Yes, crib mattresses are made of chemicals and some do off-gas when first removed from packaging. We do recognize concerns about bad indoor air quality, especially with newly built homes that are tightly sealed. If this fits your situation, look for crib mattresses that are GREENGUARD certified—this is an independent third-party test standard for mattresses that are low in VOC's (volatile organic compounds).

Since babies sleep 12+ hours a day on their crib mattress, we can understand the concern that baby has a safe sleep space. But crib mattress marketers that play on these fears to sell $400 eco options often peddle junk science—these folks claim "polyurethane foam" and "waterproof covers made of polyvinyl chloride or PVC" are dangerous, cause cancer, etc.

Most of these conspiracy theories trace their origins to a widely discredited SIDS prevention campaign by a late New Zealand forensic scientist we'll call Dr. S. He claimed toxic gases from waterproof (PVC) covers and other chemicals in mattresses caused SIDS. If you wrapped a crib mattress in a special plastic wrap, SIDS could be eliminated, Dr. S. claimed. Several companies sprung up to sell such wraps online.

After an exhaustive investigation of the toxic gas hypothesis lasting three and a half years, methodically examining every aspect of the claim both by reviewing existing research, as well as by commissioning new research, the 1998 Limerick Report concluded that there is no evidence to support the claim that fire retardants in crib mattresses cause SIDS.

But that hasn't stopped the online fever swamps in keeping this false theory alive. Dozens of crib mattress web sites still quote this discredited theory, peddling all sorts of "non-toxic" crib mattresses.

Professor Barry Taylor, of the pediatrics department at Otago University, said SIDS researchers did not wish to comment on Dr S's passing in 2014, but they viewed his legacy with regret, noting the large amounts of time and money that were spent investigating his theories.

The take-home message: conventional crib mattresses are safe.

While there is no safety issue with crib mattresses made of petrochemicals, we know some of our readers want to reduce or eliminate these items from their house for personal or ecological reasons. If that's you, we will give some recommendations for eco-friendly crib mattresses later in this chapter.

The Best Baby Crib Mattresses

We break down our picks for mattresses into these categories:

◆ Best Crib Mattress (Overall)
◆ Best Budget-Friendly Crib Mattress
◆ Best Eco Crib Mattress
◆ Best Travel/Portable Crib Mattress
◆ Best Waterproof Pad
◆ Best Changing Table Pad

The Best Baby Crib Mattress (Overall)

After comparing 15 different crib mattress brands, we pick the **Moonlight Slumber Little Dreamer** foam crib mattress ($200) as the Best Baby Crib Mattress.

The Little Dreamer features welded seams and a PVC-free, "hospital grade" fabric cover that is "water resistant." Bonus: it has two firmness zones (firm for baby, more comfy for toddler).

The mattress comes with square corners for a tight fit, an internal fire barrier (no toxic chemicals) and medical-grade foam partially made from soybeans (making it just 7 to 10 lbs.). The mattress is easy to clean and made in the U.S. The company also touts its mattresses as hypoallergenic. Priced at $200, we thought this one was a good buy as similar mattresses are creeping closer to $300 and even $400.

Got an unusual size crib? Moonlight Slumber offers custom sizes of their mattresses. That's unusual as most makers sell one standard size. Overall reader reviews of Moonlight Slumber are quite positive. Parents note that the mattress doesn't sag even after months and years of use.

8 tips to lower the risk of SIDS

Sudden Infant Death Syndrome (SIDS) is the sudden death of an infant under one of year of age due to unexplained causes. Sadly, SIDS is still the number one killer of infants under age one—over 2000 babies die each year.

So, what causes SIDS? Scientists don't know, despite studying the problem for two decades. We do know that SIDS is a threat during the first year of life, with a peak occurrence between one and six months. SIDS also affects more boys than girls; and the SIDS rate in African American babies is twice that of Caucasians. Despite the mystery surrounding SIDS, researchers have discovered several factors that dramatically lower the risk of SIDS. Here is what you can do:

Put your baby to sleep on her back. Infants should be placed on their back (*not* side or tummy) each time they go to sleep. Since the campaign to get parents to put baby to sleep on their backs began in 1992, the SIDS rate has fallen by 50%. That's the good news. The bad news: while parents are heeding this message, other care givers (that is, grandma or day care centers) are less vigilant. Be sure to tell all your baby's caregivers that baby is to sleep on his back, never his tummy.

Encourage tummy time. When awake, baby should spend some time on their tummy. This helps prevent flat heads caused by lying on their backs (positional plagiocephaly). Vary your child's head position while sleeping (such as, turning his head to the right during one nap and then the left during the next nap). Minimize time spent in car seats (unless baby is in a car, of course!), swings, bouncer seats or carriers—any place baby is kept in a semi-upright position. A good goal: no more than an hour or two a day. To learn more about plagiocephaly, go online to plagiocephaly.org.

Forget gadgets. Special mattresses, sleep positioners, breathing monitors—none have been able to reduce the risk of SIDS, says the American Academy of Pediatrics. Just put baby to sleep on her back.

Use a pacifier. Consider giving baby a pacifier, which has been shown in studies to re-

Also Great: Naturepedic Classic Organic Crib Mattress

The **Naturepedic Classic Organic Crib Mattress** is also a great pick for crib mattress, especially for a more eco-friendly option.

This mattress features closed-cell air pockets made from food-grade polyethylene. As a result, this mattress is half the weight of a traditional coil mattress.

The basic model runs $260; a dual-firmness model is $290—the firmer side for infants, the softer side for toddlers. (A coil version is also available).

In a nutshell, Naturepedic balances the best of both worlds: organic cotton filling, a firm foam or coil innerspring AND a waterproof cover. All of Naturepedic's mattresses contain no PVC's, polyurethane foam or chemical fire retardants.

duce the rate of SIDS. Why? Scientists don't know exactly, but some speculate pacifiers help keep the airway open. Okay, we should acknowledge that pacifiers are controversial—key concerns include breastfeeding interference, tooth development and ear infections. But if you introduce the pacifier after breast-feeding is well-established (around one month), there are few problems. Stop using the pacifier after one year (when the SIDS risk declines) to prevent any dental problems. While pacifiers do increase the risk of ear infections, ear infections are rare in babies when the risk of SIDS is highest (under six months old). Bottom line: Use pacifiers at the time of sleep starting at one month of life for breastfed babies. If the pacifier falls out once the baby is asleep, don't re-insert it. Stop using pacifiers once the risk of SIDS is over (about a year of life).

Don't smoke or overheat the baby's room. Smoking during pregnancy or after the baby is born has been shown to increase the risk of SIDS. Keep baby's room at a comfortable temperature, but don't overheat (do not exceed 70 degrees in the winter; 78 in the summer). Use a wearable blanket or swaddle baby with a blanket.

Bed sharing: bad. Room sharing: good. Why does bed sharing increase the risk of SIDS? Scientists say the risk of suffocation in adult linens (pillows, etc) or entrapment between bed frame and mattress, or by family members is a major contributor to SIDS. That said, *room sharing* (having baby in the same room as the parents, either in a bassinet or crib) is shown to reduce the rate of SIDS. Again, researchers don't know exactly why, but it's possible parents are more attuned to their baby's breathing when baby is nearby.

No soft bedding. Baby's crib or bassinet should have a firm mattress and no soft bedding (quilts, pillows, stuffed animals, bumpers, etc). We will discuss soft bedding more in depth in the next chapter. Also: consider using a swaddling blanket, footed sleeper or SleepSack instead of a blanket. More on these items in Chapter 3.

Make sure all other caregivers follow these instructions. Again, you might be vigilant about back-sleeping . . . but if another caregiver doesn't follow the rules, your baby could be at risk. Make sure your day care provider, grandma or other caregiver is on board.

Best Budget-Friendly Crib Mattress

Yes, you can buy a safe foam mattress for as little as $60. The **Safety 1st Heavenly Dreams White Crib Mattress** is our top pick for budget-friendly crib mattress.

Sure, it's no frills—a basic foam mattress with a single-layer vinyl cover that is easy to clean. Quality is good, but the single-layer vinyl cover will probably only last for one kid.No fancy eco materials or seamless edges, but an excellent deal if the budget is tight.

The Sealy Soybean Foam-Core crib mattress ($151.57) is a great runner up to the Safety 1st mattress. It is GREENGUARD certified to be low emission and, yes, the foam is partially made from soybeans. At just 8.3 pounds, this lightweight but firm mattress makes changing sheets easy. Bottom line: with this pick, you can get the eco-friendly features without shelling out over $300.

Best Eco-Friendly Crib Mattress

Lullaby Earth's Healthy Support crib mattress is made of poly-ethylene foam (a non-toxic, food-grade foam that requires no fire retardant chemicals) and weighs just 7 lbs. (Most other foam mattresses on the market are made of polyurethane). It features seamless edges and GREENGUARD-certification. Price: $170. A 2-Stage version of this crib mattress is $200. The Healthy Support is an excellent, lightweight option at an affordable price.

Best Travel/Portable Crib Mattress

What separate mattress do we recommend for travel or portable cribs? The answer: none. It is unsafe to purchase a separate mattress for portable cribs or play yards.

The Consumer Product Safety Commission says that when it comes to travel cribs or play yards, only use the mattress pad provided by the manufacturer (most, if not all, come with a mattress). Do not add an additional pad or mattress on top of the original mattress.

We discuss the best travel cribs earlier in this chapter.

Best Mini Crib Mattress

We like the **Dream on Me 3" Mini/Portable Crib Mattress** ($29) as the Best Mini Crib Mattress. Yes, it is firm and light! Weighing under 2 lbs., it makes for easier sheet changes in the middle of the night. Yes, it also has a waterproof vinyl antimicrobial cover. Reader feedback on this mattress

has been very positive, with folks saying it does the job at a reasonable price.

One point that can be confusing here: even though they have the same interior dimensions, mini cribs are different than portable play yards that have soft sides.

As a reminder, we urge parents NOT to buy a separate mattress for portable play yards (sometimes called travel cribs or portable cribs). Why? That's because those products come with their own mattresses or pads—the CPSC says to only use the mattress pad provided by the manufacturer (most, if not all, come with a mattress). Do not add an additional pad or mattress on top of the original mattress.

Mini cribs, however, are sometimes sold WITHOUT a mattress. In that case, we'd go for the Dream on Me.

One final caveat: some mini cribs have limitations on how THICK a mattress can be. The mattress here is 3". Be sure to read any manufacturer limitations or safety guidelines on mini cribs.

Best Waterproof Pad

In this category, we're referring exclusively to a crib mattress-size waterproof pad or mattress protector. We are not referring to travel mattresses or port-a-cribs.

Our top pick for waterproof crib mattress pad is the **SureGuard Mattress Protector** for cribs ($25.97). It comes with a 100% cotton top surface while the waterproofing material is polyurethane. It is GREENGUARD Gold Certified for low VOC's and doesn't contain any phthalates, PVC or BPA.

Caveat: readers note you have to strictly follow the washing instructions (delicate cycle) or risk losing the waterproofing.

Also Great: Carter's "Keep-Me-Dry" Fitted Quilted Crib Pad

The **Carter's Keep-Me-Dry pad** ($20) is an affordable waterproof pad that features a soft, quilted polyester top and waterproof vinyl backing. We like the all-around elastic and reinforced corners. The pad is machine washable.

Best Changing Table Pad

Changing table pads help turn a dresser or any surface into a changing table. A couple of shopping tips: look for a pad with elevated sides (see photo). This will help keep your baby on the mattress pad. A word of caution: elevated sides don't guarantee your baby won't still roll off the pad, so never walk away when changing your baby.

The best pick: **Summer Infant's Contoured Changing Pad** ($19.88); available at Amazon.com and Walmart. If you're looking for an organic or natural changing pad, consider Naturepedic's Organic Cotton Contoured Changing Table Pad for about a hundred bucks.

Last but not least, we'd like to put in a word for a couple of new types of changing pads: the **Keekaroo Soft & Cushy Diaper Changing Peanut Changer** ($130; below) and the **Skip Hop Nursery Style Wipe-Clean Changing Pad** (not pictured) While most people are used to the quilted style like our top pick above, these new pads have some distinct advantages over traditional changing pads.

First and most important, they're impermeable to liquids. No worries about liquids seeping into the pad through the stitching on the cover! And they're made of a slip resistant material that you merely wipe off. In fact, Keekaroo claims their material, a polyurethane polymer "was designed and tested for hospital use." The Skip Hop is made of PVC-free and phthalate-free foam. Finally, they are both soft and cushy and come with straps to secure baby. The Skip Hop has a toy bar too.

We do have one major issue with these kinds of changing pads: price. The Keekaroo is the most expensive. The Skip Hop is a better deal at $70. But it's hard to justify those prices when compared to our traditional changing pad above priced around 20 bucks. While most people do buy a changing pad cover for traditional changing pads this only adds about $14 each to the price; still much less than a Keekaroo or Skip Hop.

Hopefully, with more competition, prices will come down on these new foam pads. Easy cleaning is definitely a plus here.

The Best Bassinet

To encourage breast-feeding, pediatricians recommend "rooming in" with your baby for the first few weeks. That means having your baby close at hand for night-time feedings.

While baby can sleep in a full-size crib from birth, a bassinet is a handy way of bringing baby into your room until breastfeeding is established. As you'll read below, there are several different options when it comes to bassinets.

Let's go over a quick intro course to bassinets before our picks.

7 Things No One Tells You About Buying A Bassinet!

1 NO MATTER WHERE YOU PUT YOUR BABY DOWN FOR A NAP OR OVERNIGHT, FOCUS ON THE FOUR BASIC SAFETY RULES FOR SAFE SLEEP:

- ◆ Do not use any soft bedding in the crib/bassinet/cradle/Moses basket.
- ◆ Place baby to sleep on her back.
- ◆ Keep the room temperature in baby's room at about 68° F.
- ◆ Don't overdress your baby. A light blanket sleeper is all you need.

2 MANY STROLLER MANUFACTURERS SELL BASSINETS AS ACCESSORIES. If allowed by a stroller's maker, you can use these detachable stroller bassinets as free standing bassinets in your home, not just on your stroller. You'll find manufacturers like Peg Perego and Britax enable you to use their stroller bassinet as a stand-alone sleep space at home. FYI: Because bassinets have solid sides, we only recommend using them for *supervised* naps during the day time.

Stroller bassinets typically cost around $200 to $250, about the same as a free standing bassinet but with the added feature of attaching to your stroller too.

Peg Perego's bassinet (right) works with several Perego strollers and sells for $250. A stationery stand is also available for another $190.

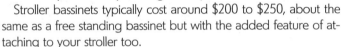

3 CRADLES ARE ANOTHER OPTION FOR NEWBORN SLEEP. If the idea of a plastic bassinet doesn't appeal to you, consider a cradle. Unlike bassinets, cradles are typically made of wood and can be rocked. Prices range from $100 to $250 or more. If you plan on having more than one child, a cradle is a very sturdy option. You can also create a family heirloom with a cradle by passing it along to others in your family. Typically a cradle comes with a mattress pad, although replacement pads are available in a variety of sizes to fit different cradles.

This Dream on Me cradle runs about $100. As is typical of cradles, the style is rather plain. Other than a sheet for the mattress pad, no other bedding should be added.

4 MOSES BASKETS CAN ONLY BE USED FOR A SHORT TIME. Moses baskets are woven baskets with liners and carry handles. You can put your newborn in a Moses basket for naps, and move your baby around the house without disturbing her. Unfortunately, these baskets are useful for only a few weeks before they reach their maximum weight limit. If you get one for a gift, it might be useful, but it probably doesn't make sense to buy one on your own.

Badger Basket makes quite a few Moses baskets like this one which run around $80.

5 **PLAY YARDS NOW COME WITH BASSINET ATTACHMENTS.** If you're going to buy a play yard anyway, consider buying a version with a bassinet attachment. You can find our top picks for play yards in the "Around the House" chapter.

Graco makes a number of Pack N Play play yards with bassinet features. This version, the Graco Pack N Play Playard Bassinet is about $75.

6 **MINI CRIBS ARE YET ANOTHER OPTION FOR NEWBORN SLEEP AND CAN BE REPURPOSED AT GRANDMA'S HOUSE.** Mini cribs are sized similarly to a cradle at about 38" long by 24" wide. For comparison, a full size crib is about 53" long and 29" wide. Mini cribs have to adhere to similarly stringent safety standards as full size cribs, so they are quite safe.

The disadvantage of mini cribs? Babies often outgrow them LONG before they are old enough to go into a toddler or big kid bed—that means you'll have to then use a full-size crib.

Some mini crib manufacturers note their mini cribs can't be used "when a child begins to climb." Well, a typical child will hit that milestone around six to ten months, when they can pull themselves up to a standing position. A mini crib has lower rails than a standard size crib—and that makes climbing out easy for infants under a year old . . . which, of course, is dangerous.

The take-home message: a mini crib does NOT replace the need for a full-size crib. A mini-crib replaces a bassinet.

Babyletto's Origami Mini Crib ($270) might be an option for moms who want their newborns to room in. But you need to take baby out of the Origami "when your child begins to climb," according to the instructions. This means you may need a full size crib by the time baby is as young as six months of age.

7 **IF YOU HAVE THE SPACE IN YOUR BEDROOM, YOU CAN JUST USE A FULL SIZE CRIB FROM BIRTH.** That's right. After all our prattling on above, you really don't have to purchase a bassinet, cradle, mini crib or Moses basket. A full size crib will do the trick . . . and save you some money!

But . . . what if you don't have room for a full-size crib in your bedroom? And you want your baby to room in to make sure breastfeeding is established during those first weeks? That's where the bassinet comes in!

The Best Bassinets

We've divided our bassinet picks into these categories:

◆ Best Bassinet (Overall)
◆ Best Bassinet Budget-Friendly
◆ Best Bassinet To Rent
◆ Best Travel Bassinet

The Best Bassinet (Overall)

After researching bassinets for the last 20 plus years, we pick The **HALO Bassinest** as the best bassinet for parents of newborns. This bassinet achieves two goals: allowing rooming in for newborns (to help with breastfeeding) while providing a safe sleep space separate from a parent's bed.

The HALO Bassinest has side walls that compress down for quick access to the baby; it also sits on a base that allows you to rotate or swivel it 360 degrees. The Bassinest includes a water-proof mattress pad and sheet; extra sheets are $15.

The Bassinest comes in four versions: a basic model for $200 (called the Essentia), a deluxe version for $290 (Premiere), the Luxe for $400. For the more expensive versions, HALO adds vibration, sounds and lullabies, nightlight and additional storage. While those frills are nice, we recommend going with the basic model—it's all most parents need. Vibration and lullabies aren't necessary for a newborn.

HALO recently debuted a lower-price Bassinest called the Bassinest Glide ($169). It features a simpler base with "gliding disks" that make it easy to move across a floor. That answers one of the big gripes about the original Bassinest: it is very hard to move from room to room. The Bassinest Glide also omits any vibration or electronics, which we think are unnecessary anyhow.

In our tests, HALO Bassinest hit all the right notes—easy to set up and use. Quality is very good. The mesh sides are a key safety features that encourages airflow. In our tests, our readers liked the fact that base legs tuck under most beds, positioning the baby right at your bedside. The Bassinest is also very quiet—when you push down the side, it doesn't make any noise.

FYI: A twin version of the Bassinest debuted recently for $470—basically, this is a larger version of the Bassinest with a divider down the middle for twins. It has the same basic features as the Bassinest.

Things we don't like about the HALO Bassinest. Yes, there a few negatives to the Bassinest to note—and as such, it may not be the perfect solution for everyone. First, it is rather heavy and bulky with a large base. As a result, you can't move it easily from room to room. It basically needs to be set up next to a bed and left there. (On the plus side, the heavy weight keeps older kiddos from accidentally knocking it over).

On the upside, the new Bassinest Glide addresses this issue if you need portability between rooms.

A few of our readers complain that the Bassinest sleeping surface is too hard—it has a thin pad and a firm surface. But that is a feature, not a bug. Infants need to sleep on a firm, flat surface.

Yes, a few folks are surprised by the tilt feature—which means the baby can roll to one side if the bassinet part is not perfectly flat. That can be caused by an uneven floor in your bedroom or by simply accidentally knocking the unit (and sometimes by a baby scooting from one side to the other). But this happens very infrequently, in our analysis.

And yes, the Bassinest can be hard to clean—to remove the cloth parts, you need to remove various screws. HALO could make this process easier.

Finally, a few folks question the value of the HALO Bassinet, considering its relatively short use period (most infants move to a full-size crib before four months of age). We see that point, but we think the benefits of rooming in with your newborn to encourage breastfeeding outweighs the costs.

Accessory to skip: HALO Bassinest Newborn Insert. While we recommend the HALO Bassinest, we say pass on their "newborn insert," a $52.99 accessory that is designed to create a smaller space inside the bassinet for newborns. This inserts attaches to the side of the bassinet and with mesh sides.

HALO takes great pains to point out that this insert is not a baby hammock, as it has a firm flat sleeping surface at the bottom. Still, we think this concept is too close for comfort to the other baby hammocks on the market—which we do NOT recommend.

We don't see the point of this accessory—a newborn is perfectly safe and secure in the Bassinest, no insert needed.

Best Bedside Bassinet, Budget-Friendly

Sometimes, the simpler the baby product, the better. Case in point: **Fisher-Price's Soothing Motions Bassinet** ($140). Basically, this is a simple bassinet with mesh sides, swing motion, vibration and lullabies. It came out tops in our testing for ease of use and overall quality.

What We Liked. This bassinet is easy to put together—assembly takes under 15 minutes. We also liked the cute extras (mobile, lights, etc.) and the mesh sides for air flow. Yes, there is even a white noise generator, which includes sounds like bird noises.

What Needs Work. Well, there are no wheels. As such, this bassinet isn't very mobile. And it is so wide, it doesn't easily fit through smaller doorways.

There's also no fold or squish down side. You access baby from the top of the bassinet. It's easier to do this if the bassinet has side that squish or fold down; this bassinet doesn't have that feature.

When you put a sleeping baby down to sleep, the bassinet can move—and that can startle some newborns.

And there is no height adjustment.

Another bummer: the sounds/lights turn off after 30 minutes. This is a battery saving feature, of course. But it also means kiddos can wake up when this stops!

Finally, consider this: you can only use this bassinet until your baby hits 20 lbs., which is a lower limit than other bassinets we tested.

Best Bassinet to Rent

If you are an experienced parent with one or two (or more) kids under your belt, so to speak, you've probably heard of Dr. Harvey Karp and his Happiest Baby books. Dr. Karp recently launched the **SNOO Smart Sleeper,** a bassinet which incorporates the soothing techniques he teaches in books and videos.

What makes it soothing? The SNOO uses white noise and motion to help rock your baby to sleep. This bassinet, which can be used up to six months of age, touts itself as being the "safest baby bed ever made."

The SNOO imitates the rhythm of the womb and when a baby wakes at night, it will automatically use sound and motion to put baby back to sleep. Used with the SNOO swaddler, it also keeps baby on his back the whole night. The SNOO includes a mattress and sheet; additional sheets are available online in the $25 range.

The SNOO sells for an astounding $1500. But there is good news: the SNOO Smart Sleeper is now available for rent! Cost: about $130 a month (or roughly $4.25 a day).

Since you most likely use the SNOO for a couple of months at best, renting the SNOO for $260 for two months makes more sense than buying it outright—unless you are planning on multiple children!

Be aware of the fine print in the SNOO rental agreement: Snoo requires a $99 refundable security charge and a minimum one month rental. The return shipping fee is $59.50. And there is also a $90 reconditioning fee (as of this writing, it is being waived). This covers the company's expense for cleaning when the SNOO is returned.

On the plus side, the rental now includes the mattress, two sheets and two swaddles.

Now that the SNOO has been on the market for a while, we are getting feedback from our readers—and the word is positive. Fans say the SNOO works as promised—and actually soothed their colicky babies.

As we probably don't have to tell you, spending $1500 for a bassinet is a bit crazy. Even renting a SNOO for two months for $300+ (when you factor in the shipping fees) is pricey, when you can buy a HALO Bassinest Glide for $170.

Bottom line: for parents who have babies with colic or who are just overly fussy, renting a SNOO is a good solution. For everyone else, the SNOO is probably overkill.

Best Travel Bassinet

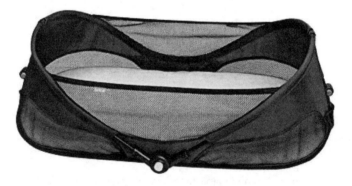

Got a road trip ahead? Here's our favorite solution for hotel rooms and holidays at the in-laws. The **Munchkin Brica Fold N' Go** travel bassinet is a decent buy at $34—it features a firm mattress with fitted sheet and mesh panels. As the name implies, it folds compactly for travel.

In our tests, this bassinet was the easiest to set up. A safety lock prevents accidental closure. The only caveat: when folded up, it won't fit in a suitcase . . . so you may have to check it if traveling by air.

FYI: Most bassinets work up to about five months of age, but the smaller Brica Fold N' Go can only be used for babies who are under three months of age and 15 pounds.

The Best Nursery Dresser

Now that you've got a place for the baby to sleep, where are you going to put baby's clothes? The juvenile trade refers to dressers, armoires, and the like as "case pieces" since they are essentially furniture made out of a large case (pretty inventive, huh?).

As you shop for baby furniture, you'll note a wide variety of dressers—three drawer, four drawer, armoires, combination dresser/changing tables, and more. In case you are new to dresser shopping, let's go over some basics.

7 Things No One Tells You About Buying A Dresser For Your Nursery!

1 **FORGET THE PRETTY FINISH. FOCUS ON DRAWER GLIDES.** The better made dressers have drawers with glide tracks on BOTH sides of the drawer for a smooth pull. Cheaper dressers have drawers that simply sit on a track at the bottom center of the drawer. As a result, they don't roll out as smoothly and are prone to coming off the track. Look at the drawer glide itself. Cheaper dressers have simple metal glides. At right, a drawer with center mount glides.

Under mounted metal drawer glides are better than center mount, but may not be as smooth as ball bearing glides (see right).

The best dressers use elaborate glide mechanisms including ball bearings or self-closing glides (you push the drawer nearly closed and it automatically/ slowly closes the rest of the way). A few nursery dresser makers use wood-on-wood glides, more commonly seen in adult furniture.

2 **LOOK CLOSELY AT THE SIDES OF THE DRAWER.** The best furniture makers use "dove-tailed" drawer joints. There are two types of dove-tail drawers: English and French (see pictures at right). Both are acceptable. What's not good? Drawers and drawer fronts that are merely stapled together.

English Dovetail   French Dovetail

3 **A THIRD QUALITY INDICATOR: CORNER BLOCKS UNDER THE DRAW-ERS.** Use a makeup mirror to look at the underside of the drawer—if there is a small block that braces the corner, that's good. Cheaper dressers omit this feature, which adds to the stability of the drawer.

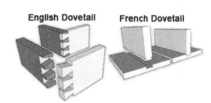

4 **THE BACK OF THE DRESSER HAS QUALITY CLUES.** Cheaply-made dressers have a flimsy piece of chipboard stapled to the back of the dresser frame. But if it's a good quality piece of furniture, a dresser back will be a solid (although perhaps only one-quarter inch thick) piece of wood that is screwed to the frame.

5 **MEDIUM DENSITY FIBERBOARD (MDF) VERSUS SOLID WOOD.** The best-made dressers have solid wood tops and drawer fronts (and some have solid wood sides).

Of course, solid wood is expensive. To make dressers more affordable, many furniture makers turn to substitute wood products such as medium density fiberboard (MDF). What is MDF? Basically, MDF is made from wood scraps that are turned into fiber and then glued together to form a solid board.

In addition to being affordable, MDF is easier to sculpt since it lacks knots or wood grain. Hence, you often seen MDF used in modern furniture groupings where a sleek, smooth aesthetic is the goal.

One downside to MDF: the glue or resin that is used to hold it together may contain formaldehyde. Back in 2008, five nursery furniture makers were sued by the state of California for unsafe levels of formaldehyde in their dressers.

Of course, not all glues are high in formaldehyde. Look for furniture manufacturers that are GREENGUARD certified to be low emission.

Our opinion: MDF isn't necessarily good or bad. The more money you spend, however, the more solid wood should be in that dresser!

6 **SKIP BUYING A SEPARATE CHANGING AREA AND USE A DRESSER.** Most folks look for dressers to do double duty: not only a place to store clothes, but also to change diapers. Basically, you need a changing area of the right height to do this—evaluate your and your spouse's heights to see what you'd need (a lower side-by-side dresser or a taller chest). Then you can purchase a changing pad for your dresser top. Some pads have non-skid bases. Changing table pads typically cost around $20.

7 **NOT RECOMMENDED: COMBINATION CRIB AND DRESSERS.** As the name implies, a combo crib and dresser is a crib with an attached dresser or changing area. This may sound like a good deal, but these combos are a safety risk, in our opinion. The hazard: babies can climb out of them too easily, based on reports to government safety databases we reviewed. Clever babies can get a toe hold on the railing or dresser drawer and push themselves up to the top of the dresser. From there, nothing good can happen.

The Best Nursery Dressers

We've broken down our picks for best dressers into these categories:

◆ Best Changing Table Dresser
◆ Best Budget-Friendly Dresser
◆ Best Dresser Splurge

The Best Changing Table Dresser

A wood dresser is a more traditional look for a baby nursery. And if you need more space for baby stuff, a six drawer dresser is a good bet.

After reviewing a half dozen different options, we think **Storkcraft's Avalon** six drawer dresser ($320) is the best bet for a wood changing table dresser. The traditional sleigh design is a classic look and the top can fit a changing pad (sold separately). Here's more:

What We Liked

◆ *Euro-glider drawers are easy to open.*

◆ *6 drawers that are 17.5" deep.*

◆ *Easy on the wallet.* Many six drawer dressers made of wood can cost a mortgage payment. This one is easier on the wallet.

What Needs Work

◆ *Dresser isn't made of solid wood.* Instead this dresser is made of engineered wood and composites. There's nothing wrong with that—it is just as safe and sturdy. The composite wood material keeps the price affordable.

◆ *Inspect immediately for any shipping damage.* This can happen with any nursery dresser, but be sure to open and inspect immediately. In our research, we found this isn't a common problem for this dresser . . . but can still happen, nonetheless!

◆ *Color can vary.* This is an issue with ordering any furniture online—depending on your monitor, the color of a dresser you see online may be slightly different in real life. This is less of an issue with the white color, of course. However, this dresser is also available in black, brown and grey . . . and may not be what you exact shade you might want.

◆ *Could be easier to assemble.* Set aside some time and patience to assemble this dresser.

Best Budget-Friendly Dresser

There are different schools of thought when it comes to finding the best baby dresser.

One popular idea: buy something that doesn't look "baby-ish" . . . which can be repurposed to another room after baby outgrows it.

For the best bang for the buck, we like dressers made of foldable fabric drawers that sit on a metal frame. Our recommendation: **Kamiler's 7 Drawer Dresser** ($80 to $100). It definitely doesn't scream "baby," yet the neutral grey color palette would fit nicely into most nurseries.

We found it easy to assemble and sturdy. The MDF top is water resistant. Also nice: adjustable feet and it can hold up to 120 lbs. of storage. Yet it's lightweight, so it can be moved around if need be (safety tip: always anchor dressers to the wall in a nursery to prevent tip-overs).

Best Dresser Splurge

If you've got the bankroll, the very best quality in dressers can be found from Canadian nursery furniture maker Natart. A double dresser from Natart typically tops $1000 (example: **Natart's Ithaca five drawer dresser** for $1400) and features top notch construction.

A close runner up to Natart is Romina, with their all solid-wood construction, and best-in-class drawer glides—smooth like butter! But it will cost you: a double dresser from Romina can run $1700 to $1900. A **Romina five drawer chest** (not shown) is $1625.

Best Eco Friendly Dresser

Romina is also our top choice for eco friendly nursery dresser. These dressers are made of solid European beech and tree sap-based organic glues, then finished with a non-toxic, water based finish (or a Bees Wax organic finish for an up charge).

No need to worry about formaldehyde emissions, since Romina's line is GREENGUARD certified. And Romina makes their furniture in Europe, not Asia. We are impressed with Romina's quality touches—corner blocks, dove tailed drawers and soft-close drawer glides. All this eco-goodness comes at a price, however. The **Imperio six-drawer dresser** runs $1625 to $1820.

The Best Glider Rocker

More than a mere rocking chair, glider rockers feature a ball-bearing system so they glide with little or no effort. They've earned a place in the nursery to help with those long hours of breastfeeding. Many are then repurposed later into a living room.

Here are some shopping tips when looking at rocker gliders.

7 Things No One Tells You About Buying A Glider Rocker!

1 YES, YOU CAN SWAP THE CUSHIONS DOWN THE LINE. Glider rockers are certainly an investment, but there is one plus when you purchase one from a major brand like Dutailier and Shermag: you can order a replacement cushion to replace a stained one or just to change the look. Dutailier has a special part of their site dedicated to replacement cushions.

Organic baby furniture

What makes nursery furniture green? As with many non-food products marketed as organic or natural, there isn't a consensus as to what that means—and that's true with baby furniture as well.

Furniture, by its very nature, isn't the most green product on earth. A toxic brew of chemicals is used to manufacture and finish most items. Example: most furniture isn't made of solid wood but veneers (a thin strip of wood over particle board). Glue is often used to adhere the veneer onto particle board for dresser tops and sides. Some glues contain formaldehyde—some baby furniture makers have been sued by the state of California for unsafe levels of this chemical.

For many folks, green means sustainable. So green baby furniture should be made from sustainable wood. But which wood is more eco-friendly? Some say bamboo is the most green (Natart's Tulip line of furniture is made from bamboo, but is very pricey). Others say rubber wood (ramin) is green since the tree it comes from (the Para rubber tree) is usually cut down anyway after it is used to produce latex.

Given all the confusion, here is our advice for green nursery furniture shoppers:

◆ *Look for solid wood furniture that is certified.* There are a handful of non-profit environmental organizations that certify wood as sustainable: the Forest Stewardship Council (FSC) is among the best known. Oeuf is an example of a FSC-certified crib makers..

◆ *Consider a water-based paint or stain.* Romina offers a "Bees wax" finish that is about as organic as it gets. Stokke's Sleepi crib features a formaldehyde-free varnish.

◆ *Avoid dressers made entirely of MDF or particle board.* The more solid wood, the better.

◆ *Consider an organic mattress.* We review mattresses earlier in this chapter.

2 **BETTER PADDING = HAPPIER PARENT.** Sure, there are some affordable $200 gliders out there—and we do like IKEA's version (see later in this section).

But heed this warning: other super bargain glider rockers have skimpy padding. You'll be spending a good amount of time in this chair, from feeding to reading bed time stories and more. Our readers are unanimous: go for the better padding, even if it is another $100 or $200. Try out the chair in person to make sure you are happy before ordering. Your bum will thank you later.

Also worthwhile: padded armrests. If that is an option for the model you are looking at, go for it.

3 **WATCH THE WIDTH.** Some bargain glider rockers are quite narrow, which might work if you are a small person. But remember you will most likely be using a nursing pillow with your newborn . . . and having the extra width to accommodate this pillow is most helpful!

Trying to follow this advice can be difficult, as many glider rockers do not list their seat width online (product dimensions may be the glider's *box* width, not the chair width). Again, trying chairs out in person is probably the best way to go.

4 **ONE WORD: LOCKS.** Consider a chair with a locking mechanism. Some brands (notably Shermag) have an auto-locking feature; when you stand up, the chair can no longer rock. Very helpful if you have a curious toddler who might end up with pinched fingers or tipping over an unoccupied glider.

5 **FOCUS ON THE CHAIR FIRST, NOT THE FABRIC OR COLOR.** With most glider rocker companies, you can choose from dozens if not hundreds of fabric colors. Hence the first task is not focusing on the fabric, but deciding on the chair *style*. Certain styles can fit better than others—chairs with deeper backs are better for taller parents. Make sure your feet can comfortably rest on the floor when you are sitting all the way back in a rocker glider. Once you've decided on the best chair style, then consider fabrics and colors.

6 **CLEANABILITY CAN BE POOR.** The Achilles heal of many rocker gliders is cleanability, or lack there of. Most glider rocker cushions lack zip-off covers that are machine washable. Hence, your only choice is dry cleaning. One solution: you can buy affordable slip covers online for around $100 (Luxe Basics sells their covers on Amazon). If your baby spits up a lot, this may be a wise investment!

7 **DON'T OVERLOOK REGULAR FURNITURE STORES FOR DEALS.** There is no federal law that says you have to buy a glider rocker for your nursery from a store with "baby" in its name! Upholstered rockers that recline are available from a wide variety of stores . . . and adult furniture stores usually have more generous sales than nursery store retailers.

The Best Glider Rockers

Up next, we'll give you our top picks for glider rockers in these categories: Best Budget-Friendly Glider Rocker, Best Glider Rocker Splurge and Best Upholstered Glider Rocker.

Best Budget-Friendly Glider Rocker

For sheer value, it is hard to beat **IKEA's POÄNG rocking chair** for $149-$269 (the more expensive version has leather cushions). A matching, non-rocking footstool is $50.

Made of "layer-glued bent beech", the POÄNG comes in ten different cushion colors with a light brown frame. There is also a darker color frame available (IKEA calls this "medium brown").

The downside? Well, if you guessed "I have to assemble it because it is IKEA," you are correct, sir!

Like most things IKEA sells, you're going to need set aside about an hour to put the POÄNG together.

Also: The POÄNG is a rocker, not a rocker-glider (as we discussed earlier). What's the difference? Well, rocker-gliders have ball bearings to enable them to rock more easily. Rockers are simpler but require more umph—if you have a c-section, it might be easier to use a rocker-glider than the POÄNG.

Despite these minuses, our readers report they are happy with the POÄNG as a stylish, yet affordable option.

Also a good bargain: **Angel Line's Windsor Glider and Ottoman** ($156). This glider rocker impressed us with its tufted look, solid wood frame and metal bearings for smooth glide. Critics say the cushions could be more, well, cushy.

Best Glider Rocker Splurge

After comparing 11 different glider rocker brands, we pick the **Dutailier Glider Recline and Ottoman Combo** as the Best Glider Rocker Splurge.

Made in Canada, Dutailier's glider rockers have been one of the most reliable recommendations we've made since we started writing about glider rockers back in 1994.

Overall, quality is excellent, as is the comfort. If you want to customize a glider rocker, this brand offers numerous options (fabrics, colors, stains, etc).

In previous editions of this book, we recommended Dutailier glider rockers as the best bet overall . . . but the

brand's prices have creeped up over the years, now making it more of a splurge.

How pricey? A glider rocker and ottoman from Dutailier will now set you back $550 to $750.

We occasionally see Dutailier models on Amazon, but Buy Buy Baby has the biggest assortment online (as of this writing). And Dutailier has also begun selling glider rockers direct on their own web site.

Is it worth the splurge? Well, Dutailier rockers can easily be reused for more than one child . . . and then repurposed to another room in the house down the road.

Best Upholstered Glider Rocker

Typically, an all-upholstered glider rocker like the **DaVinci Olive Upholstered Swivel Glider with Bonus Ottoman** would be a pretty expensive piece of furniture—similar styles in boutiques top a thousand dollars. But DaVinci (a sub-brand of Million Dollar Baby) has found a way to bring it in for a lot less than competitors—$329.

The Olive glider swivels as well as glides, comes in four colors (two with contrast piping) and includes a matching ottoman. We like the high back and the removable lumbar pillow.

Best of all: it arrives fully assembled. That's right: no assembly required!

What do our readers think? Overwhelmingly, the quality and value stand out among their comments. That said, a few complain that it doesn't work well for taller parents, given the chair's smallish dimensions. The angle of the back can be uncomfortable for some parents as well. Overall, however, we recommend this chair and its stylish look for a decent price.

Best Sleep Soother (Sound Machine)

Getting baby to sleep has been an age old dilemma. Whether you call them sound machines, white noise generators or sleep soothers, these devices offer the same sweet nirvana: soothing a fussy baby.

Types of Baby Sleep Soothers

Before we discuss our picks in depth, first let's go over the basic options for baby sleep soothers. There are two general types of baby sleep soothers: machines that play "white noise" (such as a fan sound) only and those with pre-recorded nature sounds and/or lullabies. Additional features include night lights and smart phone control. We looked for the following features when we tested baby sleep soothers:

◆ **Noise masking:** If you've got older children or live in a noisy environment and your baby wakes up because of it, you'll want a white noise machine that successfully masks the environmental noise.

glider rocker

◆ *Timer*: As we'll discuss below in our Things No One Tells You About Buying a Sleep Soother, white noise machines should not be left on in baby's room the entire night. An hour is usually enough. Hence, we only tested machines that had timers.

◆ *Volume control with a low setting:* Because babies' hearing is still developing, we recommend using the lowest volume setting possible. See our Things No One Tells You below for further explanation.

◆ *Number of available sounds*: While many babies will respond well to a simple white noise machine with the sound of a mechanical fan, some folks may want more options. For example, a soothing lullaby or nature sound might be nice to introduce baby as a "time to get ready for bedtime" sound. And when babies grow into toddlers, having more options for a restless little one may be helpful.

◆ *Ease of use:* We especially looked for soothers that have easy-to-set timers. Some have smart-phone apps to control the unit remotely, which seems like a great idea. But after testing, we discovered the apps are more promise than actual help. Apps were often difficult to set up and plagued by short Bluetooth range and random disconnections.

Things No One Tells You About Buying A Sleep Soother!

SLEEP SOOTHERS HAVE BEEN CONTROVERSIAL. Parents are always on a quest to find a way to help baby get more sleep–mainly so they can get more sleep too! Newborns typically sleep only a few hours at a time because they are growing so fast and need to eat frequently. But once your baby reaches the four-month mark, your baby can learn to soothe itself.

But it just ain't so easy! Some kids can Ferberize (the method of letting your child cry it out), but this method has its detractors and it sometimes doesn't work for every child.

Others need to keep baby asleep once she's nodded off but older siblings, dogs and street noises conspire to wake them up.

Sleep soothers that play white noise, music or nature sounds are a solution that some parents swear by. But they are somewhat controversial.

In 2014, the American Academy of Pediatrics released a study of 14 "infant sleep machines" or ISMs. The authors of the study tested their noise output at three different distances from baby's ears (no real babies were tested). They compared the level of noise to the amount of decibels that would cause noise-induced hearing loss in adults. That number is 85 decibels or more. (We don't have a level that would cause hearing loss in children–no one wants to test for that and blow out a baby's ears).

Bottom line: 13 of the 14 ISMs were capable of delivering more than 50 decibels of noise even when placed at the largest distance of 200 centimeters from a baby's ear. Since babies are more sensitive than adults, the study guesses 50 decibels would be likely to cause some hearing damage. Three of the machines were capable of more than 85 decibels of noise.

Now here's the caveat: that was a small study over seven years ago. They don't tell you which manufacturers they tested. And finally, the study authors admit there is no real world proof that infants are suffering from damaged hearing because their parents used ISMs or white noise machines.

Here's the AAP's recommendations:

◆ DO NOT place the white noise machine near baby's head. In fact, the farther away the better.
◆ DO NOT use the white noise machine at top volume, rather use the lowest volume possible.
◆ DO NOT use it all night. An hour or less is our recommendation.

BUT OTHER STUDIES SHOW THEY WORK. Another small study (using only 40 newborns aged two and seven days old) tested actual white noise machines to see if they did help infants fall asleep faster. They gave 20 babies white noise machines and compared them to a control group put to sleep with no sound machines. The result: 80% of the babies using the white noise machine fell asleep within five minutes. In the control group (no noise machine), 25% fell asleep within five minutes.

SO WHAT'S A PARENT TO DO? There are many free apps (like Decibel X for iPhone) available today that will test the decibel metric of anything. Just download the app and hold it next to the machine. Your goal is to get the sound below 50 decibels at the edge of your baby's crib.

The take-home message:

1. Only buy a machine with a timer that you can set. Run the machine less than an hour at night.
2. Place the sound machine as far away from baby as you can. Set the volume as low as possible.
3. If it's not helpful, stop using it!
4. Check back with us for future studies or information on sleep soothers.

The Best Sleep Soothers (White Noise, Nature Sounds)

After testing 17 different baby sleep soothers, we picked **LectroFan High Fidelity White Noise Machine** ($45) and **Big Red Rooster Baby White Noise Machine** ($20) as the best sleep soothers for baby.

So what made the LectroFan High Fidelity White Noise Machine and the Big Red Rooster Baby White Noise Machine our top choices?

LectroFan

This white noise machine offers ten fan noises and ten "ambient noise variations including white noise, pink noise and brown noise." In a nutshell, white noise can sound tinny to some folks—pink noise sounds more balanced to our testing ears. And brown noise takes that a step further, making more of a low hum.

This can get rather techy, so if you want to dive a bit more into the science of sounds, search YouTube for a good video

called "Colored Noise, and How It Can Help You Focus."

In our testing, we found the LectroFan does an excellent job masking environmental noises like crying toddlers (and their crying parents who've had a tough day too), dogs barking or street noise. We like the multitude of options, although once you find one that works, it's unlikely you'll change the setting much.

Other features include a 60 minute timer (it fades out rather than just stopping) and volume control (be sure to use the lowest setting possible–see discussion earlier). This machine is very simple to use, plus the noise is digitally produced so there are no repeated sound loops. Other cheaper sound machines we tested had that looping/repeating issue, which we found annoying (and so have online reviewers).

As for feedback from our readers, LectroFan gets great reviews overall, with a few complaints about a low-quality power cord. It some cases, it disconnected completely from the unit. Some readers replaced the cheaper cord and had no further issues.

Bottom line: even though the LectroFan isn't marketed directly for parents with babies, it works as an excellent white noise machine.

Big Red Rooster (BRR)

Want more than just white noise? The Big Red Rooster (BRR) is a sleep soother made especially for babies and toddlers. It comes with fewer sounds than the LectroFan (six), but includes heartbeat, lullaby, ocean, rock-a-bye and twinkle noises as well as traditional white noise.

The BRR also has a timer with three options: 15 minute, 30 minute or one hour. While it comes with an AC adapter, you can also use it with 3 AA batteries—that's a nice feature if you plan to travel (camping, hotel rooms with few outlets, etc).

On the other hand, we do have a specific baby soother machine pick for travel (see later in this section) that is smaller than the BRR.

In our testing, we found BRR very easy to use with one caveat: pushing the buttons to change the volume or choose a new sound causes a sound loud enough to wake a sleeping baby in some cases. Quieter-to-the-touch buttons would be a welcome improvement.

The Big Red Rooster (which is actually white, not red) has had a few quality control issues that we see noted in online reviews. Some folks said the AC adapter stopped working after a time (although, oddly, it still worked with batteries).

A few dissenters thought the lullabies sounded "tinny." We didn't find that in our testing—although at $20, we weren't expecting Dolby theater sound quality.

Bottom line: the Big Red Rooster sleep soother is an excellent baby sleep soother.

What about the Hatch Baby Rest?

One of the top sellers in the baby sleep soother category is the **Hatch Baby Rest Night Light and Sound Machine** ($60).

Hatch began as a small startup with an app-enabled baby scale called the Baby Grow. When founder Amy Crady Weiss worried about her newborn daughter's weight gain, she came up with the idea of a smart changing pad that includes a scale to track baby's growth metrics in an app.

After success with the Baby Grow, Hatch launched the Baby Rest in 2017. The app-enabled Baby Rest promised to combine several functions: sound machine, night light and toddler time-to-rise trainer.

The app allows you to set the lighting (dimmer, brighter, different colors) and the sound type and volume. Finally, it helps you set up routines for older babies and toddlers for bath time, bedtime and nap time.

In the last edition of our book, we expressed concerns about the Hatch's privacy policies. Those have since been revised to our satisfaction. Still, the Hatch is rather pricey compared to our other picks in this category. So if you want to go for this as a splurge (or put it on a baby gift registry), the Hatch Baby Rest is a good choice.

The Best Sleep Soother For Travel

The **LectroFan Micro2 Wireless Sleep Sound Machine** ($32) is tiny. So tiny, we didn't think it would work all that well as a sleep aid. But after testing it on various trips, were we wrong. While the sound isn't going to fill a room, it's enough to block most sounds in hotel hallways or grandma's house.

The Micro offers 11 non-looping sounds: five fan sounds, white, pink and brown noise sounds and plus ocean sound. It comes with a built-in rechargeable battery (USB) so you don't have to carry batteries with you and the volume can be adjusted in tiny increments for perfect coverage. One bummer: it comes without a timer so you'll have to turn it off yourself or leave it on all night (not our recommendation).

Best of all, the Micro weighs 6.4 ounces and is three inches tall and wide, making it easy to slip into your suitcase or bag. (A speaker flips up to direct the sound). As a side benefit, the Micro allows you to connect your smartphone via Bluetooth connectivity so you can play songs through the speaker.

What's not to like? The cord. (Why is it always the cord with LectroFan?).

Readers who've used the LectroFan Micro complained that the cord broke or became disconnected and wouldn't charge. The cord is also pretty short and irked most testers, but you can use a regular USB cord to charge it if you need more length.

Parents also mentioned the Micro has a short life if you use it continuously. If you plan to take it on occasional trips or grandma's house, it's a great option. But it doesn't have the build quality to stand up to regular use day in and day out.

The Best Sleep Soother with Nightlight

soother

Fisher-Price's SmartConnect Deluxe Soother ($50) offers a night light with ceiling projection plus a sound generator with three sounds: nature, music and pink noise (which is like white noise, but not as annoying).

We tested this model and thought it performed the best among the combo nightlight/sleep soother sound machines designed for nurseries—as long as you don't mind the somewhat glitchy companion smartphone app.

The "SmartConnect" part of this sleep soother is it's Bluetooth-enabled app. You can adjust both the sounds and the lighting effects using a smartphone. The app also allows you to set a timer, choose from three light options (amber all-over light, softer blue light and base lighting), adjust the volume and change the type of sound.

So how does this work in the real world? When it works, the app is pretty cool.

But getting it to work consistently was frustrating for us (as well as other online reviewers we found). The app occasionally cut out or froze, which required reloading. Yes, the soother itself has manual buttons and they're backlit so you can see them in the dark, but what's the point of having an app if it doesn't work all the time?

Another disappointment for some people: the projected lights don't move, they just glow steadily. We didn't see this as a major drawback in our testing.

On the plus side, you don't have to register or give Fisher-Price any personal data to use the app.

Bottom line: despite the glitchy app, we will recommend the Fisher-Price SmartConnect Deluxe Soother.

Whew! That was a lot of nursery planning. Next up: let's talk baby bedding (sheets, blankets and more!). Good news! These items are much less expensive than furniture!

CHAPTER 3

Baby Bedding & Decor

Inside this chapter

What are the best crib sheets? Blankets? What the heck is a wearable blanket? We'll answer that one, plus reveal our top picks and a chart with crib bedding brand ratings. Plus, a look at seven things no one tells you about crib sheets!

Baby blankets used to be simple—they were just, well, baby blankets. But like everything today, baby blankets have morphed into a confusing array of choices: wearable blankets, swaddling blankets, receiving blankets and so on.

Before we decipher the world of baby bedding, let's go over some shopping basic when it comes to your kiddo's linens.

7 Things No One Tells You About Buying Crib Bedding!

1 SAY NO TO CRIB BUMPERS. Yes, they look cute—but do not use bumpers in your baby's crib, cradle or bassinet.

A landmark investigation by the *Chicago Tribune* back in 2010 detailed a link between crib bumpers and two dozen infant deaths in the past decade. The article ("Hidden Hazard of Crib Bumpers," December 12, 2010) prompted the CPSC to open a review of the safety of crib bumpers. An earlier study by a Washington University pediatrician, Dr. Bradley Thach "concluded that 27 babies' deaths were attributed to bumper pads from 1985 to 2005." This study, however, has been largely ignored by both the industry and the CPSC, although it prompted the American Academy of Pediatrics to discourage parents from using bumpers.

Now we know what you're thinking: "Aren't bumpers a safety thing? What if my baby hits his head on the hard wood slats?" or "What if she gets her arm or leg stuck between the slats?" First, these issues are rare—very few kids are injured by knocking their heads against a crib's slats and even fewer get limbs stuck.

However, there are a couple of bumper alternatives if your little

baby decides getting a leg stuck in the crib slats is fun: PURE SAFETY Vertical Crib Liners and BreathableBaby Railguard. These items are either breathable mesh or firm, shock absorbing foam that don't pose a suffocation risk. Again, most folks will not need these bumper alternatives. The best advice is go without any bumpers in the crib at all.

2 **SOME CRIB SHEETS WILL SHRINK IN THE WASH—AND THAT'S A BAD THING.** Check the labels carefully on the sheet or bedding set you're thinking of buying. If a sheet recommends washing in cold water and line drying, chances are it's going to shrink. And if it shrinks, it won't fit the mattress properly. This is a suffocation hazard if the sheet should come off at one of the corners.

Once you've checked the washing instructions, look for elastic around the bottom of the entire sheet. Cheap sheets only use elastic on the ends.

Here is a list of manufacturers who make their crib sheets with elastic all around the sheet:

American Baby	Circo (Target)	Maddie Boo
BB Basics	Fleece Baby	Bobble Roos
Baby Basics	Garnet Hill	Restoration
Baby Gap	Hoohobbers	Hardware
Carousel	Land of Nod	Sweet Kyla

3 **TELL-TALE SIGNS OF GOOD QUALITY CRIB BEDDING.**

◆ *If possible, try to buy sheets with a 200 thread count.* Frustratingly, most crib sheets do not label thread count, but here's a clue: hold a sheet up to a light—if you can count the individual threads, that's probably a sheet with a low thread count.

◆ *Ruffles (on crib skirts) should be folded over for double thickness*–not a single thickness ruffle with hemmed edge.

◆ *Designs on bedding should be printed or woven* into the fabric not stamped on (like a screen printed t-shirt).

◆ *Make sure the pieces are sewn with cotton/poly thread*, not nylon, which can melt and break.

◆ *Check for tight, smooth stitching on any appliques.*

4 **NO SOFT BEDDING IN BABY'S CRIB.** This is an extension of the bumper discussion in Tip #1. Studies on Sudden Infant Death Syndrome (SIDS, also known as crib death) have linked SIDS to infants sleeping on fluffy bedding, lambskins, or pillows. A pocket can form around the baby's face if she is placed face down in fluffy bedding, and she can slowly suffocate while breathing in her own carbon dioxide.

This crib may look empty, but baby is warm and safe here.

The best advice: put your infant on her back when she sleeps. And don't put pillows, comforters or other soft bedding or toys inside a crib.

The Consumer Product Safety Commission now recommends that parents not use ANY soft bedding around, on top of, or under baby. If you want to use a blanket, tuck a very thin blanket under the mattress at one end of the crib to keep it from moving around. The blanket should then only come up to baby's chest. Safest of all: avoid using any blankets in a crib and put baby in a wearable blanket for warmth (see our wearable blankets recommendation later in this chapter).

One reader wrote to tell us about a scary incident in her nursery. She had left a blanket hanging over the side of the crib when she put her son down for a nap. He managed to pull the blanket down and get wrapped up in it, nearly suffocating. Stories like that convince us that putting any soft bedding in or near a crib is risky.

How much bedding is too much? A new father emailed us this question: "With all the waterproof liners, fitted sheets and quick change crib sheets, we're worried that our firm mattress is now becoming soft and squishy. How many layers are safe?"

Good point. We know that some parents figure it is easier to change crib sheets at 2 am if they simply pile on several layers of sheets on the crib mattress. (This way, you simply remove the top wet layer when changing the sheets). While we admire the creative thinking, we suggest NOT doing this.

Our advice: one regular sheet over a waterproof crib pad is enough. Or instead of a regular sheet, use a *waterproof* sheet (QuickZip sheet or an Ultimate Crib Sheet; see recommendations coming up) over a mattress (no additional waterproof crib pad needed then). The take-home message: don't over do it with bedding layers.

5 AVOID ELECTRIC BLANKETS AND HEATING PADS. Baby diapers often leak (sorry, fact of life) and an electric blanket or heating pad shouldn't get wet! Also, overheated babies have a higher risk of SIDS. If your baby seems cold, add an extra layer (t-shirt) under her wearable blanket for warmth. Don't turn the thermostat up over 70°, however. A too warm nursery is dangerous.

6 BE CAREFUL NOT TO OVER-SWADDLE. Take care if you are swaddling your baby, you could be wrapping her too tight.

It's fine to wrap your baby's arms snugly but leave the legs loose enough for him to move them around. Experts advise this technique to possibly prevent hip dislocation from spending hours wrapped like a mummy!

And stop swaddling after two months—your baby will need to move around and stretch out after that age.

7 LET'S TALK ABOUT HOW MUCH BEDDING YOU REALLY NEED. Start with three to four fitted sheets. This gives you enough for quick changes without doing laundry every day.

Next you'll want a couple waterproof mattress pads (the second pad is used when pad #1 is in the wash). You don't want your baby's pee to soak into the mattress or its seams.

We also recommend some light blankets. A few for swaddling, a few to throw on the floor to play on.

Everything else is optional decor: dust ruffles for the crib, curtains, etc. (Never put a curtain near the crib).

You definitely don't need diaper stackers (fancy fabric case for diapers), pillows (can't use them until about age three) and thick baby quilts. Wall hangings might be nice for decor but they aren't necessary.

An optional teething rail should be tightly secured to the crib and ONLY be used for older babies who are standing.

In the end, all you really need are sheets and blankets (or wearable blankets).

The Best Crib Bedding (Overall)

Aden + Anais makes crib sheets, blankets, towel/washcloth sets, changing pads and sleep sacks (called sleeping bags). Their classic crib sheets are made of cotton muslin ($15-$22).

Patterns are simple including leaf prints, dots, stars and dragonflies plus a few solid sheets.

What's the feedback from parents? Universally, A+A is praised for super softness and cute patterns. They wash well too, although we hear a few complaints that some items can snag in the wash. This brand is on the expensive side, especially if you choose the organic cotton option. Like most things baby and organic, there is premium to pay.

Bottom line: if you're looking for super soft, adorable prints, A+A may be the perfect option

Also Great: Carousel Designs (Baby Bedding Online)

Carousel/Baby Bedding Online is our choice for runner up best crib bedding. The company used to sell its line of bedding exclusively through retail stores at premium prices. Over a decade ago, however, they decided to change to an Internet-only sales model online at BabyBedding.com (and through Amazon as well).

Prices are on the higher side: sheets run $39 each, but let's talk quality: Carousel's sheets are 200 thread count, wash well and have all-around elastic. The site sells all its bedding as separates plus other decor items like matching window valances and lamp shades. Have a desire to outfit a nursery in the colors/logos of your favorite college football team? Yep, they have that too.

What if you want to custom design your baby's bedding? That's Carousel's secret sauce. Their website, BabyBedding.com has a cool Nursery Designer tool that allows parents to mix and match any of the patterns and colors available, using drop and drag swatches. For example, let's say you plan to get a comforter (not for use in a crib, but for play on a floor). You can pick a fabric for the front then a different fabric for the back. Or another color/pattern for the sheets. Or you might like your sheets to come in two or three different patterns. The crib skirt can also be customized.

Then you'll be able to see the final nursery online with all the different patterns and colors. When you pick your first pattern, the site will recommend some solids and patterns that go together—but you can pick anything you like. Prices are similar to Carousel's ready made designs.

Bargain tip: check out Carousel's "sale" tab, with clearance and sale items at 30% to 50% off. Bottom line: good designs, great quality and affordable prices.

Carousel still displays their sets of crib bedding online with bumpers and blankets draped over a crib rail or teether pads tied to a top rail. While it is still legal in most locales to sell items like bumpers, it would be more socially responsible if Carousel didn't merchandise these items that way.

New to the crib bedding market in recent years, **Burt's Bees** has organic cotton crib sheets for $17 for solid colors and $20 for patterns. That's a good deal—and the quality is impressive, judging from our reader feedback.

Best Budget-Friendly Crib Bedding

American Baby is one of the most affordable brands offering excellent quality 100% cotton percale and jersey sheets.

Starting at $10 per sheet (some patterns run about $15), American Baby makes traditional percale, cotton jersey and chenille sheets.

American Baby makes waterproof mattress pads, changing pad covers, crib rail covers, mini crib and cradle bedding sets. They even have a few organic cotton options. Colors and patterns are basic. Bottom line: our readers like American Baby overall and are happy with the quality and price.

Tips on eco-friendly crib bedding

Like many products sold as organic today, there is no standard for "organic" or natural baby bedding. This leaves it up to bedding manufacturers to determine for themselves what's organic. So, let's review some terms you'll see.

Many organic crib bedding makers claim their items are made from organic cotton. Organic cotton simply means cotton that's been grown with a *minimum* amount of toxic pesticides or fertilizers. That doesn't mean it is completely free of all pesticides and fertilizers.

Next let's talk sheet dyes. Conventional cribs sheets are dyed with synthetic chemicals—so how are organic bedding companies addressing this issue? Can an organic sheet be colored anything other than the natural shade of cotton (that is, an off-white)?

Turns out, the answer is yes. Organic cotton can be grown in a few colors. Yes, that's right, just like you can buy naturally orange or purple cauliflower, cotton can be cultivated in colors. Three colors are available: pink, light brown and green. Another solution: vegetable dyes. Look for manufacturers that sell baby bedding made with low-impact vegetable dyed cotton.

Of course, all this comes for a price: organic crib bedding is often 20% to 35% more expensive than conventional bedding.

Our favorite brands that offer organic crib bedding include Aden + Anais, American Baby and Carousel. FYI: not all of these brands' bedding is organic; only certain designs.

The Best Quick Change Sheets

The **QuickZip Crib Sheet** is our top pick for best quick change sheet.

What are quick change sheets? As the name implies, these sheets have a zip-off top layer to make changes quicker. You place it on the mattress like any fitted crib sheet, but if your baby's diaper leaks in the middle of the night, you don't have to struggle with removing the sheet and re-placing it. Simply zip off the top platform and zip on a clean, dry one. Voila! Minimal hassle.

Ok, that convenience comes at a price: the sheets run $46 for the sheet with base and $27 for just the zip on top. (You buy the whole set and then a few extra top sheets to use while dirty ones are in the wash).

Best Play Yard Sheet

Our pick for best play yard sheet is **American Baby Company's 100% cotton knit, fitted play yard sheet**, which fits the Graco Pack N Play bassinet/play yard mattress (as well as many other brands). The price is reasonable and they are made of organic cotton.

The Best Blankets

Our blanket recommendations break down into a few categories: Best Swaddle Blanket, Best Wearable Blanket, Best Traditional Receiving Blanket.

Best Swaddle Blanket

Our top pick for swaddle blanket (also called Swaddles) is the **Aden + Anais classic muslin swaddle**, in a four pack for $35 to $50. Excellent quality and a generous size makes swaddling easy for novices. And they come in cute patterns too!

Best Wearable Blanket

What are wearable blankets? Well, they take the place of traditional blankets, which have been banished from the crib for safety reasons.

As the name implies, your baby wears this blanket, which zips up for co-ziness. For wearable blankets, we recommend the **Halo SleepSack**, an all-cotton wearable blanket for $22.

FYI: Halo makes the SleepSack in different weights, including a lighter muslin for summer and a "winter weight" for, well, winter!

Best Traditional Receiving Blanket

Simple Joys by Carter's Baby Unisex Flannel Receiving Blankets came out tops in our testing. If you want a traditional receiving blanket, we recommend Carter's. These 100% cotton flannel blankets are great to have around the house or throw in the diaper bag. A pack of seven runs an affordable $16.

Best Milestone Blankets

Milestone blankets are a fun way to photograph your baby as the weeks and months go by, documenting all those little changes and sharing with your friends. We tried out a dozen baby milestone blankets, looking for the best included extras, quality and background design.

Luka & Lily ($27 on Amazon) is our pick in this category. We loved the handprinted watercolor style design. The super soft fleece blanket has two frames to highlight numbers/days/weeks/months. Adorable shower gift. Also nice: the blanket includes a matching bib for extra cuteness.

The Best Baby Towels

Towels are a great shower gift and we tested a dozen different options to find the very best. We looked at absorbency, softness, quality, size and, of course, cuteness! Here are our picks for best gift sets, organic towels, cute character hooded towels and a budget-friendly option.

Best Baby Towel Gift Set

After testing several different baby towel gifts, we thought this one was a winner: **Spasik's 23-piece gift set** ($24.60) Yes, you read that right: this set has 23 pieces: 20 washcloths and three hooded towels.

We thought these tools had good absorbency, plus soft fabric (and of course, cute designs). Also nice: gender neutral colors.

Best Organic Baby Towel

With smooth fabric on one side and terry loops on the other, **Burt's Bees Baby-Hooded Towels** ($25 for a two-pack) is our favorite pick for organic cotton baby towels. We found a lot of pricey organic cotton baby towels out there, but this one impressed with its overall quality and reasonable price.

We liked the 100% cotton that is GOTS-certified and made in the USA. GOTS is a textile certification program that sets standards for organic fabric. Also nice: two-sided design: smooth on one side, terry loops for more texture on the reverse.

Our biggest complaint with these towels: we wish they were a bit more absorbent. And these towels are also somewhat small in size, compared to others we tested.

Cutest Hooded Baby Towel

Hudson Baby was the winner for cutest hooded baby towel that we tested—these towels are adorable! And they are a decent quality. We love these character towels—27 designs in all! Big, soft, and cute. Good absorbency in our tests. We recommended washing it a time or two before using, to prevent fuzz. And the price is right: $9 per towel.

Best Budget-Friendly Baby Towel Set

Baby towels may be cute, but they can get pricey in a hurry. We found this set to be the best value: **Luvable Friends** ($6.82 per set) Our testers loved how absorbent these towels are—plus who could resist the cute elephant? A dozen other animal designs as well. Critics say washcloths not as nice as towels.

These towels are 75% cotton with embroidered appliqués on the hoods. That's a nice touch.

CHAPTER 4

Diaper Pails, Potty Seats, Bath, Skin Care

Inside this chapter

Which diaper pail best keeps the stink out of your home? For bath time, who makes the best bathtub, shampoo, lotion and soap for baby? We'll address these topics plus the best baby toothbrushes and toothpaste for baby and the best sunscreen in this chapter.

The Best Diaper Pail

Let's talk diaper pails—there are currently two types on the market: those that use refills (sold by the maker) and those that use kitchen trash bags. Before we get to our picks, here's a quick intro course to diaper pails and how to choose one.

7 Things No One Tells You About Buying A Diaper Pail

1 THE AVERAGE BABY REQUIRES **2300** DIAPER CHANGES IN HIS OR HER FIRST YEAR. That's right, 2300 diaper changes. A staggering figure . . . only made more staggering by figuring out what do with the dirty ones once you've changed baby. Yes, we can hear first-time parents raising their hands right now and saying "Duh! They go in the trash!" We'll get to that later.

Why so many? First time parents are inexperienced when it comes to knowing the signs baby needs a change, so they check baby more frequently. Breastfed babies also poop more often than formula fed babies. But you don't get off easy by using formula: formula-fed babies are more "odiferous" than breastfed babies.

2 DIAPER PAILS VS. REGULAR TRASHCANS: IT'S A STINKY BATTLE. We've heard from a pretty siz-able share of parents who claim they don't need a special diaper pail. A trash can works just fine for them. Maybe they don't have babies eating solids yet or drinking formula, but eventually they'll realize a specialized diaper pail isn't such a bad idea.

Diaper pails often use either deodorizers like baking soda or deodorized plastic liners to keep the stink under control. The effectiveness of such odor control varies widely.

3 **DIAPER BAGS THAT USE REFILL CARTRIDGES OF DEODORIZED PLASTIC CAN GET EXPENSIVE.** Our top choices for diaper pails both use refill cartridges of deodorized plastic to keep down the stink. And the Munchkin pail also releases a shot of baking soda on each diaper for extra deodorizing.

These refill cartridges can really add up. For example, our top choice, the Diaper Dekor Plus refill cartridge holds up to 1160 diapers per cartridge (that means if you have newborn or size one diapers, you might be able to dispose of 1160 diapers before installing a new cartridge). Cost: about $7 per cartridge. But you'll need to use more than one. And likely you won't get 1160 diapers into one cartridge as your baby grows.

So let's say the average per year is four cartridges at $7 each or $28. Then assuming you're changing diapers for three years that's $84. Add in the cost of the Plus itself ($46) and you're talking about $130 for a diaper pail.

4 **YES, DIAPER PAILS THAT USE REGULAR TRASH BAGS ARE CHEAPER, BUT THE TRADE OFF IS THE STINK.** If you choose to go with trash bag liners for your diaper pail, get ready for the smell. They will need to be replaced more frequently. And even if you get odor control kitchen trash bags like Glad OdorShield, there's no guarantee you'll be able to stand the smell after baby starts solid foods. So be aware of the trade off.

5 **SKIP THE ECO-FRIENDLY VERSIONS OF REFILL CARTRIDGES.** Great news for our eco-conscious friends: many diaper pails offer biodegradable refills. Bad news: they may not combat stink as well as the regular kind. We suggest you test out one pack of biodegradable refills rather than invest in several. Biodegradable are slightly more expensive than regular, by the way.

6 **IF YOU'RE WORRIED YOUR CLOTH DIAPERS WILL STINK UP THE NURSERY, LET US PUT YOUR MIND TO REST.** Follow these tips to keep your the nursery from stinking with cloth diapers. Scrape baby's poop from the diaper into the toilet using a flushable wipe. Throw the dirty diaper into a diaper pail. Some parents like to soak cloth diapers in a bleach solution or use a pre-soak product with enzymes (like Shout) that "predigest" the poop. Presoaking will help keep down the odor. Every few days, wash as you would your regular clothes. If you have an older washer, you may need to add bleach during the cleaning process.

7 **AVOID TOXIC DEODORANT DISKS IN YOUR DIAPER PAIL OR KITCHEN TRASH.** Older babies and toddlers are attracted to the oddest things. We recommend you avoid deodorant disks that are stuck onto the lid of the diaper pail or kitchen trash can. You don't want to find your toddler sucking on one!

Next up: our diaper pail recommendations—one for a refill pail and the other no-refills.

The Best Diaper Pail (Refill)

After comparing and testing a wide selection of diaper pails, we selected the **Diaper Dekor** brand as our top choice for best diaper pail (refills).

Here's the skinny on the Diaper Decor's three sizes and how much they hold: Mini ($25, holds 25 diapers), Classic ($30, 40 newborn diapers), Plus ($40-$45, 60 newborn diapers). And each pail has different refills with two options (regular or biodegradable). Refills run about $15 for a two-pack that wraps about 1100 diapers. (1100!) Be careful which size refills you buy: the Classic size won't fit in a Plus can.

As you might guess, the Mini is designed for lighter use (grandma's house?) while the bigger Plus version is pitched to folks who want to do less frequent emptying of the pail. The Classic and Plus are available in colors for around $5 more than the white version.

Of all the models, the Plus is most popular—but all the Dekors get generally good marks from readers. No diaper pail can completely seal out the stink and the Dekor's critics (about one in four folks who buy it) say the Munchkin Step works better. But the majority of readers are happy with the Dekor.

As for the refills, the regular ones work better at holding back the stink than the biodegradable, based on reader feedback. Our opinion: the "biodegradable" refills are horrible at blocking odor, the main reason why you'd part with the big bucks to buy one of these pails, right? So stick with the regular refills for the best odor control.

Also Great: Munchkin Step Diaper Pail Powered by Arm & Hammer

Our next favorite diaper pail is a mouthful: **Munchkin Step Diaper Pail Powered by Arm & Hammer** ($65). Let's just call it the Step.

The Step's lockable pail with deodorized bags really works well at stopping odor. Munchkin added a mechanism to sprinkle odor fighting baking soda on each diaper in the pail to improve the deodorizing power.

Reader feedback on this has been trending positive on this pail. Parents praise the lack of odor, saying it seals better than other brands. And the little shot of baking soda from the refillable cartridge seems to do the job, in our testing. It's also easy to replace the bag and remove the dirty diapers.

Perhaps the biggest complaint we hear from readers is what's called the "squish factor." You have to really push the diaper down to get it into the pail—no fun when it's a really full diaper.

And some enterprising toddlers have easily figured out how to get the door open in the base. Let's not visualize. Let's just move on.

Finally, it does take two hands to open the lid, making for tough going if you have your baby in one hand. Still with all it's faults, Munchkin's Arm & Hammer diaper pail is a great option for odor control.

Best No-Refill Diaper Pail

The **Ubbi** steel diaper pail ($65-$80) has a sliding opening with a rubber seal to keep odors in. The reason for the slide? Ubbi told us they think this keeps the smell from wafting out like other diaper pails. And the steel doesn't absorb odors like plastic. Best of all, it uses regular trash bags.

The Ubbi has received positive reviews overall, although it does get some criticism for the sliding opening. We tried it ourselves and thought the slide was a bit sticky, so you may not be able to use it one-handed. Also readers say don't overfill it—the bag can snag on the lid. But it's a lot less expensive than diaper pails that use refills (factoring in refill expense), comes in 15 different colors and patterns . . . and you can actually use this as a trash can after baby is out of diapers.

Wipe Warmers: Not Recommended

These $20 gizmos warm wipes to a comfy 90 degrees, so baby isn't surprised by a cold wipe at 2am. While this sounds like a good idea, there have been a series of safety recalls for these devices, which have caused fires, electric shock and other problems. Besides, you can just warm the wipes up in your hands for a few seconds—voila! Warm wipe without spending $20.

The Best Baby Bathtub

Sometimes, it is the simplest products that are the best. Take baby bathtubs—if you look at the offerings in this category, you'll note some baby bathtubs convert from bath tubs to step stools and then, to small compact cars.

Okay, just kidding on the car, but these products are a good example of brand manager overkill—there's even a $65 baby bathtub on the market that features a "calming whirlpool and massaging bubbles." (Summer, we are looking at you).

So let's keep it simple and stick to basic baby bathtubs. In this section, we break our bathtub recommendations into several categories, based on different parent needs:

◆ Best Bathtub (Overall)
◆ Best For Travel
◆ Best As A Gift
◆ Best Minimalist Bath Tub

The Best Baby Bathtub (Overall)

The **First Years' Sure Comfort Deluxe Newborn to Toddler Tub** is a simple tub which includes a sling and foam pads to better fit a newborn. Use the sling for newborns and then remove as baby grows. Once your child is sitting up, flip the tub from the reclined side to the straight back side and your toddler can use it. Priced at $20, our readers love this tub.

Best Bathtub For Travel

Yes, it's a giant inflatable rubber duck! **Munchkin's White Hot Inflatable Duck Tub** ($12) is great for use both at home and on the road, as it deflates for easy carrying. Also nice: textured bottom and safety disk to warn when water is too hot. And yes, it is super cute for pictures.

Best Bathtub As A Gift

If you are looking for a shower gift, the **Fisher-Price 4-in-1 Sling 'n Seat Tub** ($40) is a reader favorite . . . but it's a bit pricey, so we'll recommend it as best for a gift.

This tub is great for its extended use. Unlike inflatable baby bathtubs that only can be used by kids who can sit up (that is, six months and up), the Fisher Price 4-in-1 sling can be used by newborns, thanks to a mesh sling.

Like many Fisher-Price baby products, this one has little design touches that show the designers have kids—note the hook that lets you hang it up to dry.

Best Minimalist Baby Bathtub

Yes, we know some folks don't have big bathrooms to handle a full-size baby bathtub. If you live in a smaller apartment or condo, a more minimalist baby bathtub may work better. In that case, we'd recommend **Boon's Soak 3-Stage** bathtub ($24).

As the name implies, this can be used for three stages: newborn, infant and toddler. We like the overall design and our readers concur—it's easy to use and easy to clean. And yes, it fits most double sinks in case you don't have a bathtub in your condo.

Best Bath Sling

What's a bath sling? Basically, it's a mesh sling that enables you to give baby a bath in a kitchen sink or larger bathtub.

The **Summer Infant Deluxe Baby Bather** has three reclines and a padded head support. It also folds down so you can store it or take it to Grandma's. Parents like the portability, price ($19-$25) and small size . . . but others complained that it slips around in a big bathtub as there are no rubber grippers on the bottom.

Potty Seats

Potty seats come in two flavors: floor models and inserts. Inserts are molded (and sometimes padded) seats made for smaller bottoms. They are installed on top of the regular toilet seat. Floor models are traditional self-contained units with a base and seat.

Some potty seats start out as floor models and then the seat can be removed and used as an insert on the regular toilet. Our advice: go for the insert only. Yes, you'll need a step stool for your little one to climb up, but it's much easier to transition to a regular toilet if your child is already using one. And think about how excited your child will be to use the same toilet as his parents (trust us, it is a big deal).

The Best Potty Seat

After comparing and testing dozens of potty seat (and cleaning up a lot of messes!), we picked the **Baby Bjorn Toilet Trainer** as the best potty seat.

The Baby Bjorn is a seat insert that attaches to a full-size toilet seat. It comes equipped with a unique adjustment dial to fit most toilet seats. It also includes an angled splash-guard (handy to guide pee into the toilet bowl) and a contoured, molded seat for tushy comfort. Price: $35.

In the budget-friendly category of potty seats, we think the **Munchkin Sturdy Potty Seat** ($10) is a good

bet. Our toddler testers loved this contoured potty seat with non-skid edge. Great for travel. Fits best on round toilets, but ok for elongated ones as well.

Best Floor Potty

Floor potties aren't our first choice when toilet training (we prefer toilet inserts), but we know quite a few readers love them. So here's our pick: **Nuby My Real Potty Training Toilet** ($30). Yes, this one looks like

an adult toilet—and that's the point. Toddlers love mimicking adults. This potty is easy to clean and even makes a flushing sound.

Skin, Teeth & Hair Care

New for this edition, we review the best baby shampoo, lotion and soap, plus the best diaper rash cream. Also: we pick our favorite baby toothbrush and toothpaste.

The Best Baby Shampoo & Soap

We lathered up 20 babies with over 20 different brands of baby shampoo/body wash to find the Best Baby Shampoo—and the winner is **Puracy Natural Baby Shampoo & Body Wash** ($23 for a two-pack).

The best shampoo for baby should be tear free and gently clean with the fewest natural ingredients that are hypoallergenic—and without using potentially carcinogenic chemicals (such as formaldehyde-releasing 1,4-dioxane), sulphates or phthalates.

We prefer scent free or lightly scented shampoos and don't recommend trendy herbal ingredients (like lavender). Why? These can cause potential allergic reactions. Yes, it is ironic: many "natural" and "organic" baby care shampoos and lotions contain HIGHLY allergenic ingredients (example: almonds, chamomile). Avoid any products with milk, almonds or peanuts (also called arachis oil).

FYI: Baby shampoos can typically be used as body wash on most babies. If your baby has eczema, check out our recommendations for best baby soaps below.

Priced at 72¢ per ounce, Puracy is made with coconut-based cleansers, which based on our independent research are gentler on baby's skin and scalp than traditional detergents. The ingredients also include sea salt (yes, Himalayan Pink sea salt), pink grapefruit oil and a bunch of natural, plant based and biodegradable preservatives.

But what do parents think? Is it gentle on baby's skin? Is it "tear free"? Yes, most of our readers thought the shampoo was gentle with few reports of rash or other irritations—and that was verified with our own hands-on tests.

However, we should point out that a significant minority of our readers didn't think it was as "tear free" as stalwarts like Johnson and Johnson's Baby Shampoo.

Interestingly, the company addresses these complaints by saying this:

"When it comes to being 'tear-free,' we did test this product to be gentle and non-burning to the eyes. We first tested it on ourselves (employees) and only afterward on our little ones. We made many revisions along with many discussions before labeling our product as such. Our formula does not contain any eye numbing agents like most tear-free shampoos.

"Instead, it contains a very gentle blend of cleansers and moisturizers. If you notice any discomfort, it is possible that the cleansers are attempting to clean the mucous from your eyes. This could result in some friction (less mucous acting as a lubricant) and, therefore, discomfort. It is typically very short-lived and eradicated by rinsing out with some fresh water."

Bottom line: despite the small numbers of folks who think this shampoo isn't as tear-free as it should be, Puracy is an excellent choice for parents looking for a safe, effective baby shampoo.

Also Great: Aveeno Baby Wash and Shampoo

Aveeno Baby Wash and Shampoo is a great second choice for baby shampoo. Aveeno's claim to fame is that it "cleanses without drying," thanks to its soap-free and tear-free formula that includes oatmeal.

Our readers tell us that the Baby Wash and Shampoo works fine for babies with normal skin, but those with eczema or very dry skin may find it too drying. Our own tests confirmed this—Aveeno Baby Wash worked well, is affordable ($11.88, which is about 36¢ per ounce—50% less expensive than our top pick) and has a pleasant smell. Another bonus: Aveeno Baby Wash is widely available in grocery stores and at big box discounters.

Yes, Aveeno is now owned by Johnson & Johnson, but traces its roots to 1945 when it debuted its first product (soothing bath treatment). The Aveeno Baby care line was launched in 2001. Bottom line: Aveeno Baby Wash and Shampoo ($8.97) is a great option for baby shampoo if you can't find our top pick . . . or think it is too pricey!

Best Budget-Friendly Baby Shampoo

If you had to pick just one iconic brand synonymous with baby care, **Johnson's Baby Shampoo** would probably fit the bill. First debuting in 1953, Johnson's Baby Shampoo runs 24¢ per ounce ($6.40 per bottle), which makes it one of the most affordable baby shampoos on the market (about 30% less expensive than our top pick, Puracy).

To say Johnson's "no more tears" formula was successful is an understatement—as recently as the late 90's, Johnson's had a whopping 75% share of the baby shampoo market.

The smell of Johnson's Baby Shampoo is also iconic—the perfume may remind generations of grandparents of baby bathtime, but some find it overwhelming.

We're betting most people have had their hair washed at least once with Johnson's Baby Shampoo. And besides the price, it's the "no more tears" formula and familiar smell that attract parents.

In the past few years, Johnson's was plagued by controversy over the chemicals in their baby shampoo. Those ingredients under question included formaldehyde-releasing chemicals, phthalates and other potential carcinogens. The good news: Johnson's reworked its formula in 2014 and dropped the questionable ingredients . . . or reduced them to trace amounts.

Let's be honest: Johnson's Baby Shampoo will not win awards for the most all-natural ingredients. Making it mild and tear-free requires chemicals like 1,4-dioxane, which has been linked to cancer in animal studies. Johnson's says their new formulation reduces that chemical to a trace mount (one to four parts per million).

We realize that for many readers the fact that Johnson's Baby Shampoo still contains preservatives like Phenoxyethanol and dyes like Yellow #6 will turn them off to the brand—that's understandable.

In our hands on testing, we found Johnson's Baby Shampoo worked well—the only caveat is that parents tell us it left some babies with hair feeling dry. We didn't personally see that, but we realize that is a perception for some folks.

Best Shampoo Splurge

Do the grandparents want to splurge a little on items for baby? Then you might want to add **Mustela Stelatopia** baby foam shampoo to your baby registry. At $3.06 per ounce (or $15 a bottle), it's no one idea of a bargain, but readers who use it tell us they love it.

Yes, Mustela is from France, but interestingly, at least in France, the brand is like a French version of Johnson & Johnson's (that is, a basic, inexpensive option).

So what do parents like about Mustela? The biggest deal: many parents swear Mustela cleared up or at least improved their babies' cradle cap. What's cradle cap? The Mayo Clinic defines cradle cap as "crusty or oily scaly patches on baby's scalp." This common condition doesn't hurt baby or itch, it just looks unpleasant. Mustela appears to have some curative effect for quite a few parents we've interviewed.

One caveat to Mustela's use for cradle cap: it is no quick fix. A few weeks of continued use is required to see a decline in cradle cap plaques.

Our tests of Mustela as a baby shampoo were positive—the smell is pleasant but not overwhelming. It doesn't irritate the eyes. We also like that Mustela baby shampoo comes in several different forms: liquid, gel or foam. You can also use it as a body soap.

Best Treatment for Cradle Cap

If you haven't been around newborns much, you may be surprised to find that some babies can develop weird skin conditions. Most of them are benign and go away on their own.

Cradle cap is definitely in the "no big deal" category—it is basically patchy scales or flakes on baby's scalp. It freaks out some parents who don't like how it looks . . . and we can understand that.

Dr. Ari Brown, pediatrician and co-author of the *Baby 411* book series has a recommendation: olive oil. That's right, head to the kitchen and grab the can of olive oil. Doesn't matter if it's extra virgin either. We recommend **Zoe Organic Extra Virgin Olive Oil** ($13 for a 33 oz. tin) in case you want a specific brand pick.

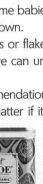

It's a great olive oil for cooking and works as a cradle cap cure too. Just massage it into baby's scalp, leave for a little while and use a comb to lift up the plaques. Then you can shampoo out the oil during regularly scheduled bath time. Also, as we mentioned above, many parents swear by Mustela Baby Shampoo for relief of cradle cap.

Best Soap for Babies with Eczema

What is eczema? It's a skin condition that causes itchy, red and inflamed skin. Some babies are born with it; others develop it after birth. About 30 million Americans suffer from eczema.

Eczema can be related to certain allergies (including food allergies). We recommend visiting with both a dermatologist and an allergist if your child's condition is severe. In the meantime, our top recommended soap for babies with eczema, mild or severe is plain old **Dove**. That's right. Stick with a mild, moisturizing soap with no dyes or strong scents. Dove fits the bill and is very affordable at around $1 per bar.

Other great soap options are made by **Cetaphil** ($5.40 per bar), **Vanicream** ($4 per bar) or **CeraVe** ($7.50 per bar). But stick with bar soaps, no liquids. To create liquid soap, manufacturers add alcohol as an ingredient and alcohol can have a drying effect. Anti-bacterial soaps can be drying as well. Follow it up with the lotion/cream recommendations above.

Best Baby Lotion

Parents often assume they need to put lotion on their baby every day, but unless your baby has very dry skin or eczema, you really only need a moisturizer after baby's bath (and you only need to bathe a newborn every three or four days).

Our top choice for a basic lotion: **Aveeno Baby Calming Comfort Moisturizing Lotion**. ($8.20, 46¢ per ounce). If you prefer to use a lotion without petroleum or mineral oil, consider **Cetaphil Baby Daily Lotion**. It's a bit more expensive at 52¢ an ounce.

If your baby has eczema (see below for discussion), the general advice is "lube 'em up." That's right, use the thickest, greasiest stuff you can stand. Our Dr. Ari Brown, co-author of Baby 411 recommends **Vaseline Intensive Care Jelly Cream** ($1.27 per ounce) as her top choice.

Other cream options: **Eucerin** (lanolin is an ingredient—may cause an allergic reaction; 73¢ per ounce), **CeraVe** (85¢ per ounce) and **Cetaphil** (64¢ per ounce). As Dr. Brown notes: "You need to lube your child up several times a day. As soon as you get your child out of the bathtub, apply the moisturizer (I'm serious—have the tube ready)."

Best Diaper Rash Cream

After testing 13 over-the-counter diaper rash remedies on actual baby butts and consulting with pediatricians who fight the diaper rash battle every day, we pick **Desitin.** Around for over 40 years, Desitin is a diaper rash cream that often tops pediatrician surveys for diaper rash creams. Our informal poll of pediatricians also confirmed Desitin is still among the top diaper rash creams recommended to parents.

Desitin comes in several varieties: Maximum Strength is probably the most popular. Maximum strength has a whopping 40% zinc oxide, beating out Balmex and other zinc oxide options.

Desitin's web site has helpful graphics that illustrate the different severity levels of diaper rash. Also helpful: advice on how much to use on your baby and discount coupons.

What is the downside to Desitin? Desitin isn't called "paste" for nothin'! It is stickier than other creams like Balmex—and that makes it harder to apply, in our tests. And the smell? Well, let's just say it funkier than Balmex.

Speaking of **Balmex Diaper Rash Cream** ($14.50), this brand is our pick for moderate rashes.

The best diaper rash cream creates a moisture barrier that keeps baby's skin from being irritated (moisture + diaper + skin = diaper rash). After testing, we believe the best diaper rash cream is more creamy than sticky, making it easier to apply.

Balmex contains one of the most effective moisture barriers: zinc oxide. Balmex has 11% zinc oxide as its active ingredient plus inactive ingredients like beeswax, mineral oil and microcrystalline wax. Balmex also claims one special ingredient: evening primrose extract, which the company claims helps "inhibit enzymes in stool that are known to irritate skin."

Balmex is priced at as little as 91¢ per ounce in a 16 ounce jar or, if you prefer tubes, you can buy it for about $1.56 per ounce.

Does it work? Our readers swear by it, according to our message boards and email feedback. Parents tell us they like the creamy texture; it's not as sticky as many other zinc oxide diaper rash cream—and we would agree with this after road-testing several diaper rash creams ourselves for this article. The scent isn't bad either.

Best Budget-Friendly Diaper Rash Cream

Yes, it's old school but effective: **Vaseline Petroleum Jelly** is our pick for best budget-friendly diaper rash treatment.

The humble jar of Vaseline Petroleum Jelly in your bathroom has a long and storied history . . . all the way back to 1859. A British chemist, Robert Chesebrough, was traveling through Titusville, PA where petroleum was first discovered. While touring the oil fields, Chesebrough noticed that the grunts doing all the oil drilling were using a byproduct of the process to moisturize and heal cuts and burns. Light bulb!

Once the idea hit him, it took Chesebrough five years to get petroleum jelly to the state he wanted. He purified it three times: filtering it and distilling it to clean the substance, then de-aerating it to remove air bubbles. This triple process removes all impurities so it's safe for everyone's skin, including your baby's. (Not all petroleum jellies are guaranteed as pure, hence our recommendation of the Vaseline brand.)

So how does petroleum jelly help with diaper rash? Petroleum jelly isn't really a moisturizer for your skin per se. Instead, it's very good at holding in moisture—or in the case of diaper rash, keeping moisture out, like pee and poop.

If your baby is suffering from diaper rash Vaseline should be your first line of defense. It's cheap at a mere 33¢ per ounce and easy to find. And it will keep urine and poop off baby's sensitive skin, allowing it to heal.

For our eco-friendly readers, we realize it is easy to diss Vaseline. If the thought of using a petroleum product on your skin is a non-starter, there are "un-petroleum" diaper rash remedies to consider (see earlier in this section). Just remember, these other options may cost considerably more than Vaseline and aren't necessarily any more effective!

Best Diaper Rash Cream for Severe Rashes

Sometimes, you have to bring in the big guns. If your little one's diaper rash goes from mild to severe overnight, we suggest the oddly named but effective **Boudreaux's Butt Paste** ($6.68). Based on our testing, it works effectively to stop severe diaper rash. Boudreaux is available in three formulas, including maximum strength with 40% zinc oxide.

Boudreaux's ingredients are simple. The original formula contains: zinc oxide (16%), castor oil, mineral oil, paraffin, peruvian balsam, white Petrolatum (petroleum jelly).

The natural aloe version switches out the mineral oil and petrolatum and adds aloe vera, beeswax, carnauba wax, citric acid, and hydrogenated caster oil. However, it's more expensive than the regular and maximum strength versions—the natural aloe is $1.75 per ounce

The only complaints we hear are that Butt Paste itself is an unappealing beige color (like putty) and a few babies have had a skin reaction to it, based on reviews posted to parenting message boards.

Also Great: Triple Paste

Another great option for tough-to-tackle diaper rash is **Triple Paste,** which previously was available only by prescription. It contains zinc oxide, petrolatum, corn starch, lanolin, stearyl alcohol, beeswax, bisabolo, cholesterol, glycerine, oat kernal extract and polysorbate 80. It's expensive ($30 for a 16 oz. tub) but our testers say it does the job. A few parents complained it was too thin and has an unpleasant smell. FYI: If your baby has a diaper rash caused by a yeast infection, we would recommend **Triple Paste AF**, an anti-fungal version.

Best Baby Toothbrush

After researching, reviewing and testing 15 baby toothbrushes, we pick the **Jordan Step 1 Baby Toothbrush** ($14) as the best baby toothbrush.

The Jordan Step 1 has soft bristles, a grippy ergonomic handle, and comes in cool colors. We like the visual marking on the bristles to show parents how much toothpaste to use (only about the size of a grain of rice for 6-12 month olds).

Another plus: the Jordan Step 1 is affordable: four brushes for $14. Our testers were happy overall with the brush although some complained the handle was too big for tiny hands and wished the bristles were a bit softer.

Other baby toothbrushes we tested didn't last as long or lacked soft bristles. We also thought gimmicky toothbrushes shaped like bananas or sharks were nice but too expensive—often 30% more than our top pick. There's no reason to waste money on this, especially since toothbrushes need to be replaced every three months.

Want an electric toothbrush? In our tests, the **Oral-B Kids Battery Powered Toothbrushes** ($5.91) performed the best. As you'd guess, you can choose from just about any character for these toothbrushes . . . and, yes, the Disney Frozen version is quite popular.

Be aware this brush vibrates but does not spin—which is fine, as it cleans just as well. And it is a bit loud—so give it a test spin before you do the first brushing so there are no surprises! In our testing, both toddlers and parents preferred this brand of electronic toothbrush.

Also Great: Dr. Brown's Infant to Toddler Toothbrush

Dr. Brown, most famous for their baby bottles, also makes excellent toothbrushes in our opinion. The **Dr. Brown's Infant to Toddler brush** has a soft, flexible handle shaped like an elephant with an elongated trunk. The "ears" stick out to the side so your baby can't shove the brush into her mouth too far. It's priced at $8, with Dr. Brown's Natural Baby Toothpaste included in the purchase. You can also buy just the toothbrush separately.

We're not impressed with Dr. Brown's fluoride-free toothpaste (see our recommendations later in this chapter) so we'd recommend going with just the separate toothbrush if you like this brand. Another issue: a few of our testers (and other parents in online reviews) complained the bristles fell out, a potential hazard to your baby. Others thought the bristles weren't soft enough.

However, most of our testers were pleased with Dr. Brown's baby toothbrush brush overall, so we'll recommend it as a runner-up pick.

Not recommended: Baby Finger Toothbrushes

We tested five different versions of the finger toothbrush, a silicon device that slips over your finger. It typically has soft silicone bristles to massage/brush baby's gums, and later, teeth. After extensive testing and conversations with both parents and pediatricians, we decided not to recommend any of these baby finger toothbrushes. Here's our reasoning:

◆ *Baby finger toothbrushes are very thin and rather delicate, so they didn't last long.* Even babies with only one or two teeth quickly chew the silicone up, requiring replacement.

◆ *In our tests, babies thought it was pretty funny to bite down on them.* Not such a huge problem when they don't have teeth, but, oh boy, when trying to brush even one new tooth, babies could inflict some serious pain! (If you're breastfeeding, you know all about that!). The take home message: once babies have teeth, baby finger toothbrushes aren't easy to use or effective.

◆ *You don't need them.* Dentists and pediatricians agree that gauze squares will wipe clean your baby's gums and later teeth just fine for the first six to nine months or so. Then you can look for a suitable baby toothbrush like those we recommend above.

Bottom line: skip the baby finger toothbrushes.

Best Baby Toothpaste

Parents often ask our resident pediatrician, Dr. Ari Brown, what should I brush my child's teeth with? The simple answer: a fluoride toothpaste. What about those special baby or toddler toothpastes?

We don't recommend them for two reasons. First, they often do NOT have fluoride. Second, baby and toddler toothpastes are very sweet with fruity flavors. In our testing, flavored toothpastes encourage kids to suck on the toothbrush—making it a challenge to actually clean the teeth!

Fluoride is important for cavity-free teeth and is recommended by both pediatric dentists and pediatricians. Yes, there are lots of articles in the fever swamps of the Internet claiming fluoride is dangerous. We understand as a parent you might be concerned that your child is getting too much fluoride from drinking water and toothpaste. If you have such concerns, speak with your pediatrician—she'll have accurate information about fluoride exposure in your area.

Crest Pro-Health Toothpaste is our top choice for best toothpaste. Note we didn't say Kid's Crest—we recommend the adult version. It contains no Triclosan (an antibacterial additive used to combat gingivitis and plaque build up that has become controversial recently). It does contain fluoride, in a form called Stannous Fluoride, which offers good protection from plaque and gingivitis as well as cavities. The best things about Crest? It's affordable (46¢ per ounce) and available everywhere.

Also Great: Tom's of Maine Wicked Cool Fluoride Toothpaste

If you'd prefer a natural alternative, **Tom's of Maine Natural Wicked Cool Fluoride Toothpaste** is another great choice, although it costs more then Crest (about $2 per ounce). While it does come in strawberry and orange-mango, we don't recommend sweet flavors—kids tend to suck on their toothbrushes making brushing more difficult. The Wicked Cool flavor does not contain artificial dyes, sweeteners or flavors.

Best Sunscreen for Babies & Toddlers

After testing 23 sunscreen and sunblock options available for babies and toddlers, as well as doing extensive research into sunscreen chemistry, we pick **Coppertone Ultra Guard 50** as our top choice for the best sunscreen for babies. (FYI: Sunscreen is for babies older than six months of age).

In our opinion (we've been writing about babies and toddlers for 24 years), the best sunscreen is easy to put on a squirming baby or toddler, doesn't smell overwhelming and performs the best in third-party tests. And it must be affordable—you'll be reapplying this often to the sensitive skin of babies and toddlers.

Coppertone Ultra Guard checks off every box: it offers broad spectrum coverage (both UVA & UVB; see below for more info) with a SPF of 50; is available widely in stores and online; comes in large quantities (8 oz) and has very little smell.

In our tests, we think this sunscreen strikes the right balance for babies and toddlers: it doesn't feel too heavy or sticky when applied and is water resistant for about 80 minutes. (We still recommend parents reapply sunscreen every one to two hours whether your child is in a pool or not.) The lack of scent is a major plus with babies or toddlers, who can be picky, as we all know!

Coppertone Ultra Guard runs about $1.37 per ounce online and at stores like Target and Walmart; slightly more in grocery stores. (We've seen on sale for less from time to time). That puts it on the affordable end—sunscreen ranges in price from 50¢ to $5 an ounce.

FYI: Coppertone makes a version of this sunscreen under the WaterBabies brand that works equally well.

What's the best SPRAY sunscreen for babies? Answer: NONE.

We don't recommend spray sunscreen for babies or toddlers. That's because these are difficult to apply evenly. There has been little research done into the health effects on babies or toddlers of inhaling spray sunscreen fumes. To stay on the safe side, we suggest just using lotion.

Best Budget-Friendly Mineral-Based Sunscreen

Mineral based sunscreen can be pricey, we know! Good news: we found **Babyganics** sunscreen ($16.58 for a two-pack of 6 oz. bottles) to be both effective AND easy on the wallet—about $1.38 per ounce. In some cases, this sunscreen was 45% to 65% less per ounce than others we tested.

We loved how well this sunscreen worked, with no fragrances or nanoparticles. It is water resistant to 80 minutes. Critics note it is greasy and difficult to rub in.

Best Sunscreen For Babies With Sensitive Skin

We tried out several popular baby sunscreens that say they are good for sensitive skin. After testing, we thought **Baby Bum** was the best bet for those babies with sensitive skin. This smooth sunscreen won over our testers with its effectiveness: 80 minutes water resistant and broad spectrum UVA/UVB protection. The ingredients (coconut oil, shea butter and cocoa butter) made babies with sensitive skin happy, said our testers.

Best Baby Sun Hat

Sunscreen is just one arrow in your quiver when it comes to protecting baby from the sun's harmful rays. A good sun hat is just as important.

Besides looking terribly cute, hats help keep sun off baby's face, neck and ears—and that's something pediatricians recommend since babies under six months aren't old enough yet to wear sunscreen.

Consider these quick tips for finding the best baby sun hat:

◆ *Baby hats come in three basic styles: wide brim, safari-style and bucket hats*. Each has its fans—for smaller babies, safari-style hats help keep sun off the back and ears. Older babies do better with wide brim or bucket hats.

◆ *Look for adjustable sizing with toggles.* All the hats in this article were recommended by our readers for their ease of adjustability.

◆ *How compact does it fold?* The best baby sun hats collapse into a small shape for transport.

◆ *Consider throwing an extra hat in your diaper bag for those surprise sunny days.* We love having a spare hat around for just such occasions.

After asking our readers for their favorites and doing independent research on our own, here are the baby sun hats we'd recommend.

Best Wide Brim Hat

SimpliKids UPF 50+ UV Ray Sun Protection Wide Brim Baby Sun Hat ($15-$19). Loved this super cute hat that dries quickly with adjustable drawstring with toggle for sizing. 20+ colors and patterns. Caveat: a bit floppy.

Best Safari-Style Hat

i play. by green sprouts Baby Girls' Sun Hat ($10.50- $21). One of our favorite brands, this hat has a longer section to cover the neck and a baseball-hat style brim. Love the adjustability. Caveat: sizing can run small.

sun hats

Best Budget-Friendly Baby Sun Hat

Durio Baby Sun Hat ($10 to $12). Love this bucket-style hat with great bang for the buck. Nice quality with 50+ UPF protection and contrasting inside fabric.

Best Baby Scale

Watching your baby's weight is an important part of a newborn's growth and development. We tested nine baby scales, checking for ease of use, accuracy and affordability. Here are the winners.

Best Budget-Friendly Baby Scale

We know, why spend a fortune on a baby scale when you use it for a short period of time? We hear you—and you don't have to spend a fortune to find an accurate, easy to use scale. For best budget-friendly baby scale, we think **Beuerer BY80** ($37.70) has the best bang for the buck. Love the large, backlit LCD display.

Best Multi-Function Baby Scale

If you are looking for a baby scale that can covert to one that can be used by older kiddos and even adults, we'd suggest the **MOMMED baby scale** ($52). We tried out a few models that claim to be convertible, but we thought this one was the best bet.

We liked the longer-use design of this scale, which morphs into a scale for toddlers, kids and even adults up to 220 lbs. Also nice: it can be used for height measurements for infants.

Best App-Enabled Baby Scale

Most baby scales we tested had one glaring omission when it came to features: no way to automatically track weight in a smartphone app. And yes, there are expensive scales that do this, but we thought **GreaterGood's Smart Baby Scale** ($50) did a great job at a price that is much easier on the wallet.

This excellent scale sends measurements to an easy-to-use app via Bluetooth to track your baby's weight. Very accurate. We liked the compact design with folding tray. The scale weighs down to tenth of an ounce.

Best Nasal Aspirator

What's the second most common reason parents call a doctor for infants? Nasal congestion! (#1 is fever). To the rescue come nasal aspirators, which promise relief for unhappy kiddos.

But do they really work? We tried out several gadgets that promise relief for nasal congestion and consulted with pediatricians about best practices. Here are our picks—and a simple remedy that doesn't involve a gadget! As always, we recommend consulting with a doctor about your baby's congestion and whether an aspirator is recommended to use for your baby.

Parent Favorite

The **NoseFrida Snot Sucker** (their words, not ours) is a low-tech solution ($15) to relieve congestion. One end goes in baby's nostril. Then this is attached to a tube, which a parent sucks on to remove mucus. Yes, there is a filter to prevent this from backing up into your mouth! We know, yuck. NoseFrida has a cult-like parent following—fans just love this thing since it is effective and non-invasive. And there are no batteries to worry about.

Simple remedy: Saline drops/sprays

If you ask pediatricians what they'd recommend to treat nasal congestion in infants and toddlers, they will universally recommend saline nose spray. **Little Remedies Nasal Spray** ($4.19) is a good example. Saline drops or sprays are a mix of salt and water and that's the easiest (and most gentle) way of breaking up mucus in the nose. Not only are saline drops affordable, they don't run the risk of side effects.

Getting overzealous when using a nasal aspirator like the NoseFrida can irritate the lining of the nose and possibly cause nosebleeds.

CHAPTER 5

Baby Clothes, Diapers, Wipes

Inside this chapter

What the heck is a "Onesie"? How many clothes does your baby need? How come such little clothes have such big price tags? We unravel these mysteries in this chapter, plus give our top brand picks for baby clothes. Next, let's talk diapers—how to save and top brands for both disposable and cloth.

Baby Clothes

So you thought all the big-ticket items were taken care of when you bought the crib and other furniture? Ha! It's time to prepare for your baby's "layette," a French word that translated literally means "spending large sums of cash on tiny clothes." But, of course, there are some creative (dare we say, sneaky?) ways of keeping your layette bills down.

At this point, you may be wondering just what does your baby need? Sure you've seen those cute ruffled dresses and sailor suits—but what does your baby really wear everyday?

Meet the layette, a collection of clothes and accessories that your baby will use daily. While your baby's birthday suit was free, outfitting him in something more "traditional" will cost some bucks. In fact, a recent study estimated that parents spend $13,000 on clothes for a child by the time he or she hits 18 years of age—and that sounds like a conservative estimate to us. Baby clothes translate into a $20 billion business for children's clothing retailers.

7 Things No One Tells You About Buying Baby Clothes

1 **IGNORE BABY STORES' RECOMMENDED LISTS.** Surprise, many stores load up their recommended baby clothes lists with unnecessary items (baby kimono, anyone?). See our "Baby Bargains" Layette later in this chapter for the real deal.

2 **SIZING—YEAH, IT'S CONFUSING.** Most baby clothes come in a range of sizes rather than one specific size ("newborn to 3 months" or "3-6 months"). For first time parents buying for a newborn, we recommend you buy "3-6 month" sizes (instead of newborn sizes). Why? Because the average newborn will grow out of "newborn" sizes way too fast. The exception to this rule: preemies and multiples, who tend to be on the small side.

No matter how big or small your newborn, a smart piece of advice: keep all receipts and tags so you can exchange clothes for larger sizes—you may find you're into six-month sizes by the time your baby hits one month old! (Along the same lines, don't wash all those new baby clothes immediately. Wash just a few items for the initial few weeks. Keep all the other items in their original packaging to make returns easier).

3 **YOUR BABY WILL OUTGROW CLOTHES MUCH FASTER THAN YOU THINK!** Babies double their birth weight by five months . . . and triple it by one year! On average, babies grow ten inches in their first year of life. Given those stats, you can understand why we don't recommend stocking up on "newborn" size clothes.

Also: remember, you can always buy more later if you need them. In fact, this is a good way to make use of those close friends and relatives who stop by and offer to "help" right after you've suffered through 36 hours of hard labor—send them to the store! FYI: our supply list should last for the first month or two of your baby's life.

4 **YOUR BABY'S DEVELOPMENT FACTORS INTO CLOTHING.** If you're new to this baby thing, you may be wondering how to pair the right clothing with your baby's developmental stage (if you're back for another round, think of this as a refresher). Here's a little primer on ages and stages.

◆ **0-3 months:** Newborns aren't even lifting their heads and they aren't able to do much besides eat, sleep and poop. Stick with sleepers, wearable blankets, and nightgowns for these guys. They don't need overalls or shirts and pants. Look for items sized by weight if possible since 0-3 month sizes can be all over the board.

◆ **3-6 months:** By the end of this stage your little one will be rolling over, sitting up and sleeping somewhat less. Still need those sleepers, but you're probably going to expand the wardrobe to include a few more play clothes. Two new items you will need now: bibs and socks. Depending on your baby's growth, you may find that you're buying nine and 12-month sizes.

◆ **6-12 months:** Finally, your baby is crawling, standing, maybe even cruising. At the end of a year she's likely tried those first tentative steps! Play clothes are a layette mainstay during these months. You'll also need good, no-skid socks that stay on (or very flexible shoes). You may find you're buying into the 18-month sizes.

5 **YOU'RE GOING TO SPEND QUALITY TIME WITH YOUR WASHER.** You may wonder, if you follow our list, how much laundry will you do? The answer: there is no answer. Factors such as whether you use cloth or disposable diapers (cloth can leak more; hence more laundry) and how much your baby spits up will greatly determine the laundry load. Another factor: breast versus bottle-feeding. Bottle-fed babies have fewer poops (and hence, less laundry from possible leaks). An "average" laundry cycle with our layette list would be every two to three days, assuming breast feeding, disposable diapers and an average amount of spit-up. Hint: if your washing machine is on its last legs, this might be something to upgrade before baby arrives.

6 **SECOND-HAND BABY CLOTHES = BIG SAVINGS.** Especially when you're talking about infant clothing. After all, infants don't do much damage to their clothes. They aren't playing in puddles, sucking down OtterPops or finger painting yet. So you can bet the wear and tear on used infant clothing is minimal.

Yes, there are national resale chains that specialize in kids clothes—Once Upon a Child (onceuponachild.com) is a reader favorite. But a quick Google search should uncover local stores.

Safety tip: make sure any second-hand clothes you buy don't have hazards like drawstrings or easy-to-detach buttons or bows.

7 **ONE SIZE DOES NOT FIT ALL.** A six month-size t-shirt is a six-month-size t-shirt, right? Wrong. For some reason, baby clothing companies have yet to synchronize their watches when it comes to sizes. Hence, a clothing item that says "six-month size" from one manufacturer can be just the same dimensions as a "twelve-month size" from another.

All this begs the question: how can you avoid widespread confusion? First, open packages to check out actual dimensions. Take your baby along and hold items up to her to gauge whether they'd fit. Second, note whether items are pre-shrunk—you'll probably have to ask (if not, allow for shrinkage). Third, don't key on length from head to foot. Instead, focus on the length from neck to crotch—a common problem is items that seem roomy but are too tight in the crotch.

Finally, forget age ranges and pay more attention to labels that specify an infant's size in weight and height, which are much more accurate. To show how widely sizing can vary, check out the following chart. We compared "six-month" t-shirts from six major clothing makers (sold on Amazon.com) plus two popular web sites, Hanna Andersson, and Baby Gap. Here's what these six-month t-shirts really translated to in terms of a baby's weight and height:

What a six month t-shirt really means

MAKER	WEIGHT	HEIGHT
BABY GAP	17-22 LBS.	27-29"
CARTER'S/OSHKOSH	12.5-16.5 LBS.	24-26.5"
GYMBOREE	17-22 LBS.	25-29"
HANNA ANDERSSON	14-21 LBS.	26-30"
GERBER	16-20 LBS.	26-28"
LITTLE ME	12-16 LBS.	24-27"
LUVABLE FRIENDS	16.5-20.5 LBS.	26.5-28.5"
SPASILK	12-18 LBS.	24-26.5"

Here's another secret from the baby clothing trade: the more expensive the brand, the more roomy the clothes. Conversely, cheap items usually have the skimpiest sizing. What about the old wives' tale that you should just double your baby's age to find the right size (that is, buying twelve-month clothes for a six-month old?). That's bogus—as you can see, sizing is so all over the board that this rule just doesn't work.

The "Baby Bargains" Layette

Let's talk quality when it comes to baby clothes.

First, you want clothing that doesn't shrink. Look at the washing instructions. "Cold water wash/low dryer setting" is your clue that this item has NOT been pre-shrunk. Also, do the instructions tell you to wash with "like colors?" This may be a clue that the color will run. Next check the detailing. Are the seams sewn straight? Are they reinforced, particularly on the diaper area?

Go online and check message boards for posts on different brands. On our boards (Babybargains.com), parents comment frequently on whether a brand shrinks, has plenty of diaper room, falls apart after a few washings, etc. Spend a little time online to get some intel on the best brands—and which ones to avoid.

Now, let's get to the list:

◆ **T-Shirts.** Oh sure, a t-shirt is a t-shirt, right? Not when it comes to baby t-shirts. These t-shirts could have side snaps, snaps at the crotch (also known as infant bodysuits, Onesies, creepers) or over-the-head openings. If you have a child who is allergic to metal snaps (they leave a red ring on the skin), you might want to consider over-the-head t-shirts. (FYI: While some folks refer to Onesies as a generic item, the term Onesie is a registered trademark brand by Gerber.)

By the way, is a t-shirt an outfit or an undergarment? Answer: it's both. In the summer, you'll find Onesies with printed patterns that are intended as outfits. In the winter, most stores just sell white or pastel Onesies, intended as undergarments.

How many? T-shirts usually come in packs of three. Our recommendation is to buy two packages of three (or a total of six shirts) of the side-snap variety. We also suggest buying two packs of over-the-head t-shirts. This way, if your baby does have an allergy to the snaps, you have a backup. Later you'll find the snap-at-the-crotch t-shirts to be most convenient since they don't ride up under clothes.

◆ **Gowns.** These are one-piece gowns with elastic at the bottom. They are used as sleeping garments in most cases. (We'll discuss more pros/cons of gowns later in this chapter.)

How many? This is a toss-up. If you want to experiment, go for one or two of these items. If they work well, you can always go back and get more later.

◆ **Sleepers.** This is the real workhorse of your infant's wardrobe, since babies usually sleep most of the day in the first months. Also known as stretchies, sleepers are most commonly used as pajamas for infants. They have feet, are often made of flame-retardant polyester, and snap up the front. As a side note, we've seen an increase in the numbers of cotton sleepers in recent years. Another related item: cotton long johns for baby. These are similar to sleepers, but don't have feet (and hence, may necessitate the use of socks in winter months).

One parent emailed us asking if she was supposed to dress her baby in pants, shirts, etc. or if it was OK to keep her daughter in sleepers all day long. She noted the baby was quite comfortable and happy. Of course, you can use sleepers exclusively for the first few months. We certainly did. As we've said all along, a comfortable baby is a happy parent!

How many? Because of their heavy use, we recommend parents buy at least four to eight sleepers.

 ◆ ***Blanket Sleepers/wearable blankets.*** These are heavyweight, footed one-piece garments made of polyester. Used often in winter, blanket sleepers usually have a zipper down the front. In recent years, we've also seen quite a few fleece blanket sleepers, their key advantage being a softer fabric and a resistance to pilling.

Another option is a wearable blanket or swaddling blanket. See near the end of Chapter 3 for our top recommendations. You may want to put a t-shirt on baby and then wrap her up in a swaddling blanket or wearable blanket.

How many? If you live in a cold climate or your baby is born in the winter, you may want to purchase two to four of these items. As an alternative to buying blanket sleepers, you could put a t-shirt on underneath a sleeper or stretchie for extra warmth.

 ◆ ***Coveralls.*** One-piece play outfits, coveralls (also known as rompers) are usually cotton or cotton/poly blends. Small sizes (under 6 months) may have feet, while larger sizes don't.

How many? Since these are really play clothes and small infants don't do a lot of playing, we recommend you only buy two to four coveralls for babies less than four months of age. However, if your child will be going into daycare at an early age, you may need to start with four to six coveralls.

 ◆ ***Booties/socks.*** These are necessary for outfits that don't have feet (like gowns and coveralls). As your child gets older (at about six months), look for the kind of socks that have rubber skids on the bottom (they keep baby from slipping when learning to walk).

How many? Three to four pairs are all you'll need at first, since baby will probably be dressed in footed sleepers most of the time.

◆ ***Sweaters.*** How many? Most parents will find one sweater is plenty (they're nice for holiday picture sessions). Avoid all-white sweaters for obvious reasons!

 ◆ ***Hats.*** Believe it or not, you'll still want a light cap for your baby in the early months of life, even if you live in a hot climate. Babies lose a large amount of heat from their heads, so protecting them with a cap or bonnet is a good idea. And don't expect to go out for a walk in the park without the baby's sun hat either.

How many? A couple of hats would be a good idea—sun hats in summer, warmer caps for winter. We like the safari-style hats best (they have flaps to protect the ears and neck).

◆ ***Snowsuit/bunting.*** Similar to the type of fabric used for blanket sleepers, buntings also have hoods and covers for the hands. Most buntings are like a sack and don't have leg openings, while snowsuits do. Both versions usually have zippered fronts.

FYI: Snowsuits and buntings should NOT be worn by infants when they ride in a car seat. Why? Thick fabric on these items can compress in an accident, compromising the infant's safety in the seat. So how can you keep your baby warm in an infant car seat? There are car seat covers that fit over the top of the car seat to keep baby warm. Cozy Cover (Cozy-Cover.com, $20), makes a variety of styles and fabrics to protect your child from the cold or the sun.

How many? Only buy one of these if you live in a climate where you need it. Even with a Colorado winter, we got away with layering clothes on our baby, then wrapping him in a blanket for the walk out to a warmed-up car. If you live in a city without a car, you might need two or three snowsuits for those stroller rides to the market.

◆ **Kimonos.** Just like the adult version. Some are zippered sacks with a hood and terry-cloth lining. You use them after a bath.

How many? None. We recommend you pass on the kimonos and instead invest in good quality towels.

◆ **Saque Sets.** Two-piece outfits with a shirt and diaper cover.
How many? Forget buying these as well.

◆ **Bibs.** These come in two versions, believe it or not. The little, tiny bibs are for the baby that occasionally drools. The larger versions are used when you begin feeding her solid foods (at about six months). Don't expect to be able to use the drool bibs later for feedings, unless you plan to change her carrot-stained outfit frequently.

How many? Skip the drool bibs. The exception: if your baby really can't keep dry because he's drooling the equivalent of a bathtub full every day, consider buying a few of these. When baby starts eating solid foods, you'll need at least three or four large bibs. One option: plastic bibs for feeding so you can just sponge them off after a meal.

◆ **Washcloths and Hooded Towels.** OK, so these aren't actually clothes, but baby washcloths and hooded towels are a necessity. Why? Because they are small and easier to use . . . plus they're softer than adult towels and washcloths.

How many? At first, you'll probably need only three sets of towels and washcloths (you get one of each per set). But as baby gets older and dirtier, invest in a few more washcloths to spot clean during the day.

◆ **Receiving Blankets.** You'll need these small, cotton blankets for all kinds of uses: to swaddle the baby, as a play quilt, or even for an extra layer of warmth on a cold day.

How many? We believe you can never have too many of these blankets, but since you'll probably get a few as gifts, you'll only need to buy two or three yourself. A total of seven to eight is probably optimal.

Baby Clothes to Avoid

◆ **Clothing that Leads to Diaper Changing Gymnastics.** It's pretty obvious that some designers of baby clothing have never had children of their own. What else could explain outfits that snap up the back, have super tiny head, leg and arm openings, and snaps in inconvenient places (or worse, no snaps at all)? One mother we spoke with was furious about outfits that have snaps only down one leg, requiring her baby to be a contortionist to get into and out of the outfit.

Our advice: stay away from outfits that don't have easy access to the diaper. Look instead for snaps or zippers down the front of the outfit or on the crotch. If your baby doesn't like having things pulled over his head, look for shirts with wide, stretchie necklines.

◆ **Shoes for newborns.** Developmentally, babies don't need shoes until after they become quite proficient at walking (around 11 to 14 months). In fact, it's better for their muscle development to go barefoot or wear socks. While those expensive baby Merrells or Air Jordans might look cute, they're really a supreme waste of money.

Once your baby (now a toddler) masters walking, *then* you need shoes. Here's our thoughts.

First, look for shoes that have the most flexible soles. You'll also want fabrics that breath and stretch, like canvas and leather—stay away from vinyl shoes. The best brands we found were recommended by readers. *Robeez* (robeez.com, a division of Stride Rite) have soft, skid-resistant soles and are machine washable. They start at $24 for a basic pair. Another reader recommended New Zealand-made *Bobux* shoes ($35, bobux.com). These cute leather soft soles "do the trick by staying on extremely well," according to a reader. Finally, we also like *PediPeds* (pediped.com). The soft-soled shoes are hand stitched and most are made of leather. They are sized from 0 to five years and start at $15.

◆ **Drool bibs.** These tiny bibs are intended for small infants who drool all over everything. Or infants who spit-up frequently. Our opinion: they're pretty useless—they're too small to catch much drool or spit-up.

When you do buy bibs, stay away from the ones that tie. Bibs that snap or have Velcro are much easier to get on and off. Another good bet: bibs that go on over the head (and have no snaps or Velcro). Why? Older babies can't pull them off by themselves.

Stay away from the super-size vinyl bibs that cover the arms, since babies who wear them can get too hot and sweaty. However, we do recommend you buy a few regular-style vinyl bibs for travel. You can wash them off much more easily than the standard terry-cloth bibs.

◆ **A toss-up: gowns.** The jury is still out on whether gowns are useful. We thought they were a waste of money, but more than one parent we interviewed mentioned that they used the gowns when a baby had colic (that persistent crying condition; see our other book *Baby 411* for a discussion). Folks believe that the extra room in the gown made her baby more comfortable. Still others praise gowns for their easy access to diapers, making changes easy, especially in the middle of the night. Finally, parents in hot climates say gowns keep their infants more comfortable. So, you can see there's a wide range of opinions on this item.

The Best Baby Clothes Brands

Walk into any store and you'll see a blizzard of brand names for baby clothes. Which ones stand up to frequent washings? Which ones have snaps that stay snapped? Which are a good value for the dollar? We asked our readers to divide their favorite clothing brands/stores into three categories: best bets, good but not great and skip it.

The Best Bets tend to be clothes that were not only stylish but also held up in the wash. The fabric was usually softer and pilled less. Customer service also comes into play with the best brands. Hanna Andersson is a great example of a company that bends over backwards for their customers. Gymboree, on the other hand, seems to be less satisfactory for many parents, souring them on the brand. Keep in mind, some brands are pricey, so look for sales and second hand deals. Or just point Grandma to these sites!

Good but not Great clothes were pretty good, just not as soft or as stylish as Best Bets. The Skip-It brands were most likely the poorest quality: they shrunk in the wash, pilled up or fell apart. Inconsistent sizing was also a problem with brands like Gerber and George by Walmart.

Garage & Yard Sales
Nine Tips to Get The Best Bargains

It's an American bargain institution—the garage sale. Sure you can save money on baby clothes online or get a deal at a department store sale. But there's no comparing to the steals you can get at your neighbor's garage sale.

We love getting email from readers who've found great deals at garage sales. How about 25¢ Onesies, a snowsuit for $1, barely used high chairs for $5? But getting the most out of garage sales requires some pre-planning. Here are the insider tips from our readers:

1 **CHECK CRAIGSLIST FIRST.** Many folks advertise their garage sales a few days before the event— zero in on the ads/posts that mention kids/baby items to keep from wasting time on sales that won't be fruitful. Neighborhood message boards like Next Door are also good.

2 **BECOME A GPS NINJA.** Plot your route to avoid doubling back, factoring in travel time.

3 **START EARLY.** The professional bargain hunters get going at the crack of dawn. If you wait until mid-day, all the good stuff will be gone. An even better bet: if you know the family, ask if you can drop by the day before the sale. That way you have a first shot before the competition arrives. One trick: if it's a neighbor, offer to help set-up for the sale. That's a great way to get those "early bird" deals.

4 **DO THE "BOX DIVE."** Many garage sale hosts will just dump kids clothes into a big box, all jumbled together in different sizes, styles, etc. Figuring out how to get the best picks while three other moms are digging through the same box is a challenge. The best advice: familiarize

Some of these brands sell direct; others just through retailers.

Best Bets

Baby Gap	(800) GAP-STYLE	gap.com
Carter's	(770) 961-8722	carters.com
First Impressions		macys.com
Flap Happy	(800) 234-3527	flaphappy.com
H & M		hm.com
Hanna Andersson		hannaandersson.com
Janie and Jack		janieandjack.com
Kissy Kissy		kissykissyonline.com
Little Me	(800) 533-5497	littleme.com
LL Bean		llbean.com
Boden All Baby		bodenusa.com
Old Navy		oldnavy.com

clothes

yourself with the better name brands in this chapter and pluck out the best bets as fast as possible. Then evaluate the clothes away from the melee.

5 CONCENTRATE ON "FAMILY AREAS." A mom here in Colorado told us she found garage sales in Boulder (a college town) were mostly students getting rid of electronics, clothes and other junk (sadly, a used beer pong table isn't useful in a nursery). A better bet was nearby Louisville, a suburban bedroom community with lots of families.

6 HAGGLE. Prices on big-ticket items (that is, anything over $5) are usually negotiable. Another great tip we read in the newsletter *Cheapskate Monthly*: to test out products, carry a few "C" and "D" batteries with you to garage sales. Why? Some swings, bouncers and other gear use such batteries. Pop in your test batteries to make sure items are in good working order!

7 SMALL BILLS. Take small bills with you to sales—lots of $1's and a few $5's. Why? When negotiating over price, slowly counting out small bills makes the seller feel like they are getting more money. A wad of 20 $1's for a high chair feels like a more substantial offer than a $20 bill.

8 DON'T BUY A USED CRIB OR CAR SEAT. Old cribs may not meet current safety standards. It's also difficult to get replacement parts for obscure brands. Car seats are also a second-hand no-no—you can't be sure it wasn't in an accident, weakening its safety and effectiveness. And watch out for clothing with drawstrings, loose buttons or other safety hazards.

9 BE CREATIVE. See a great stroller but the fabric is dirty? And non-removable so you can't throw it in the washing machine? Take a cue from one dad we interviewed. He takes dirty second-hand strollers or high chairs to a car wash and blasts them with a high-pressure hose! Voila! Clean and useable items are the result. For a small investment, you can rehabilitate a dingy stroller into a showpiece.

OshKosh B'Gosh	(800) 692-4674	oshkosh.com
Sarah's Prints	(888) 477-4687	sarasprints.com
Tea collection		teacollection.com
Wes & Willy		wesandwilly.com
Zutano		zutano.com

Good But Not Great

Children's Place		childrensplace.com
Good Lad of Philadelphia		goodlad.com
Target (Little Me, Carter's Just One You, Halo, Circo)		target.com

Skip It: Gerber, Hanes, Disney, Carter's Just One Year at Target, George by Walmart.

Top Picks For Day Care, Weekends & Special Occasions

What clothing brands are best? Well, there is no one correct answer. An outfit that's perfect for day care (that is, to be trashed in Junior's first painting experiment) is different from an outfit for a weekend outing with friends. And dress-up occasions may require an entirely different set of clothing criteria. Hence, we've divided our clothing brand recommendations into three areas: good (day care), better (weekend wear) and best (special occasions). While some brands make items in two or even three categories, here's how we see it:

Day Care & Play. For everyday comfort (and day-care situations), basic brands like Carter's, Little Me, and OshKosh are your best bets. We also like the basics (when on sale) at Baby Gap (Gap Kids) for day-care wardrobes. For great price to value, take a look at Old Navy and Target.

Weekend Outings. What if you have a miniature golf outing planned with friends? Or a visit to Grandma's house? The brands of better-made casual wear we like best include Baby Gap and Flapdoodles. Also recommended: Jake and Me (now part of the Gap), and Wes and Willy. For online sites, we like the clothes in Hanna Andersson and Boden's All Baby as good brands, especially on sale.

Special Occasion. Yes, holidays and other special occasions call for special outfits. We like Janie and Jack (janieandjack.com) for that!

The Best Toddler Pajamas

Our top pick for best toddler pajamas is **Burt's Bees Unisex Pajamas** (2-piece set). These PJs performed well in our testing, are made of organic cotton and are reasonably affordable at $16 (some patterns/sizes are lower).

We researched 15 different brands of cotton toddler two-piece pajamas to see which were softest, shrunk least and didn't break the bank. Of those, we narrowed the list down to the top five choices, based on our reader feedback, online best-seller status and availability. We purchased samples of each brand and then starting the testing: washing, measuring for shrinkage and gauging softness.

After we tested the pajama samples (see below for details on how they were tested), we crowned a winner: Burt's Bees Unisex Pajamas were among the softest and had no shrinkage after washing. The price was surprisingly reasonable, roughly between ten and twenty bucks per set—it varies by size and pattern. Another plus: they are the only ones we tested that are made of organic cotton and they are Global Organic Textile Standard (GOTS) approved.

What's not to like? The company sews a tag onto the back outside neckline and pants—a few of our readers' toddlers found this to be a tad itchy, especially near the stitching.

But with that tiny caveat, we think Burt's Bees toddler pajamas are the best.

The Best Budget Toddler Pajamas

The crown for the best budget-friendly PJ's goes to **Simple Joys By Carter's.**

The brand sells 3-piece sets of PJs for $27 ($9 each) Caveat: some shirts have appliques which may be itchy.

Also Great: Amazon Essentials Toddler 2-Piece Pajamas

Amazon's own brand is another good budget-friendly PJ pick—we liked the cute designs and overall quality. The negatives: some designs are screen printed so they feel a bit rough on the outside of the garment. Another bummer: Amazon Essentials PJs shrunk the most (7%-9%), about double that of other brands. On the plus side, the sizing is more generous (that is, larger) to start.

The Best Toddler Pajama Splurge

Soft, soft, soft! **Aden + Anais pajama** sets aren't cheap ($25-$49), but they were judged the most soft in our tests. And shrinkage was at a minimum. Of course, A+A is famous for their cute designs, carried over from their excellent swaddle blanket line to pajamas.

Also Great: Hanna Andersson Toddler Pajamas

Priced at a whopping $42-$46 for a two piece set, **Hanna Andersson** toddler pajamas are definitely expensive. But readers who are fans of this brand tell us the super soft organic cotton fabric is very durable. Mostly available at Hanna Andersson's site and stores, check brand's sale section for good deals. A great gift idea.

Shopping Tip: Planning for Shrinkage

Yes, cotton shrinks. But shrinkage varies by brand.

When we tested toddler pajamas, we were surprised to see that even when we followed the washing instructions scrupulously, shrinkage occurred whether the pajama brand was super affordable or outrageously expensive. The shrinkage was as much as 9% in some cases.

And oddly the pants didn't always shrink at the same rate as the tops.

In case you're curious, the Amazon Essentials toddler pajamas shrank the most in our survey: between 7% and 9%. Burt's Bees and Aden + Anais shrank the least.

Regardless, you'll be better off buying the next size up to account for the shrinkage. Especially if you like to throw all the clothes in together and wash them on "normal" rather than delicate. As parents, we often forgot to follow washing instructions to a T—and then paid the price when a beloved pair of pajamas shrunk too much in an initial washing.

What about shopping for pajamas at yard or church sales? Second hand pjs are a great idea for infants and young toddlers.

Children under three probably won't wear out their pajamas the way kids four and up will. So you may be able to find some great buys at second hand stores. Keep in mind you don't want to buy anything with snags or strings. And sizes will not always tell the truth as cotton shrinks. Hold them up to your kiddo or if you really want a work out, try them on him/her.

The Best Diapers: Cloth vs Disposable?

The great diaper debate still rages on: should you use cloth or disposable? Fans of cloth diapers argue cloth is better for the planet. On the other hand, those disposable diapers are darn convenient—and the choice of 96% of parents in the U.S.

Considering the average baby will go through 2300 diaper changes in the first year of life, this isn't a moot issue—you'll be dealing with diapers until your baby is three or four years old (the average girl potty trains at 35 months; boys at 39 months). Yes, you read that last sentence right . . . you will be diapering for the next 35 to 39 MONTHS.

Now, in this section, we've decided NOT to rehash all the environmental arguments pro or con for cloth versus disposable. Fire up your web browser and you'll find plenty of diaper debate on parenting sites. Instead, we'll focus here on the FINANCIAL and PRACTICAL impacts of your decision.

Let's look at each option:

◆ **Cloth**. Prior to the 1960's, this was the only diaper option available to parents. Fans of cloth diapering claim that babies experienced less diaper rash and toilet trained faster. From a practical point of view, cloth diapers have improved in design over the years, offering more absorbency and fewer leaks. They aren't perfect, but the advent of diaper covers (no more plastic pants) has helped as well.

Another practical point: laundry. You've got to decide if you will use a cloth diaper service or launder at home. Obviously, the latter requires more effort on your part. Meanwhile, we'll discuss the financial costs of cloth in general at the end of this section.

Final practical point about cloth: most day care centers don't allow them. This may be a sanitation requirement governed by state day care regulators and not a negotiating point. Check with local day care centers or your state board.

◆ **Disposables**. Disposable diapers were first introduced in 1961 and now hold an overwhelming lead over cloth—about 95% of all households that have kids in diapers use disposables. Today's diapers have super-absorbent gels that lower the number of needed diaper changes, especially at night (which helps baby sleep through the night sooner). Even many parents who swear cloth diapers are best often use disposables at night. The downside? All that super-absorbency means babies are in no rush to potty train—they simply don't feel as wet or uncomfortable as babies in cloth diapers.

The jury on diaper rash is still out—disposable diaper users generally don't experience any more diaper rash than cloth diaper users.

Besides the eco-arguments about disposables, there is one other disadvantage—higher trash costs. In many communities, the more trash you put out, the higher the bill.

The financial bottom line: Surprisingly, there is no clear winner when you factor financial costs into the diaper equation.

Cloth diapers may seem cheap at first, but consider the hidden costs. Besides the diapers themselves ($100 for the basic varieties; $200 to $300 for the fancy ones), you also have to buy diaper covers. Like everything you buy with baby, there is a wide cost variation. The cheap stuff (like Dappi covers) will set you back about $3 to $5.

And you've got to buy several covers in different sizes as your child grows. If you're lucky, you can find diaper covers second-hand for as little as $2. Of course, some parents find low-cost covers leak and quickly wear out. As a result, they turn to the more expensive covers—a single Mother-Ease cover is $14-$20, for example. Invest in a half dozen of those covers (in various sizes, of course) and you've spent another $300 to $500 (if you buy them new).

What about laundry? Well, washing your own cloth diapers at home may be the most economical way to go, but often folks don't have the time or energy. Instead, some parents use a cloth diaper service. In a recent cost survey of such services across the U.S., we found that the average is about $1000 to $1200 a year. While each service does supply you with diapers (relieving you of that expense), you're still on the hook for the diaper covers. You'll make an average of eight changes a day (more when a baby is newborn, less as they grow older), so be sure you're getting about 60 diapers a week from your service.

Proponents of cloth diapers argue that if you plan to have more than one child, you can reuse those covers, spreading out the cost. You may also not need as many sizes depending on the brands you use and the way your child grows.

So, what's the bottom line cost for cloth diapers? We estimate the total financial damage for cloth diapers (using a cloth diaper service and buying diaper covers) for just the first year is $1100 to $1300.

By contrast, let's take a look at disposables. If you buy disposable diapers from the most expensive source in town (typically, a grocery store), you'd spend about $700 to $800 for the first year. Yet, we've found the best deals are buying in bulk from the discount sources we'll discuss shortly. By shopping at these sources, we figure you'd spend $450 to $550 per year (the lowest figure is for private label diapers, the highest is for brand names).

The bottom line: the cheapest way to go is cloth diapers laundered at home. The next most affordable choice is disposables. Finally, cloth diapers from a diaper service are the most expensive choice.

10 Keys To Saving Money on Diapers

1 **THINK PRICE PER DIAPER.** Stores sell diapers in all sorts of package sizes—always compare diaper prices per diaper, not per box.

2 **BUY IN BULK.** Don't buy those little packs of 20 diapers—look for the 80 or 100 count packs instead. You'll find the price per diaper goes down when you buy larger packs. That's why grocery stores are usually the most expensive place to buy diapers—they sell diapers in smaller packages, with the highest per diaper price. Online discounters often sell packs of more than 200 at even bigger discounts.

3 **GO FOR WAREHOUSE CLUBS.** Sam's (samsclub.com), BJ's (bjs.com) and Costco (costco.com) wholesale clubs sell diapers at incredibly low prices. For example, Costco sells a 192-count package of Huggies Little Snugglers stage 1 for just $39.99 or about 21¢ per diaper. We also found great deals on wipes at the wholesale clubs. The downside to these warehouse clubs?

You buy a membership to shop at clubs, which runs about $45 (Sam's) to $60 (Costco) a year. And clubs don't stock the usual sizes of diapers—some carry "size 1-2" diapers, instead of just size 1 or 2. Readers are frustrated with this combined sizing, according to our message boards.

4 **BUY STORE BRANDS.** Many readers tell us they find store brand diapers to be equal to the name brands. And the prices can't be beat—many are 20% to 30% cheaper. Chains like Target and Walmart carry in-house diaper brands, as do many grocery stores. Warehouse clubs also carry in store brands: Costco's Kirkland, BJ's Little Bundles and Sam's Club's Member's Mark.

5 **ONLINE DEALS MAY BEAT IN-STORE PRICES.** If you've got Amazon Prime, sign up for Amazon Family (it's free) to get 20% off "Subscribe & Save" deals on diapers. Not to be outdone, Walmart now offers free two-day shipping on diapers with no membership fee. And Walmart aggressively prices diapers to be competitive with Amazon.

6 **DON'T BUY DIAPERS IN GROCERY STORES.** We compared prices at grocery stores and usually found them to be sky-high. Most were selling diapers in packages that worked out to over 30¢ per diaper. Of course, sales and coupons can lower those prices—some grocery chains aggressively price diapers as a loss leader.

7 **COUPONS.** Yep, it doesn't take much effort to find high-value coupons for diapers. If you have to make a late-night diaper run to the grocery store, use these to save. We've got diaper coupons on our web site (http://bit.ly/diapercoupons).

8 **ASK FOR GIFT CARDS.** When friends ask you what you'd like as a shower gift, you can drop hints for gift cards from stores that sell a wide variety of baby items—including diapers and wipes. That way you can get what you really need, instead of cute accessories of marginal value.

9 **FOR CLOTH DIAPER USERS, GO FOR INTRODUCTORY OR TRIAL DEALS.** Many suppliers have special introductory or trial packages with built-in discounts. Before you invest hundreds of dollars in one brand, give it a test drive first.

10 **BUY USED CLOTH DIAPERS.** Many of the best brands of cloth diapers last and last and last. So you may see them on eBay or cloth-diaper message boards. Buy them—you can get some brands for as little as a buck or two. As long as you know the quality and age of the diapers you're buying, this tip can really be a money saver.

The Best Diapers

We break down our diaper picks into several categories:

◆ Best Disposable Diaper Overall
◆ Best Budget-Friendly Disposable Diaper
◆ Best Disposable Diaper To Buy at 2am
◆ Best Eco-Friendly Disposable
◆ Best Cloth Diapers

The Best Disposable Diaper

After extensive research into 18 different diaper brands, surveying our readers about their diaper favorites and evaluating several diaper leakage lab tests, we pick **Pampers Swaddlers** as the best disposable diaper. (If you're a cloth diaper fan, don't worry we cover that topic later).

Pampers Swaddlers checks all the boxes we look for in a diaper—great leak protection (as judged by independent tests), excellent reader feedback for overall fit and performance and wide availability with affordable pricing.

Yes, there are some bells and whistles here that you don't see in generic diapers (Pamper's color-changing wetness indicator), but what we care about is performance and fit. On that score, Pampers Swaddlers is excellent.

A box of 164 count Size 1 Pampers Swaddlers runs $37 (or roughly 23¢ cents per diaper) on Amazon (you can slice that price down by a penny or more per diaper by being a member of Amazon Prime, sign up for the free Amazon Family program and use Subscribe & Save.).

FYI: Walmart sells the same diapers for 23¢ per diaper as of this writing. (Amazon and Walmart are in a fierce battle over diaper prices, so these prices can change daily!)

Pampers does sell a couple of variations on the Swaddlers, including Swaddlers Sensitive (for babies with sensitive skin). Those are also excellent diapers, but more expensive ($45.61 for a box of 174 diapers or about 26¢ a diaper).

The Best Budget-Friendly Disposable Diaper

We conduct rolling price checks on diapers, both online and offline, chain stores and warehouse clubs. We then take the lowest priced diapers and compare them to lab tests for effectiveness.

The winner this year is **Luv's Ultra Leakguards**—on Amazon, these diapers are as low as 11 cents per diaper ($28.92 for a box of 252 diapers).

As for other bargain diapers, we would also recommend generic diapers like **Walmart's Parent's Choice** and **Target's Up & Up.** Club picks like **Costco's Kirkland Supreme** diapers can also be quite a deal.

Fans of Target say their diaper promo sales (example: buy $125 worth of diapers, get a $20 or $25 gift card) drop prices under 10¢ per diaper for top brands like Huggies. Target's Cartwheel app also regularly features diaper deals.

Of course, a disposable diaper deal that leaks is no bargain. That's why Luv's Ultra Leakguards tops our list of bargain choices, based on fit and leak testing. A close second would be **Huggies Snug & Dry** when they are on sale on Amazon or Walmart.

We realize we are talking cents per diaper savings and that may not seem like much. But pennies add up when you're talking about buying 2300 diapers in your baby's first year.

Total annual savings of Luv's Ultra Leakguards at Amazon versus Pampers Swaddlers would be $300+. That's more than 50% less money on diapers! Heck, just following that one tip paid for this book many times over!

Best Eco-Friendly Diaper

How is that even possible—to be both eco-friendly and disposable? Our top pick for best eco-friendly disposable, **Bambo Nature**, manages that and more.

Made in Denmark, Bambo Nature backs up its environmental talk with certifications: the diapers are FSC-certified, Nordic Ecolabel and the EU's Ecolabel. Other eco-friendly diapers talk eco-friendliness but rarely back it up with third-party testing.

These diapers tick just about every box for sustainability and eco-friendliness. While we don't have room here for a full run-down, Bambo Nature's web site lays out the features in detail.

Bambo Nature diapers scores at the top for performance— very little leakage, strong absorbency and comfort/fit. Too often we see expensive green diapers that tout their eco credentials but do an average to poor job of stopping leaks.

So what's the catch? Well, if you said price, give yourself bonus points. Like many other eco-baby gear picks, all the environmental goodness will cost you. Even on Amazon size 1 Bambo

Nature diapers run $11.77 for a box of 28 diapers—or about 42¢ each. Ouch.

Another caveat: the sizing of European diapers is a bit different from the USA. Basically, the Bambo Nature diapers run large compared to Pampers or Huggies.

Best Cloth Diaper

Ask ten cloth diaper aficionados for their favorite cloth diapers and you'll probably get 11 different answers! That's because there are so many different options out there it can be confusing. And then there is the learning curve.

So let's cut through the clutter and give you a pick, assuming you are a first-time cloth diaperer and looking for a simple solution: **BumGenius First Year Original One-Size 5.0 cloth diaper**.

Also known as the BumGenius Freetime, this diaper is the easiest for first-timer cloth diaperers—as an all-in-one, you don't need to buy separate covers or inserts. Basically, you pop the entire diaper in the wash.

Best of all, BumGenius adjusts to fit babies from seven to 35 lbs. So what's not to like? Well, BumGenius must be line-dried, and that can take a while (especially in humid climates). Also: the diaper is a bit bulky. These diapers run $21.95 each.

Also Great Cloth Diaper: Rumparooz One-Size Cloth Pocket Diaper

If you consider yourself a more advanced cloth diaper, we would suggest the **Kanga Care Rumparooz One-Size Cloth Pocket Diaper** ($26). Rumparooz is a one-size diaper that adjusts to fit babies six to 35 lbs. What our readers love about this cloth diaper is Rumparooz's attention to detail and high quality materials. You can customize the absorbency via different liners (the diaper comes with a microfiber "6r soaker" insert).

An inner and outer elastic barrier stops nearly all leaks. Overall, excellent quality. What's not to like? Well, you do have to deal with those inserts, which can be a pain. The Rumparooz is bulky and a few readers complain it doesn't fit toddlers well, despite the claimed 35 lb. weight limit.

Best Diaper Wipes

Diaper wipes are diaper wipes, right? What's the difference?

Actually, there can be large differences in diaper wipes. To find the best, we extensively surveyed our parent readers to find the best bets.

In the past few years, we've seen a new crop of eco-friendly wipes join the market. These wipes drop the typical wipe chemicals (disodium phosphates? Phenoxyethanol?) for a mix of more natural ingredients free of chemical perfumes or dyes. Many of these new wipes are "water-based."

We break down our diaper wipe picks this way:

◆ Best Diaper Wipe (Overall)
◆ Best Eco-Friendly Diaper Wipe

Best Diaper Wipes (Overall)

Amazon Mama Bear 99% Water Diaper Wipes are our choice for the best diaper wipe. Readers praise these wipes for overall quality and value. And yes, they are unscented.

A 72 count box (six packs) on Amazon run just 4¢ per wipe—that's less than half of the price of name-brands. FYI: Amazon's wipes come in three versions: scented, unscented and water wipes.

Also Great: Pampers Sensitive Diaper Wipes

Pampers Sensitive Diaper Wipes also score high with our readers, who like the very soft texture. Compared to Pampers' other wipes, these are somewhat thicker and come unscented. The price is about 3¢ on Amazon. In stores, these wipes run 2.6¢ to 3¢ wipe. Another bonus: these wipes are so popular, you can typically score coupons to drop the price further.

Costco fans tell us their **Kirklands Signature Diaper Wipes** are a winner and we agree—these wipes perform just as well as the name brands at a price (2.2¢) that is hard to beat.

Best Eco-Friendly Diaper Wipes

What if you took out all the chemicals in wipes and just left water? That's the essence of **WaterWipes**, which we recommend as an eco-friendly wipe. These wipes run $42.99 for a box of 720 wipes (or roughly 6¢ per wipe).

As the name implies, these wipes are 99.9% water with the balance being grapefruit seed oil. Readers love their simplicity, especially for babies who've developed rashes from standard wipes.

A few caveats: some of the chemicals in standard wipes keep them from molding. So it doesn't come as a surprise that we hear more than a few complaints about molding with WaterWipes—this would be a case where we suggest NOT ordering in bulk . . . or at least store them in a cool/dry place if you go for a large box. And don't use these wipes in wipe warmers.

Critics note that these wipes can also be drippy, irking more than one reader.

Those caveats aside, we still like WaterWipes for folks who desire a simple wipe for babies with super-sensitive skin. Or just use a washcloth dipped in water—can't get much cheaper or simpler!

CHAPTER 6

Feeding Baby

Inside this chapter

F eeding baby comes with many decisions . . . and it's own array of gear. We'll go over everything from bottles to high chairs, breast pumps to formula plus baby food in this chapter!

The Best Breast Pumps

This category can be confusing, with an array of options that start at $20 and go over $300. Before we get to our picks, let's go over some basic things to learn about pumps.

7 Things No One Tells You About Buying a Breast Pump

1 **BREAST PUMP 101 : THE THREE BASIC TYPES OF PUMPS (AND WHAT THEY DO WELL).** Even if you exclusively breastfeed, you probably will find yourself needing to pump an occasional bottle. After all, you might want to go out to dinner without the baby (yes, that is possible). Maybe you'll have an overnight trip for your job or just need to get back to work full or part time. Your partner might even be interested in relieving you of a night feeding (it can happen).

The solution? Pumping milk. Whether you want to pump occasionally or every day, you have a wide range of options. Here's an overview:

◆ **Manual Expression:** OK, technically, this isn't a breast pump in the sense we're talking about. But it is an option. There are several good breastfeeding books that describe how to express milk manually. Most women find that the amount of milk expressed, compared to the time and trouble involved, hardly makes it worth using this method. A few women (we think they are modern miracle workers) can manage to express enough for an occasional bottle; for the majority of women, however, using a breast pump is a more practical alternative. Manual expression is typically used only to relieve engorgement.

◆ **Manual Pumps:** Non-electric, hand-held pumps are operated by squeezing on a handle. While most affordable, manual pumps are generally also the least efficient—you simply can't duplicate your baby's sucking action by hand. Therefore, these pumps are best for moms who only need an occasional bottle or who need to relieve engorgement.

◆ *Mini-Electrics:* These breast pumps (most work either with batteries or an A/C adapter) are designed to express an occasional bottle. Unfortunately, the sucking action is so weak that it often takes twenty minutes per side to express a significant amount of milk. And doing so is not very comfortable. Why is it so slow? Most models only cycle nine to fifteen times per minute—compare that to a baby who sucks the equivalent of 50 cycles per minute!

	BREAST PUMPS	Which pump works best in which situation?			
			Manual	Mini-Elec.	Professional	Rental*
Do you need a pump for:						
A missed feeding?			■	◆		
Evening out from baby?			■	◆		
Working part-time.			■	◆		
Occasional use, a few times a week.			■	◆		
Daily use; full-time work					●	●
Premature or hospitalized baby?					●	●
Low milk supply?					●	●
Sore nipples/engorgement?			■		●	●
Latch-on problems or breast infection?					■	●
Drawing out flat or inverted nipples?			■	◆	●	●

Key: ■ = Good ◆ = Better ● = Best
*Rental refers to renting a hospital-grade pump. These can usually be rented on a monthly basis.
Source: Medela.

◆ *High-End Double Pumps (aka Professional Grade):* The Mercedes of breast pumps—we can't sing the praises of these work horses enough. In just ten to twenty minutes, you can pump both breasts. And high-end double pumps are much more comfortable than mini-electrics. In fact, at first I didn't think a high-end pump I rented was working well because it was so comfortable. The bottom line: there is no better option for working women who want to provide their babies with breast milk.

2 THAT "FREE" ACA BREAST PUMP MAY NOT WORK BEST FOR YOU. Yes, as a new mom, you may qualify for a free breast pump with your health insurance, thanks to the Affordable Care Act. So what's the catch? (You knew there would be a catch.) That "free pump" is determined by your insurance carrier—and that's whatever breast pump they decide to cover. So, they could give you a cheap, underpowered mini-electric . . . or a top-of-the-line professional grade electric pump. In the former case, you may find yourself needing to purchase a breast pump out of pocket.

3 IT MAY MAKE MORE SENSE TO RENT THAN BUY. Rental pumps are what the industry refers to as hospital-grade or piston electric pumps. They are built to withstand continuous use of up to ten times a day for many years. The interior parts are sealed to prevent contamination from one renter to the next.

Compared to purchased pumps, rentals have much more powerful motors and can often empty both breasts in 10 to 15 minutes without hurting breast tissue.

We recommend renting first before buying, just so you can get the hang of it and determine if you really need a breast pump for long-term pumping. They usually rent from $65 to $90 per month, plus the cost of a collection kit.

4 DON'T PURCHASE A USED PUMP. We're big proponents of saving money, but somethings you must draw the line at for safety's sake. One is never, ever buy a used professional grade electric pump. Some pumps can actually collect milk in the pump mechanism—that can expose your baby to bacteria and pathogens from another mother's breast milk.

So, let's state it clearly: DO NOT PURCHASE A USED BREAST PUMP. The risk of exposing your baby to any pathogens isn't worth the savings. Of course, it is fine to re-use your own breast pump for another child down the road. Just replace the tubing and collection bottles to make sure there are no bacteria left over from previous uses.

5 NEXT DECISION: HOW TO STORE THAT MILK. You have options: plastic bags, plastic bottles and ice cube trays. Plastic bags designed for breast milk storage are the cheapest option—we recommend several brands later in this chapter such as Lansinoh (pictured right).

If you prefer plastic bottles, Medela makes plastic bottles ($11 for six five-ounce bottles) that are compatible with all their breast pumps.

Milkies Milk Trays (lower right) is our last recommended storage product. They look like old fashioned ice cube trays, but they include lids to help avoid freezer burn. The cubes come out as long cylinders, perfect for a baby bottle. Cost: $20.

6 WHEN IT COMES TO BREAST PUMPS, DON'T SKIMP ON QUALITY. It's important to buy a pump you can successfully use. Invest in quality, speed and comfort. Yes, you can find a $20 breast pump in a discount store . . . but if it is slow, painful and inefficient, it's no bargain.

7 HIRING A LACTATION CONSULTANT IS A WISE INVESTMENT. Successful breast feeding and pumping is not just about the pump. A lactation consultant (either affiliated with your doctor or with a hospital) can help make sure you're using that pump correctly. It should not hurt! Lactation consultants can help troubleshoot problems, enabling your breastfeeding and pumping to be as successful as possible. We strongly suggest using a lactation consultant's services.

Up next, our picks for best pump (overall), best cordless pump and best manual pump.

The Best Breast Pump (Overall)

What's the best breast pump? We surveyed our parent readers and interviewed five lactation consultants to find the best bets. Which was easiest to use? Easy to clean? Lightweight? Here are the ones we'd recommend.

Medela is to breast pumps what Apple is to smartphones—they pretty much set the standard. So when Medela launches a new model, like the **Pump in Style with MaxFlow,** it's big news. The MaxFlow ($200) is Medela's first major revision of its mainstay breast pump in years . . . and the company has done its homework. Gone is the bulky, heavy pump—now, it's a sleek, one pound motor that is built off the technology of Medela's hospital-grade pump (the Symphony).

The MaxFlow is also Medela's first closed system pump, which makes it much easier to clean. And as you'd expect from Medela everything here from the flanges to the breast shields are designed with comfort in mind.

What We Liked. This pump is super easy to use. And comfortable. It includes a battery pack (8 AA batteries not included) for portable pumping.

The MaxFlow is easier to clean than past models. Yes, just three parts—that's it. Medela's previous pumps had many more parts. Also nice: the pump includes cooler bag, microfiber pump bag and four bottles with lids.

We think this pump is great for travel or pumping on the go—that lightweight (1 lb.) is a major plus.

And of course, there is the excellent brand track record. Medela has set the standard for breast pumps since the 1990's.

What Needs Work. Well, no pump is perfect. Here are the drawbacks to the MaxFlow:

◆ *Must use Medela's "PersonalFit" connectors.* This pump is not compatible with third-party connectors. And it isn't even compatible with Medela's older pump parts. So if you need replacement parts, be sure to order the correct ones!

◆ *Hard to tell what suction level the pump is set at.*

◆ *A bit loud.*

◆ *No timer.* It would be nice to see how long you've been pumping.

◆ *Battery pack isn't rechargeable.* That means you could go through quite a few AA batteries if you plan to do a lot of pumping on the go. If this is an important feature to you, you may want to consider a cordless breast pump with rechargeable battery—which we will discuss next!

Best Cordless Breast Pump

Pumping on the go is part of life—whether you need to pump at the office or in the car while stuck in traffic. For the best cordless breast pump, we'd recommend ***Spectra Baby USA S1 Plus*** ($200).

We liked the rechargeable battery, which lets you pump on the go. Quiet, small and efficient, this pump does an excellent job. Also great: a pumping timer, night light and easy to clean design.

What Needs Work. While this is our an excellent breast pump, be aware of these caveats:

- *The Spectra pump has hit or miss compatibility with other brand's bottles* (Avent, yes, Dr. Brown's no, etc.). Yes, you can buy adapters to fit Medela bottles, but they are a pain to use in our opinion. Spectra's collection bottles get mixed reviews—the ounce markings rub off after a run through the dishwasher, for example.
- *The wide neck collection bottles can tip over easily*—take care.
- *Spectra's customer/warranty service is inconsistent*. For every report we see that praises Spectra, we see another mom complaining the company was slow to respond to warranty claims or general customer service inquiries.

Best Manual Breast Pump

Breast pumps are like tools—you need the right one to do a certain job.

Take engorgement, for example. A manual breast pump is a quick (and affordable) way to deal with this sometimes painful condition.

Manual breast pumps are also great for an occasional (very occasional) bottle.

Our top pick for best manual breast pump is the incredibly simple ***Haakaa Manual Breast Pump*** ($13) from New Zealand. In our testing, the Haakaa beat out several other veteran manual pump brands for overall quality.

This is an excellent manual pump, great for relieving engorgement. Easy to use—just squeeze and attach. And the flange fits all breast sizes, plus the pump is lightweight for travel. Caveat: our mom readers note that it may take some trial and error at the beginning.

Breastfeeding Help: Nursing Pillows, Bras, Nipple Shields, Cream

Breast pumps are an important tool for nursing moms, but there are quite a few other helpful accessories. In this section, we give you picks for the best nursing pillow, nursing bras, nipple shields and nipple cream. Let's go!

The Best Nursing Pillow

After researching and reviewing ten different nursing pillows, we pick the **My Brest Friend pillow** ($35) as the best nursing pillow.

When it comes to nursing pillows, the key word is support—the My Brest Friend (MBF) nursing pillow offers excellent support for both mom and baby, better than any other pillow we tested. The cushion is firm foam with support for arm and elbow. My Brest Friend has a padded, wrap around waist belt with slightly elevated backrest; "silent release" strap; removable, washable cover; firm foam cushion and convenient attached pocket.

MBF makes three versions of the pillow: the Original has a 100% cotton cover, the Deluxe has a "plush" fleece fabric and the Organic has an organic cotton cover. The company notes the Deluxe "slipcover stays fresh through dozens of washes" . . . which seems like an odd claim. Anyway, the Original and Deluxe versions come in a variety of patterns and solid colors. Additional covers are available for purchase.

My Brest Friend has many fans among our readers for a variety of reasons. Moms tell us they like the back support, and lactation consultants note the pillow encourages better posture. The strap and buckle mean you can stand up or adjust the pillow position for different holds (football, cross cradle).

Some versions of the MBF pillow have two "bumps" to help position baby's head closer to the breast. While many parents found these useful, some thought they got in the way. (One mom recommended turning the pillow over if you don't like the bumps—the underside is completely flat.)

So what's not to like about the MBF? The biggest complaint: the waist strap didn't fit everyone and some thought it was uncomfortable (MBF recommends their Twins Plus Deluxe Nursing Pillow for curvy moms). Despite a few drawbacks, we recommend the My Brest Friend nursing pillow as our top pick for the best nursing pillow.

Also Great: Boppy Nursing Pillow and Positioner

Boppy has been making pillows for babies and moms since 1989. The original version was intended as a support pillow for babies when they weren't being held. Now they've expanded its uses to include tummy time for babies and nursing support. The Boppy itself is filled with polyester fiberfill and upholstered in a poly/cotton blend fabric (90% poly, 10% cotton). We'll talk about slip cover options for the Boppy below.

The **Boppy Nursing Pillow and Positioner** comes in three flavors: the Bare Naked, Classic and Luxe. All three designs are made in the classic curved design with an opening at one end. The Bare Naked comes without a slip cover (you can purchase one separately) and sells for $30.

The Classic design is the same as the Bare Naked except it comes with a printed slip cover in ten different patterns. The covers are a polyester/cotton blend that zips off for cleaning. Price: $40. The Luxe comes with a "minky" slip cover (like a soft velour on top and regular poly/cotton underneath) and runs $50.

All three versions of the Boppy pillow are machine washable and the covers are as well. Just be sure to remove the cover before washing the pillow. Additional covers are available starting at ten bucks for a Classic cover, more for the organic version or Luxe version. And if you're worried your baby might have a leaky diaper on occasion, Boppy sells a water resistant cover that goes under a regular slip cover.

What do parents think about the Boppy? It has a very devoted following among our readers who note it worked well for nursing but then could also be used to support baby during tummy time and eventually for sitting up. However, long time fans are unenthusiastic about the quality of the slip covers. And while most said the Boppy fit fine and helped support baby during nursing, a minority of moms felt it was too small to stay in place comfortably.

We think the Boppy is an acceptable alternative to the My Brest Friend pillow if you are looking for a pillow that has other potential uses. It's also smaller and more compact than MBF and comes in a wider variety of colors. You can toss the whole thing into the washing machine, so that's a plus too.

FYI: Boppy also makes a nursing pillow called the Best Latch that straps around your waist similar to the My Brest Friend. It has two different surfaces: one firm, one soft. It is thicker than the Boppy and bulkier, which made it harder for some moms to use in our testing. If this style appeals to you, we recommend the My Brest Friend instead.

The Best Nursing Pillow for Twins

Our top pick for best nursing pillow for twins is the **My Brest Friend Twins Plus Deluxe Nursing Pillow**. Priced at $55.98, it offers enough room to nurse two babies at a time. Like the regular version of My Brest Friend (MBF), the Twin Plus has a washable pillow cover, adjustable back support, waist belt and accessory pocket. The company also recommends the Twins Plus for curvy moms.

While most moms liked the Twins Plus in our testing, there were complaints that the cover was poorly made and the zipper broke. Also: this pillow is very large—some moms couldn't get a tight fit with the belt.

These complaints aside, for nursing your twins at the same time, we found this pillow works well—at least when babies are small and not very active. Once they get bigger and more mobile, it can be tough to keep them on the pillow.

Curvy moms told us the My Brest Friend Twins Plus Deluxe Nursing Pillow definitely fits better than the regular MBF pillow.

Best Nursing and Pumping Bras

After testing seven different options, our recommendation for the best nursing bra is **Bravado! Designs Silk Seamless Maternity and Nursing Bra** ($39).

Bravado! has been making excellent quality nursing bras for over 20 years. We like the soft fabric, wireless and seamless design, and easy to release clip. Yep, you can get this bra unhooked for baby in a split second! Included with their bras, Bravado! has foam inserts to calm the "headlight" effect and handle mini leaks. For bigger leaks, you might want a more substantial pad. See later in this section for recommendations.

Bravado also makes a great bra for those with large breasts up to a cup size M, the **Bravado! Essential Embrace bra** ($14-$31). We like its soft cotton lining and smooth exterior microfiber fabric. It comes with a free bra extender and Bra Conversion Kit, so you can transform it into a regular, non-nursing bra later. Some readers noted that the sizing was a bit on the small size for this bra, so consider ordering it in two sizes if you want to be cautious.

If you're on a tight budget and looking for a less expensive option for a nursing bra, we recommend **HOFISH Nursing Maternity Bralettes** (3-pack for $29-$34). This is quite a deal. Included in the price are foam pads, three bra clips (to turn it into a sport style bra) and three bra extenders. Yes, that is a good deal, but here are the trade-offs: the quality is only average say our testers . . . and the foam cups were annoying and tend to fall apart after a few washings, according to our tests.

Also Great: Simple Wishes Hands Free Breastpump Bra

Hands-Free pumping means just what it says: you can literally pump breast milk without holding the bottles in your hands. Yeah, it sounds obvious, but until a few years ago, there were no hands-free pumping bras. The only option was to sit at a table while nursing and hold the pumping flange/bottles with your hands. You couldn't hug your toddler or eat a snack. And your arms got tired or you might find yourself slumping–all bad things for expressing milk.

Our top pick for best hands free pumping is the **Simple Wishes Hands Free Breastpump Bra** ($35). Designed like a bustier, this cotton/spandex bra closes with a velcro back panel that can be adjusted for a better fit. To hold in the flanges of your favorite breast pump (it works with Medela, Avent, Lansinoh and Spectra pumps), the Simple Wishes uses four overlapping layers of fabric to keep your flange/bottles attached while you pump.

While we came across the occasional complaint that the Simple Wishes was not very durable, most moms in our testing like the soft fabric and customizable fit. Bottom line: we recommend the Simple Wishes Hands Free Breastpump Bra.

Best Nursing Pads

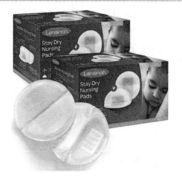

There are two options with nursing pads: disposable and reusable. Common sense tells you that reusable breast pads make the most economical sense, particularly if you plan to have more children. Still, if you aren't a big leaker, don't plan to breast feed for long or just need something quick and easy when you're on the go, disposables are handy.

When we polled our readers recently on this subject, the majority preferred disposables. **Lansinoh Disposable Nursing Pads** ($17 for 100 count) were by far the favorite, followed by Johnson & Johnson, Curity, Evenflo and Medela.

What's the secret to Lansinoh's disposables nursing pads? The same type of super absorbent polymer that makes your baby's diapers so absorbent. That makes them super thin too so you aren't embarrassed by telltale "bulls-eyes" in your bra.

Moms also love the individually wrapped pads because they can just grab a couple and throw them in the diaper bag on the way out of the house. Interestingly, moms were divided on whether they like contoured or flat pads or those with adhesive strips or without–you may have to sample a few varieties to see what works best for you.

If you prefer reusable, washable pads, **Bamboobies** and **BabyBliss** are our top picks.

So how many nursing pads will you need? With disposable pads, buy the smaller package—don't buy the Costco-sized box. You may not need that many or may not like the brand. As for reusable pads, we recommend starting with three pair. That gives you one to wear, one to wash and an extra just in case.

Best Nipple Cream

Cracked nipples from nursing or pumping or both? We feel your pain. So let's talk relief.

Surprisingly, you don't have to buy a separate cream to heal cracked nipples. Lactation consultants recommend moms rub sore nipples with their own expressed breast milk. And it works! But (there's always a but), some moms tell us they want a moisturizing product or don't feel breast milk is helping.

In that case, we recommend **Earth Mama's Nipple Butter** ($7.50) for sore nipples. This beloved nipple cream is a wonderful moisturizer. Lanolin-free and no GMO's. No petroleum, parabens or artificial fragrances. The slight chocolate-like scent turns off some, however.

Lanolin is another option to consider for cracked nipples. Our mom readers seem to be less than enthusiastic about lanolin because it's expensive, can be allergenic and is often difficult to apply (too thick and sticky). That said, it works for others. We did find a great source for an affordable lanolin-based ointment: **Corona Multi-Purpose Ointment** ($14 for a 14 ounce jar—$1 per ounce!). Yes, it is designed for horses—but it works great for humans as well, say our readers!

Best Nipple Shields

Sometimes referred to as a breast shell, a nipple shield is a piece of thin plastic placed over mom's nipple and surrounding tissue (areola). It typically has four holes in it that allows breast milk to pass to your baby. You would use a nipple shield if you have sore, cracked and/or bleeding nipples.

Nipple shields are a temporary solution that should allow your nipples to avoid further damage and give you time to heal. Shields can also be used to help women who have flat or inverted nipples and are experiencing difficulties nursing.

Our top recommended nipple shield is **Medela's Contact Nipple Shield** ($8 for a two-pack). It comes in small, medium or large sizes. We like this type of nipple shield because it has a cutout that allows more skin to skin contact between mom and baby. Medela also makes a traditional nipple shield that is completely round without a cut out.

Best Gel Pack

What to do when engorgement sets in? Your significant other may be impressed with the size and scope of your problem, but it's darned uncomfortable. So what's a girl to do? Grab an ice pack, which also can help with sore nipples.

But wait—what if you have trouble with let down, a plugged duct or mastitis (breast infection)? A warm compress can help with these issues.

When we went looking for our top recommendation for a gel pack, we wanted to find one that could be frozen *or* warmed—the ultimate soother for any situation. We also wanted a pack that was comfortable, preferably with a circular shape to lay easily on a breast. Our top pick for best gel pack for the nursing mom is **Lansinoh's Thera-Pearl 3-in-1 Breast Therapy Pack** ($9.78).

The Lansinoh pack comes with two gel packs and two covers that snap on over the packs. You can put them in the microwave to warm them up or store them in the refrigerator or freezer. The unique round shape with the opening allows you to use the pack (when warmed) around the flange on your breast pump to stimulate let down.

One caution: parents told us it is too easy to explode your gel pack in the microwave, so be sure to follow directions carefully. We doubt you want to be cleaning goo off the inside of your microwave.

Which brings us to a complaint about the Thera-Pearl packs: some of our testers were disappointed that the packs didn't stay warm long enough to be helpful (by contrast, an electric heating pad might be more effective).

As for the cool function, most of our testers said these packs were excellent frozen.

Other cheaper/DYI options to consider: in a pinch you can grab a bag of frozen veggies from the freezer. Clean, chilled and crushed cabbage leaves can also relieve pain. (Our resident lactation consultant notes you should change the wilted leaves every 15 minutes for 45 minutes, and repeat three times daily. Thanks to Linda Hill, RN.) Still another trick to consider if you're trying to encourage let down is a hot shower plus breast massage. Check with your lactation consultant or pediatrician for more tricks.

The Best Baby Bottle

Nothing is more intimidating upon visiting a baby superstore than the WALL OF BOTTLES. The mere sight has been known to make grown adults cry. Who knew there were so many choices for such a simple item?

Let's break down the basics of baby bottles and then give you our picks.

7 Things No One Tells You About Buying Baby Bottles!

1 **THE NIPPLE IS REALLY MORE IMPORTANT THAN THE BOTTLE.** There are three basic types of baby bottle nipples: orthodontic, flat-topped and bell-shaped.

Which is best? All of them claim to be "closest to mom's breast," but here's our advice. If you're breastfeeding and only intend to give your baby an occasional bottle, these babies tend to do best with bell shaped nipples. With babies who are bottle fed from the get-go, any of the nipple shapes will likely work well.

Orthodontic

2 **NIPPLES HAVE DIFFERENT FLOW RATES.** When you're buying your first nipples/bottles, be sure you're using newborn nipples. This means the hole in the nipple is small, allowing a slow flow. If you use a nipple for older babies, you'll find your newborn gagging and sputtering.

Some parents find their babies get used to the newborn nipple and never need to change to the nipples for older babies. And you'll only need 2 oz. bottles if you're feeding a newborn—that's the right amount at first.

Flat-topped

3 **YOU'LL WANT TO BUY ENOUGH BOTTLES TO GET THROUGH A COUPLE DAYS WITHOUT WASHING.** Who wants to wash bottles the first day you get home from the hospital? If you're bottle feeding baby every two to four hours, that's quite a few bottles—as many as 24 bottles per day! For parents who are breastfeeding, three to six bottles is the max you'll need. Because you don't want to start bottle feeding until breastfeeding is well established (a few weeks, usually), get a couple 4 oz. and 9 oz. bottles.

Bell shaped

4 **BABY BOTTLES DON'T NEED TO BE STERILIZED AFTER EVERY USE.** Ok, maybe sterilize them when you first open the package. But after that, you can just put baby bottles in the top rack of the dishwasher or wash them by hand in hot, soapy water. There is no proven benefit to sterilizing baby bottles. Hint: get a dishwasher basket to keep bottles and tops in place in your dishwasher.

5 **WE RECOMMEND SILICONE NIPPLES, NOT LATEX.** Nipples are made of either silicone or latex. Silicone nipples are stronger, last longer, don't have any flavor, are heat resistant and may resist bacteria better than latex, according to our research. Latex is a natural product (and allergenic for some) and is softer than silicone. Bottom line: we like silicone better overall.

6 **THE CAUSE OF LEAKY BABY BOTTLES MAY BE . . YOU!** Before you return that leaky baby bottle to the store, consider how you are tightening the bottle. We see lots of complaints from parents that a particular baby bottle leaks, but when we ask manufacturers about this problem, they point out that parents often over tighten the bottle, which (ironically) can cause leaking.

Some baby bottles also have vents to allow air to escape the bottle and keep baby from swallowing that air leading to colic and discomfort. While the venting is a great idea, it complicates how the bottle is put together. Consult the bottle's instructions on assembly (and yes, there are even YouTube videos) especially if you are a first-timer!

7 **LOTS OF LITTLE PARTS = CLEANING FRUSTRATIONS.** Sometimes simpler is better. Baby bottles with lots of gaskets, vent tubes and more, mean you have to clean more small parts. And it's easier to lose those parts in a dishwasher.

Example: **Comotomo**. A rising favorite among some parents, Korean import Comotomo's baby bottles have *five* separate parts, including a "fastening top ring" and "fastening ring bottom" that sit between the nipple and bottle.

We break down our bottle recommendations into four areas: best bottle (overall), best glass bottle, best bottle warmer and best bottle sterilizer.

Best Baby Bottle (Overall)

After consulting with numerous certified lactation consultants, surveying more than a thousand of our readers and researching dozens of baby bottles, we've chosen **Avent** as the best baby bottle.

Compared to other bottles, we crowned Avent the best bottle for its well-designed nipple, which is clinically proven to reduce colic (uncontrollable, extended crying that starts in some babies around one month of age). Avent bottles are perhaps the most popular baby bottles on the market today. Many parents swear by them for being easy to clean (easier than the multi-piece Dr. Brown's bottles). Feedback from readers is excellent.

Avent makes two types of baby bottles: Anti Colic with AirFree Vent and Natural. The big difference between the bottles is their nipples. The Natural is breast-shaped plus it has "Comfort Petals," which are supposed to make the nipple softer and more flexible. The Anti Colic version has a one piece vent to keep air out. FYI: you can't use the Natural nipples on the Anti Colic bottles or visa versa.

Lest you think the Natural bottles aren't "anti colic," never fear. The nipple itself has a twin valve, anti-colic system to keep baby from ingesting too much air. Regardless, both types are compatible with Avent's breast pump, the Comfort Double. While both the Anti Colic and the Natural are available in the BPA-free plastic, only the Natural comes in a glass version.

Prices vary depending on the number of bottles, size and type (but generally they are priced in the middle of the pack). If you find them pricey, there is some good news: they go on sale frequently. Example: a starter set for about $36. A 9 oz bottle runs $7.20 each (in a three pack).

You can get a starter set if you don't know which sizes to buy. They even offer one that includes a microwave sterilizer.

Avent bottles are perhaps the most popular baby bottles on the market today, along with Dr.

Brown's. Many parents swear by them for reducing colic and gas and being easy to clean. Overall, feedback from readers is excellent.

The biggest complaint about Avent: the measurement markings on the side rub off after a few months of use. This understandably frustrates parents who've shelled out this much for a bottle, only to discover it's now hard to measure out formula and water.

Some readers report trouble with leaking, although this may be because some folks over-tighten the top. (Avent addresses this issue on their web site with graphics on how much to tighten). Leaks can also occur with the Anti Colic bottle if the gasket ring is incorrectly installed. Make sure the blue side is always facing down. And while there is no separate gasket for the Natural bottles, the nipple has to be set into the bottle correctly or it too can leak.

Overall, these complaints are minor compared to the effusive praise the bottles receive from readers. We highly recommend them.

Also Great: Dr. Brown's

Dr. Brown's baby bottles ($6) are neck and neck with Avent when it comes to popularity. Dr. Brown's big selling point is its two-piece vent system which keeps air out of the milk or formula ensuring the nipple never collapses. They claim this type of venting (called "positive-pressure flow") reduces colic, spit-up and gas.

Dr. Brown's makes four types of bottles: the Original (the flagship), a wide-neck version, the Options polycarbonate bottles and Options glass bottles. Their newest bottle, Options, is so named because the bottle gives parents the (wait for it) "option to use it with or without the internal vent." Since colic starts around three weeks of age and ends around three months, we guess Dr. Brown's wanted to give parents of older babies the option of using the bottle without the vent.

Overall feedback from parents is excellent. They aren't perfect though. The biggest complaint: cleaning all those parts. Of course, if it cures your baby's colic, it's worth it.

Best Glass Baby Bottle

Nobody beats **Evenflo's** glass baby bottles, in our opinion. They are affordable, available in several sizes and quantities and the best choice for folks who don't want plastic. Price: about $5-$6 per bottle.

We also like **Philips Avent Natural Glass Baby Bottles**—very good quality, albeit a bit more pricey at $9-$10 a bottle.

Best Bottle Warmer

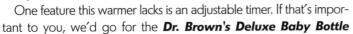

Avent's Fast Bottle Warmer ($40), which warms a room temperature bottle in about four minutes, is our pick for the best bottle warmer. This model took the crown in our recent tests of bottle warmers—just 4 minutes to warm a room temperature bottle to serving temperature. And a bag of frozen expressed breast milk was ready in just 9 minutes on the unit's highest settings. That was a land speed record compared to other units. We found it heats bottles quickly and evenly.

Critics note it lacks a timer or auto shut-off. On the plus side, Avent's Fast Bottle Warmer can warm baby food jars and all types of baby bottles (not just Avent).

Best Budget-Friendly Bottle Warmer

The *First Years 2-in-1 Simple Serve Bottle Warmer* ($15) earns our best budget-friendly pick—it is much easier on the wallet than fancier bottle warmers that can run three or four times the price! Loved this affordable yet functional bottle warmer that has an auto shut off. Compact size. Caveat: time to heat is slower than others we tested.

One feature this warmer lacks is an adjustable timer. If that's important to you, we'd go for the *Dr. Brown's Deluxe Baby Bottle Warmer* ($30). This feature-packed bottle warmer has auto shut-off and timer. We liked the LCD panel with heat adjustment settings. Critics note it needs frequent cleaning.

Best Bottle Sterilizer

Yes, earlier we pointed out that you really don't need a bottle sterilizer—just pop the bottles in the dishwasher; it's safe! But if you still want a sterilizer, we pick the **Avent Express II Microwave Steam Sterilizer** as the best bottle sterilizer. This model holds up to four Avent bottles for $22.

Simple to use, this sterilizer pops in your microwave. Two minutes later, you have sterilized bottles. Also works for pacifiers. No electronics to break!

For the best electric bottle sterilizer, we'd recommend **Philips Avent 3-in-1 Electric Steam Sterilizer** ($75). With a six minute run time, this easy-to-use sterilizer uses steam to clean up to six bottles. Worked well and easy to clean. Critics note you still have to dry bottles.

If that model is too pricey, we'd suggest the **Dr. Brown's Deluxe Bottle Sterilizer** as a more budget-friendly alternative at $47. This excellent sterilizer has electronic controls that are simple to use. We liked how easy it is to load . . . plus it can be used to sterilize small toys as well. Dissenters note bottles come out wet—hence, you might need a drying rack like those below!

Best Baby Bottle Drying Rack

It's cute. And functional. We tested a half dozen different solutions for drying baby bottles before settling on the **Boon Drying Rack Lawn** ($20) as the best bet. This clever design holds bottles and add-on accessories in blades of "grass." But the rack itself isn't dishwasher-safe.

If you need room to dry more bottles, we'd suggest the **Munchkin High Capacity Drying Rack** ($12.79) for this job—the double-decker Lazy Susan has folding pegs to hold bottles and cups. It comes with a removable drip tray that can either catch water draining from the unit—or flip it over and it works as a drain into a sink.

One caveat: this rack can be fragile—don't overload or it may collapse! When folded for storage, this rack has several loose parts . . . which will inevitably get lost, at least in our kitchen.

Best Baby Bottle Brushes

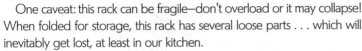

What are the best baby bottle brushes? To find out, we purchased 8 bottle brushes and put them to the test. Which were easiest to use? Did the best job cleaning bottles? Here are the ones we recommend.

Our top pick is the **Dr. Brown's Bottle Brush** ($4) Loved this dishwasher-safe brush, with suction cup base that allows for air drying. Only caveats: the handle could be more grippy. And the nipple brush end is not very effective.

Another excellent pick is the **OXO Tot Bottle Brush** ($8)—it's pricey but lasts a long time. Our testing confirmed: it works well. We loved the long, grippy handle. But the bristle nipple brush is too short—and breaks too easily.

One more caveat to the OXO Tot Bottle Brush: the base collects water. You have to drain the base and frequently wash its two parts to avoid mold. That's more washing than we think a baby bottle brush should require.

Best Breast Milk Storage Bags

If you're planning to breastfeed your baby, storing expressed breast milk is mission critical. We tested several milk storage bag options, checking for leaks and ease of use. Then we interviewed seven lactation consultants about their top picks. Here are the best bets for breastmilk storage bags.

When polling experienced moms about freezer bag storage for breast milk, the winner hands down is **Lansinoh** ($13.88 for a 100 count box). These bags allow you to attach them directly to the breast pump and they work with Lansinoh, Medela, Ameda and Avent pumps. Lansinoh storage bags have a double zipper seal to prevent leaks. You can store them in the freezer stacked flat to save space as well.

Also recommended: **Medela Breast Milk Storage Bags** ($15 for 100 count). We loved these bags, which can stand up for filling. The double zipper is excellent . . . but critics note they don't lay as flat as others. The bags are not microwave safe.

Finally, we'd also recommend this parent favorite: **Kiinde Twist Pouch Breast Milk Storage Bags** ($11 for a 40 count box). These storage bags are unusual—they are part of a system that includes bottles and nipples (sold separately). And parents we interviewed universally praised Kiinde's bags. They are quite a time-saver: the same bag goes from freezer to bottle (after thawing, of course).

What are the drawbacks to the Kiinde Twist? Well, the entire system (bags + sleeves + nipples+ cap) is rather pricey. And these bags are bulky when stored in a freezer.

The Best Baby Formula

Baby formula is a $6.25 billion a year business in the U.S. But is there any nutritional difference between brands of formula? We'll answer that question and give our picks for best baby formula next.

7 Things No One Tells You About Buying Infant Formula!

1 **GENERIC FORMULA INCLUDES EXACTLY THE SAME NUTRITION AS NAME BRAND FORMULA.** That's right, the federal government mandates that all baby food include the *same* nutritional ingredients. So what's the difference between formulas? Some name brands include additional ingredients to help with digestion, such as pre-biotics. They aren't necessary ingredients, so we recommend trying less expensive generic formulas like Bright Beginnings, Member's Mark (Sam's

Club), and Parent's Choice (Walmart). These are all made by PBM Products.

2 **PREMIXED FORMULA WILL COST YOU.** Formula 101: there are three types of formula: powdered, liquid concentrate and ready-to-drink (pre-mixed). Liquid concentrate and ready-to-drink premixed formula is very expensive—50% to 200% more than powdered formula. A word to the wise: start your baby on powdered formula, not liquid concentrate or ready-to-drink. Why? Because babies get used to the texture of whatever they try first (powdered formula tastes different). Start on ready-to-drink formula and baby may refuse powdered formula.

3 **YOUR TODDLER DOESN'T NEED TODDLER FORMULA.** In an attempt to keep parents buying formula way past the time kids need it, some formula manufacturers have created "toddler formulas." These toddler formulas claim to contain more calcium, iron and vitamins, but nutritionists and pediatricians point out that toddlers should be getting most of their nutrition from solid foods, not formula.

Toddlers should ideally only be drinking about two cups of whole milk a day. Whole milk should be served to toddlers between 12 and 24 months of age. At age two, switch to skim or 1% milk. By the way, whole milk is significantly less expensive than formula. No toddler needs "toddler formula" (unless instructed by your pediatrician for a health condition).

4 **FORMULA MAKERS LIKE SIMILAC AND ENFAMIL HAVE FREQUENT BUYER CLUBS YOU CAN JOIN FOR COUPONS AND OTHER FREEBIES.** Similac's program is called StrongMoms Rewards while Enfamil has Family Beginnings. Of course, there is a trade off for all those freebies—formula companies want your personal info (email address, street address, birth date, etc). But no one said you have to use your main email address. Create another Gmail email address for joining clubs like this.

5 **WHERE YOU SHOP CAN MAKE A DIFFERENCE IN THE PRICE OF FORMULA.** Yes, Amazon sells formula at good prices. And you've probably discovered that chains and warehouse clubs offer great prices on formula as well. But did you realize that some locations of the same chain, say Walmart, offer lower every day prices than other locations in the same town.

Yes, this really happens. One reader stopped by a Walmart location in a different part of her home town and discovered that she was paying $6.61 per can at her local Walmart while this other Walmart location 20 minutes away was selling that same can for $3.68!

6 **YOUR PEDIATRICIAN GETS LOTS OF FREE SAMPLES.** That's right, the formula companies bombard pediatricians with samples and most pediatricians don't have lots of room to store them. Don't be afraid to ask if your doctor has free samples. (But don't start your newborn on ready-to-drink or liquid concentrate formulas, see tip #2 above!).

7 **DON'T FORGET TO FACTOR IN THE COST OF BOTTLED WATER!** What, you say? Don't you just mix tap water with powered formula? No, bottled water is recommend by both the American Academy of Pediatrics and the American Dental Association. That's because tap water can contain *too much* fluoride, which is a problem (discolored teeth).

If your tap water contains .3 ppm or less fluoride, tap water is okay (ask your local water department for fluoride levels). But if fluoride levels are HIGHER than that, you should use bottled water.

formula

And not just any bottled water: purified, demineralized, deionized, distilled or reverse osmosis filtered water is recommended. Also: be sure to boil that bottled water before mixing with powered formula. For a full discussion of formula and how to prepare it, see our *Baby 411* book.

Next, our recommendations for best baby formula (overall), best name brand formula and best organic formula.

The Best Baby Formula (Overall)

After comparing and testing over 15 baby formulas, **Walmart's Parent's Choice** infant formula is our top choice for best baby formula.

Parent's Choice is made by PBM Products, a privately owned formula manufacturer based in Georgia. This formula is sold under the Parent's Choice label on formula for sale in Walmart stores.

We picked Parent's Choice because it is the least expensive generic cow's milk formula with iron that is available everywhere in the U.S (with no club membership required). Other chains carry PBM-made generic formula (see below for a list), but Parent's Choice is consistently cheaper at Walmart than other stores.

Insider tip: all formula sold in the U.S. must meet the SAME nutritional and safety guidelines mandated by the government. So that expensive name brand formula you see is virtually the same as the affordable store brand generic—same basic ingredients, same nutrition, and so on.

If you belong to a warehouse club, here's some good news: you'll find even cheaper prices on generic formula there. Sam's Club's Members Mark and BJ's Berkley & Jenson formulas are also made by PBM Products.

Let's take a look at prices for generic (store-brand) powdered formulas available at chain stores and warehouse stores, from cheapest to most expensive (priced per ounce of dry powder):

Sam's Club Members Mark:	48¢/oz.
Costco Kirkland Signature:	49¢/oz.
BJ's Berkley&Jensen:	52¢/oz.
Walmart Parent's Choice:	57¢/oz.
Target Up&Up:	59¢/oz.
CVS Health:	68¢/oz.
Walgreens Well Beginnings:	86¢/oz.

Wow! You can spend 86¢ per ounce of basic powdered formula . . . or 48¢ per ounce. Why pay almost twice as much for the same thing?

Remember that baby formula is very promotional—it goes on sale all the time. And then there are coupons, which you can find with a five second Google search. So here's an expert bargain shopper tip: record the best formula price per ounce in your phone. Then when you see a "sale", divide the sale price by the ounces in the container. If it is below your strike price, buy!

Best Name Brand Baby Formula

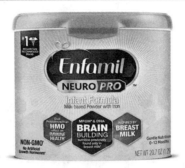

If you prefer a name-brand infant formula, our top pick is **Enfamil**. They offer a great club program (Enfamil Family Beginnings) with freebies and coupons. You'll find Enfamil pretty much anywhere in a wide variety of options including Gentlease (for gassy, fussy babies), Reguline (constipation), A.R. (reflux), ProSobee (soy), and allergy formulas. (Heads up: only use specialized formula as directed by your pediatrician).

Yes, Enfamil also has some non-GMO versions. We found the least expensive basic, powdered Enfamil runs about $1.25 to $1.35 per ounce online. Costco had it for $1.03 per ounce.

Also great: **Similac** is another name brand we recommend. Their flagship formula is Similac Advanced. We didn't think it possible, but Similac has even more "specialty" formulas for sensitive kids, those with allergies and assorted other issues. They also offer non-GMO versions as well as organic formula.

Best Organic Formula

Earth's Best infant formulas (cows' milk, soy and sensitive) are our top pick for best organic baby formula. Their formulas are certified by the USDA to be organic, do not include corn syrup, and have added pre-biotic fiber.

FYI: Earth's Best does add DHA and ARA plus lutein. What is DHA and ARA? Long-chain fatty acids, DHA and ARA are present in breast milk and thought to aid in cognitive development. In formula, DHA and ARA are synthetically made . . . and that's controversial in some organic parenting circles.

Despite that, we recommend Earth's Best—it's easy to find in grocery stores and online. We've seen it online for as little as $1.42 per ounce.

Best Formula Dispenser

Munchkin's Formula Dispenser ($4) pours easily into narrow baby bottles, making this the best bet. We liked the extra single serving dispenser for short trips. This the only dispenser we tested that didn't require banging on the bottom like a ketchup bottle—a potential recipe for disaster if you bang too hard. Pretty much all the formula came out in one stream; better than any of the others we tested.

The Best Baby Food

At the tender age of four to six months, you and your baby will embark on a magical journey to a new place filled with exciting adventures and never-before-seen wonders. Yes, you've entered the SOLID FOOD ZONE.

7 Things No One Tells You About Buying Baby Food!

1 **NO MATTER WHAT BRAND YOU BUY, ALL "STAGE 1" BABY FOOD IS PRESERVATIVE- AND ADDITIVE-FREE.** But . . . that doesn't mean they're using organic ingredients. Once you move to later stages, however, many baby food makers start adding extra sugar and salt.

2 YOU DON'T HAVE TO BUY BABY FOOD. JUST USE THIS . . .

That's right, you can make most baby food at home with a food processor you might already own. Just buy veggies and fruit from your favorite grocery store or farmer's market, steam and mash or puree. You may need to add a bit of water, but that's it. Voila! Baby food. If you want to buy a food processor, we give you a recommendation later in this chapter.

You may still want to purchase a bit of commercial baby food for those days when you aren't eating at home, however. It's pretty convenient to pop open a pouch or cup and feed baby wherever you are.

After baby has mastered pureed food, you'll want to move up to food with more texture. At this stage, you can start feeding baby what you're eating albeit slightly mashed. A detailed discussion on what to feed baby when is in our sister book, *Baby 411*.

3 FEED FROM A BOWL, NOT FROM THE PACKAGING (JAR, POUCH OR CUP). If you feed from the jar, bacteria from baby's mouth can find its way back to the jar, spoiling the food much more quickly. Also, saliva enzymes begin to break down the food's nutrients. The best strategy: pour the amount of baby food you need into a bowl and feed from there (unless it's the last serving in the jar). Refrigerate unused portions.

4 BUYING THE BEST QUALITY FOOD WON'T BREAK THE BANK. The average baby eats 600 jars of baby food until they "graduate" to adult foods. Sounds like a lot of money, eh? Well, that only works out to $240 or so in total expenditures (using an average price of 40¢ per jar). Hence, if you go for better-quality food and spend, say, 15% to 20% more, you're only out another $36 to $48. And feeding baby food that tastes more like the real thing makes transitions to adult foods easier.

How about organic baby food? Well, there is no scientific data that shows any health benefit for organic baby food. For most parents, the issue is about exposure to pesticides. Organic foods are certified synthetic pesticide-free, but may still use certain "natural" pesticides and fungicides. See Certifications below for further discussion.

5 AVOID UNPASTEURIZED MILK, MILK PRODUCTS AND JUICES. And no honey under age 1. Babies don't have the ability to fight off serious bacterium like e. coli. Avoid these hazards by feeding your child only pasteurized dairy and juice products. Also: steer clear of feeding honey to children under one year of age. Botulism spores can be found in honey— while not harmful to adults and older children, these spores can be fatal to babies under age 1.

6 **SHHHH! BABY APPLESAUCE = ADULT APPLESAUCE.** Lets' take a look at a jar of baby applesauce.

Now here's what adult applesauce looks like.

What's the difference? They basically contain the same thing— applesauce. The only difference: applesauce in a jar with a cute baby on it costs several times more than the adult version. On Amazon, you can buy the Gerber baby applesauce for 26¢ per oz. and the Mott's Applesauce for 13¢ per oz. (One caveat: make sure the regular applesauce is NOT loaded with extra sugar; you can find many examples that don't have that).

One of our key Baby Bargains Commandments is "shop for things without baby in their name." Baby food is a good example!

7 **"NEXT STEP" FOODS FOR OLDER BABIES AND TODDLERS ARE A WASTE OF MONEY.** Baby food makers tout "Graduates" foods for older toddlers, but here's the truth: baby doesn't need it.

Pediatricians note you can start feeding your baby the same food you eat when they reach nine to 12 months of age. When baby is ready to eat pasta, just serve him small bites of the adult stuff. Bottom line: babies should learn to eat the same (hopefully healthy) foods you are eating, with the same spices and flavors.

Baby food certifications: what is organic?

In the U.S., the USDA oversees the program that certifies food as organic. There is a List of Allowed and Prohibited Substances, which is used by certifying agents (along with a host of other requirements) to certify that food is being organically produced.

Organic is defined by the USDA as "products that have been produced using cultural, biological, and mechanical practices that support the cycling of on-farm resources, promote ecological balance, and conserve biconvexity in accordance with the USDA organic regulations."

"This means that organic operations must maintain or enhance soil and water quality, while also conserving wetlands, woodlands, and wildlife. Synthetic fertilizers, sewage sludge, irradiation, and genetic engineering may not be used."

For many organic shoppers, that last part is their most important reason for buying organic.

Once an agricultural product has been certified, it can then carry the USDA Organic Seal.

In our opinion, the word organic in baby food has been so common-place in recent years that shoppers forget its limitations. When it comes to "organic," we are reminded of a line from one of our favorite movies: "I do not think it means what you think it means." (Yes, that's a *Princess Bride* reference.)

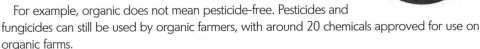

For example, organic does not mean pesticide-free. Pesticides and fungicides can still be used by organic farmers, with around 20 chemicals approved for use on organic farms.

Ironically, sometimes these organic pesticides require higher rates of application than synthetic chemicals!

The take home message: reducing your baby's exposure to environmental toxins is a goal for all parents. And organic food is one way to do that—if you can afford it. But realize organic food isn't the be-all, end-all to keeping baby healthy!

The Best Baby Food

That's right, after sampling more than our fair share of commercial baby food, we recommend **Earth's Best** as the best baby food for your baby.

Earth's Best has been around for over 25 years and it's hard to beat this company for quality and price. Put simply, Earth's Best tastes like real food. It's certified organic too. And it can be found nearly everywhere: online, in grocery stores and at chains like Target.

The price is reasonable at about 32¢ per ounce, and they offer occasional coupons. (For comparison, we priced other organic baby food around 40 cents per ounce; non-organic baby food from Gerber is around 20 cents per ounce).

At first, Earth's Best was only available in glass jars, but they've recently added a line of pouches.

Also Great: Plum Organics

Plum Organics was one of the first baby food companies to come out in pouches, which have since become all the rage. Plum Organics' fans came for the easy-to-pack pouches (no glass jars that can shatter), but stayed for the quality, organic baby food. JUST Fruit (about 32¢ per oz.) and JUST Veggies (about 46¢ per oz.) are made without ad-

ditives—just fruit and veggies.

Plum Organics' Second Blends (about 30¢ per oz.) include interesting combinations like blueberry, pear and purple carrot. Stage 3 Meals (about 70¢ per oz.) and Mighty 4 Blends (about 30¢ per oz.) are complete meals in a pouch with "fruits, veggies, protein and grains." Prices vary often according to how many packs you buy. Some veggie options can be more expensive than fruit options.

Parents tell us they like the JUST Fruit and Second Blends best. By the time kids are ready for Stage 3 and Mighty 4, they should really be eating what you're eating (not baby food). FYI: Plum Organics has expanded its offerings to include snack items and formula.

Hints on Making Your Own Baby Food

Making your own baby food is clearly on the rise. In fact, the New York Times reported last year that commercial baby food sales have declined 4% per year since 2005 (measured in volume consumed). Yes, some of that might be because of a decline in births, but the commercial manufacturers of baby food are plenty worried. They're trying to improve sales with new flavors and "sexy" packaging (not our adjective, the Times said that).

Our own pediatrician expert and co-author of *Baby 411*, Dr. Ari Brown, applauds parents who want to make their own food:

"It's actually preferable to offer food from your table. That way, your baby will get used to your cooking! Yes, you can use seasonings, herbs and spices. Just limit the amount of salt and use iodized salt if you must add it. It's not that hard. Trust me, I'd never make it on 'Top Chef' but even I could make baby food."

So grab a food processor and go for it. We review baby food processors next.

Once you've decided to make baby food, how do you store it so it doesn't spoil? Surprisingly, there are more options for baby food storage than you might think.

First, you need something small. Two to four oz. portions are considered ideal for babies just starting out with solid food. Then you have to decide how to store it. Do you want to freeze or refrigerate extra servings? Do you want to be able to microwave them to bring them up to room temperature? Do you prefer glass to plastic? How about single use or reusable storage? And finally, consider whether you'll need to travel with baby food—some options are easier to take with you than others.

There are three basic choices for baby food storage:

Freezer trays. We know, you're asking, "why can't we just used an ice cube tray?" Good question. You could, but you'll have to remove the baby food blocks once they freeze and store them in a freezer bag to prevent freezer burn. Specialized baby food freezer trays, on the other hand, have a lid that helps avoid freezer burn. These are usually BPA-free silicon trays divided into single, 2 oz. serving with a plastic top. Freezer trays are just for freezing—you pop the serving out of the tray and warm it in a microwave safe bowl or defrost it in the fridge.

Storage sets. No doubt you've been using plastic or glass storage containers with snap-on lids for years. Now they make special sets just for baby food. These containers often have measurements marked on the side of the container, leak-proof lids and stacking storage trays. Individual containers can be defrosted and heated in the microwave. The only issue: if you want to freeze a large batch of baby food, storage sets have a major limitation—you can't remove portions from these sets once they are frozen to put in freezer bags and free them up for more batches.

Feeding pouches. You may have seen commercial baby food in pouches (like Sprout and Ella's) at the grocery store. Now you can buy the pouches yourself and fill them with your own foods. You have two choices with pouches: single use (recyclable) or reusable. The pouches can be frozen (don't overfill, though!) or refrigerated, but not microwaved. Instead, you'll have to warm them in a hot water bath.

So now that you know a bit more about baby food storage, check out our reviews of brands you can buy for your own home made baby food.

Best Baby Food Storage

OXO Tot Baby Blocks ($20) is our top pick for baby food storage. Sold in sets of ten with 2 to 4 oz. containers with trays, Baby Blocks have handy measurement markings and can be washed in the dishwasher, warmed in the microwave and frozen as well. One caveat: careful cleaning is needed to make sure food doesn't stick in the seal (or that the seal doesn't pop out). Overall, however, Baby Blocks are a winner for ease of use and durability.

Also Great: KIDDO FEEDO, WeeSprout

Yeah, it is a goofy name, but we thought **Kiddo Feedo's silicone baby food storage containers** ($15) were the best option for silicone food storage. Why silicone? You can actually cook baby food in the silicone container (the maker says they can be heated up to 400 degrees). Food is easier to remove from silicone than it is from glass or plastic when frozen.

Silicone food containers can also be used after your baby is done with baby food—they are great for mini muffins or mini popsicles!

What about glass containers? After trying out several glass baby food storage options, we liked **WeeSprout's glass containers** best—easy to clean and stack. Loved the measurement markings and writable lids. Critics say they aren't completely leak-proof.

baby food storage

Best Food Processor for Baby Food

Making your own baby food has been trending for the last couple of years, so let's look at some key tools for this task: a food processor, food mill and steamer. The basic decision here: should you buy a specialized baby food processor? Or not?

First, some basics about shopping for these kitchen gadgets.

7 Things No One Tells You
About Buying A Food Processor for Baby Food!

1 **BABY ONLY EATS PUREED FOODS FOR A SHORT PERIOD OF TIME.** That's about six months or so. After that, your baby (around one year of age) can eat regular adult table food (cut into smaller bites, of course). Hence the utility of a *specialized* baby food processor is limited; a regular food processor will give you more bang for the buck since it can blend, chop and grind things like pastry dough, nuts and cheese.

2 **TO FIGURE OUT THE BEST FOOD PROCESSOR FOR YOUR FAMILY, DECIDE HOW MUCH FOOD YOU WANT TO MAKE.** If you're planning to freeze a month's worth of carrots for your little one, consider a regular food processor. You'll be able to puree from 12 to 20 cups of baby food in a full size processor. Some models have smaller bowls that can be used for fewer servings. If you're only interested in a few day's worth of food, the two to four-cup capacity processors will work just fine. And if a single meal is all you need, consider an affordable manual food mill.

3 **CONSIDER THE SIZE OF YOUR KITCHEN.** Do you have room for another appliance on your counter? If you already have a food processor, don't add to the clutter and expense with a specialty baby food processor. If you have limited counter space and don't already have a processor, here's where a steamer/processor might make more sense. The capacity is small and most steamer/processors aren't as well made as a heavy duty food processor, but one might do the trick and save some space.

4 **IF POSSIBLE, GO LARGE.** If you have the money, you'll find that larger processors are useful for other cooking needs. We make pie crust, puree sauces, mix bread dough and more in our Cuisinart. But if price is a consideration, hand-crank food mills are under $20 and will do the job for the small amount of time you'll be making baby food puree.

5 **GOOD NEWS: FOOD PROCESSORS SHOULD LAST A LONG TIME.** Most high end food processor are meant to be workhorses. So if you're buying a food processor to use for more than baby food, spend the money to get good quality. This means a heavy base with a strong motor. That's another reason to stay away from some of the "baby food" processors. They don't have the same high quality motor and rugged construction.

6 **COMBINATION PRODUCTS DON'T ALWAYS WORK OUT.** Steamer/processors are like a lot of combination products. Most of them don't really do multiple tasks well. Or they break. Cuisinart, for example, makes a baby food steamer/processor. But our reader reviews are rather unimpressive, mainly because the steamer sometimes stops working. That's why our top pick is a processor-only appliance.

7 **YOU REALLY DON'T NEED LOTS OF EXTRA BLADES OR ATTACHMENTS.** Basically, you'll be able to do almost anything with the main blade plus the shredding and slicing disks. Yes, some processors have extra blades and attachments that sound cool. But do you really need a french fry cutting disk? Or a special storage box? Stick with the basics and you'll be just fine.

In this section, we review the following baby food tools:

◆ Best Food Processor for Baby Food.
◆ Best Food Mill.
◆ Best Steamer/Processor.

Best Food Processor for Baby Food

We've tested a dozen food processors for making baby food. The winner: **Cuisinart Elite Collection 2.0 12-cup food processor** ($215, model CFP-24DCNPC), a full featured food processor with four different blades and disks. It includes a smaller 4-cup bowl, which would be perfect for pureeing smaller amounts of food for baby. Just pull out your veggie steamer basket and a pot, steam your preferred veggies then pop them in the Cuisinart. Ta-dah! you've got pureed baby food.

Some fruits are soft enough that you won't need to cook them first (we're looking at you, bananas). And you can vary the consistency easily by hitting the pulse button a few time for chunks. But the beauty of buying a traditional food processor (rather than a baby food steamer/processor) is you can use it for so much more around the kitchen: pie crust, bread dough, chopping nuts, grating cheese and more.

You may have noticed that there are several "baby food steamer/processors" for sale in cooking stores and online. For the most part, these combo appliances are rather disappointing and don't rate very well with parents. However, we know some folks are still tempted to buy one—so below, we have a our recommendation for the best of these steamer/processors as well as

food processor

the best manual food mill. For the most part, these combo appliances are rather disappointing and don't rate very well with parents.

Also Great: Cuisinart Chopper/Grinder

Looking for a smaller solution to your baby food making quest? Or just don't want to spend $100+ for a fancy processor? Consider the **Cuisinart 4-Cup Food Chopper**. This is a real workhorse that can not only puree baby's food, but also chop herbs, grind spices and other mundane kitchen tasks. At $60, The Chopper is a great option to consider.

Best Food Mill

If you lack space in your kitchen but still want to make your own baby food, consider a food mill like the **OXO Good Grips Food Mill** to help puree baby's food. This hand crank model may look like a blast from the past, but it does the job with just a little elbow grease. At $49, it isn't cheap, but it will last and parents love it. Use it to make mashed potatoes and other purees when you're done with the baby food stage.

Best Baby Food Steamer/Processor

Yes, we think these specialized baby food makers are a waste of money. But . . . we know some folks still want a specialized baby food steamer/processor, especially if a relative is insisting on giving you one as a gift. Our pick is the **Homia Dansa Baby Food Maker** ($90). This affordable baby food processor has seven functions: sterilize, cook, juice, warm, defrost, puree and chop. The LCD panel is easy to use and the bowl is dishwasher safe. We liked the three basket system which allows you to steam three items at once. It also warms baby bottles.

The Best Sippy Cups

The sippy cup is one of those Instagram milestones for baby, graduating from a bottle to drinking like a big kid. But if you hand a baby a glass full of water, you can guess what will happen. Enter the sippy cup.

Here's your Sippy Cup 411. Sippy cups are supposed to teach toddlers how to drink from a cup. At about a year of age, most babies can hold a cup in their hands. At this point, you have three choices: a sippy cup with a spout, sippy cup with a straw or one of the newer, rimless training cups.

Our recommendation: sippy cups with a straw or a rimless training cup. (Read below for why we don't recommend a sippy cup with spouts).

An excellent sippy cup should be easy to assemble, easy to clean and easy to use—that is, for a child to draw liquid from the cup. And let's talk about spills: The whole point is for your child to feed herself without spilling it all over the floor.

Good news: the nation's best scientists have been working overtime to create all manner of valves, gaskets and gizmos to keep liquid in sippy cups—and off your floor. Yet how successful are these cups in real life? We torture-tested 14 of the most popular sippy cups to pick a winner.

7 Things No One Tells You About Buying A Sippy Cup!

1 WHENEVER YOU CAN, TRY HELPING YOUR CHILD USE A REAL CUP, NOT A SIPPY CUP. Especially when you're eating at home, the quickest way to teach your child to drink from a cup is to use a real cup. Now we don't recommend you just hand your child a full cup of milk in a standard cup, rather you should be helping her. That's right, hold the cup for her. You can control spills and make sure baby doesn't start gulping down too much liquid.

2 PRO TIP: NOT ALL SIPPY CUPS ARE DISHWASHER SAFE. Sippy cups today come with gaskets and valves that keep liquid in the cup and off your floor. That's great—but the downside is cleaning. While most of the cups we recommend are dishwasher-safe, there are a few exceptions: stainless steel cups, for one.

Another key point: remember to dry all the parts thoroughly. Trapped moisture can lead to mold.

3 HANDLES ARE GOOD FOR BEGINNERS. Little hands can't always hold onto a wide sippy cup so give them a little help in the form of handles. Most sippy cups have options with handles— some, like our top pick from **OXO Tot Transitions Straw Cup**, have removable handles. Hence you can start with cups with handles and then transition to handle-less mode!

4 GET A BRUSH TO CLEAN THE STRAW. One of the frustrations about buying a sippy cup with a straw is cleaning those reusable straws. They can get gunked up, especially when you don't clean the cup out immediately.

Usually, the straw is two parts: a silicone tip and a harder plastic body, so you want a brush that's gentle on the silicone, but can handle the harder plastic too. Our favorite is a set of three different size brushes from **Hiware** (pictured). You get two brushes of each size and can clean brushes as small as 6mm up to 12 mm. They are dishwasher safe (top rack) too.

5 WEIGHTED STRAW CUPS—SKIP 'EM! What's a weighted straw sippy cup? This is a cup with a flexible straw to which a weight is added at the bottom. Munchkin makes one of the most popular weighted straw cup, the **Munchkin Click Lock**. Because the flexible straw is weighted, if you tip the cup up to drink, the weight always keeps the end of the straw in the liquid.

You might think to yourself "this is a great idea! No matter how my baby holds the cup, she'll be able to drink the liquid." Yes, that's true, but when your baby graduates to a regular cup, likely she will dump the entire cup upside down on herself or your kitchen floor. In other words, you aren't helping your child learn to gently tilt the cup a little bit to drink. You may as well give her a baby bottle.

Another thing to remember, these weighted straws are difficult to clean. Munchkin includes a flexible straw brush, but it's so tiny it is very easy to lose. And to thoroughly clean the straw, you have to remove the weight from the end of the straw. Again, you could lose this small part. So overall, we don't recommend this type of cup.

6 INTRODUCE WATER FIRST IN A SIPPY CUP, THEN WHOLE MILK AT 12 MONTHS. Dr. Ari Brown, our resident pediatric expert and co-author of our best selling *Baby 411* book, recommends babies start drinking water at around six months of age. This is a great time to introduce a straw sippy cup with handles. Your baby will likely not immediately take to a sippy cup, rather she may treat it like a new toy. But you can help her by bringing it up to her mouth and helping her put the straw in her mouth.

It can take up to six more months before your baby gets the hang of a sippy cup. If you are weaning from formula or breast milk around one year of age, you should be switching to whole milk. And at this point, Dr. Brown recommends presenting whole milk only in a cup, not a bottle.

7 SAY NO TO . . . JUICE! Let's look at the numbers. An 8 oz. serving of Tree Top Apple Juice contains 26 grams of sugar. An 8 oz. serving of Coca Cola also has 26 grams of sugar. The American Heart Association's recommended daily amount of sugar for a 12 month old child is only 17 grams of sugar per day. The take-home message: skip the juice!

Would you hand your 15 month old a can of Coke? Then why hand them a cup full of juice? Even 100% juice is really just a form of liquid sugar. The American Academy of Pediatrics came out with a policy statement in 2017 saying that juice is "absolutely unnecessary for children under one." Here's why:

◆ *Juice provides little nutrition.* Vitamin C has to be added to many juices to give them any nutritive value.
◆ *Juice is filling, which decreases a child's appetite for more nutritious foods.*
◆ *Drinking juice throughout the day (especially in a bottle or spouted sippy cup) causes sugar buildup on the teeth.* This, in turn, creates high dental bills.
◆ *A sugar-loaded diet causes diarrhea.*

So, by all means, fill those sippy cups but stick to water or milk (formula, breast or whole).

The Best Sippy Cup

After researching and testing 14 different sippy cups, we pick the **OXO Tot Transitions Straw Cup** with Removable Handles (20 for a 2-pack) as the best in class.

OXO Tot's Transitions Straw Cup is the best cup for parents transitioning baby from the bottle or breast to the kitchen table. It comes with a silicone straw tip, hinged lid, and removable handles. Plus, the OXO has a rare feature in straw sippy cups: measurement markings on the side so you can see how much baby is drinking.

During our shake and leak testing, the OXO performed perfectly. Even though it has a tiny vacuum-release hole in the lid under the straw, no liquid dribbled out. It also comes with a flip lid for extra protection when tossed in diaper bag for travel. The flip lid is removable if needed.

Available in two sizes (6 oz. with handles, 6 oz. without handles and 9 oz. without handles), the biggest negative with the OXO Tot Transitions Straw Cup is the price. At ten bucks per cup ($9.99 for the 9 oz. version with no handles), it's substantially more than its runner up, the Nuby.

Another negative: The OXO cup has six parts to clean (see picture right from our tests)—which is more than other cups. Of course, this includes the removable handles and the removable flip lid (not all cups have those features). The parts are dishwasher safe. Replacement straws are available on OXO's web site, two for $3.

Like most straw sippy cups, the OXO Tot Transitions Straw Cup does have a learning curve. Parents complained that getting liquid from the cup was difficult at first, although many said their kids got the hang of it over time.

Despite these drawback, we still think OXO Tot is the best in class. Overall, we think this is the top option for parents and toddlers transitioning away from breast or bottle.

Also Great: Nuby No-Spill Cup with Flex Straw

The **Nuby No-Spill Cup with Flex Straw** ($8 for three) performed well in our shake and leak test. It comes with a soft silicone straw top (removable for cleaning) as well as an attached hard plastic straw extending into the cup itself.

But let's talk frankly about getting liquid out of these cups. Even our top pick, the OXO, is difficult to get the hang of at first. With any no-leak straw cup, the straw itself has a gasket to stop leaks. To get it to work, your child will have to push the straw up to the top of his mouth, compressing the straw, then suck. Kids are pretty adaptable and learn quickly in most cases, but we can imagine some initial frustration.

In the case of the Nuby, we found this to be the one of the easiest straw to suck from. Other straws required more force or the straw was too narrow. We also liked Nuby's silicone straw top: it's comfortable in the mouth but can stand a lot of toddler chewing. The shape of the cup makes it easier for little hands to hang on, but we wish it had handles like Nuby's spouted version. You can buy replacement straws from Nuby's web site for $2.70.

So what do parents think about the Nuby? It's affordability is a major plus. These cups are significantly less expensive than our top pick, the OXO Tot. And parents are impressed that the Nuby doesn't leak. You can shake it like a Polaroid picture, but you won't get any liquid out.

sippy cups

That's impressive compared to other cups we tested.

On the other hand, it's a bit difficult to master the valve in order to drink. In fact, even some *parents* couldn't do it. Others noted that kids who didn't get it at first were quick learners, so patience and persistence should help. Many folks liked the slow flow from these cups since it slows down those kids who chug their drinks.

Best Rimless Sippy Cup

After testing a few of the new "rimless" cups, we have picked the **Munchkin Miracle 360 Sippy Cup** ($11 for a two-pack) as our top choice for Best Rimless Sippy Cup.

Rimless cups are the next developmental step after straw sippy cups. They look and behave like a lidless cup, but have a control valve that keeps your toddler from spilling the entire contents when you're not looking. These are a great idea for those days when temper tantrums rule the house. Even if your little one threw this cup across the room, the amount of liquid spilled would be minimal.

The Munchkin Miracle 360 allows your child to sip from any side of the cup (hence the 360 moniker) just like a regular cup. It comes with only three main parts (plus a thin, clear gasket at the top of the cup— see picture at right from our testing), is dishwasher safe (top rack) and has a softly textured surface for easy holding. Smaller versions come with handles if your child's hands are too small to grasp comfortably. Your child activates the cup when she puts light pressure from her lips to the edge of the cup/gasket. When released, the gasket automatically closes.

While the cup is pretty good at containing liquid, you can get some leakage with vigorous shaking or if you leave it on its side for a long period of time. Parents also complained the cups can grow mold under the gasket (which can be hard to clean) and the control valve. Careful cleaning and drying is necessary to keep the cup mold free.

However, if your child is at least 12 months old and ready for the transition from a straw sippy to a more realistic low-leaking cup, the Munchkin Miracle 360 is the best option.

Best Budget-Friendly Sippy Cup

First Years Take & Toss Spill-proof Straw Cups are budget-friendly yet sturdy enough to be used for up to a year before throwing them out, based on our testing. These cups retail in stores for $2.68 for four cups, lids and straws.

These 10 oz. cups are made from BPA- and BPS-free plastic and can be washed in the dishwasher. While they are reusable, the First Years' selling point is they are cheap enough that you won't be bummed if you lose one. And if you have a toddler at home, you know that is going to happen.

Our readers are pleased overall with these cups, although they caution to put the lid on first, then put the straw in the lid. If you snap on the lid with the straw already in it, the seal creates a vacuum which pushes liquid out of the straw and all over you.

Also, the Take & Toss cups aren't completely spill proof, as the straws don't have a gasket to hold back the liquid. So we suggest these cups for older toddlers who aren't spiking their cups like a football.

But for the price and performance, First Years Take & Toss Spill-proof Straw Cups are great for older toddlers.

Best Eco-Friendly Sippy Cup

Most sippy cups are made of plastic. The good news: most cups on the market today are free of chemicals like BPA. And some are BPS-free (another type of plastic some folks have concerns about).

But we hear you—plenty of our readers are worried that even "safe plastics" may have unknown long-term health impacts . . . not to mention they aren't very earth-friendly.

If you're looking for an eco-friendly alternative, try a stainless steel sippy cup. Example: Munchkin, maker of our top choice for rimless sippy cup (the Miracle 360) makes it with a stainless steel base. The **Munchkin Miracle Stainless Steel 360** ($14.79) is insulated and the company claims this will keep drinks cool for up to 15 hours. Our testers concur! These cups are impressive.

The lid and control valve are still made of plastic like the original version of the cup. The company has included a plastic cap for travel.

We love that the lids are interchangeable between the stainless steel and plastic versions. Another plus: stainless doesn't retain odors so if you forget to clean them out (guilty!), you don't have to worry the container will absorb any funky smells. And unlike the straw cup mentioned above, these cups can be washed in the dishwasher.

What's not to like? The Munchkin Miracle Stainless Steel 360 is large and heavy, and prone to leaking. Remember this when you throw one in your bag or car (some readers recommended packing them in a zip lock bag just in case). A few folks complained about a metallic taste, so if you're sensitive to that, consider sticking with plastic cups.

Overall, this is a great option if you want to reduce the plastic in your life. We recommend the Munchkin Miracle Stainless Steel 360 cups.

Why didn't we recommend a sippy cup with spout?

Good question! We do not recommend cups like this one at right.

Here are the reasons why. Transitioning from breast or a bottle to a cup is a big step for toddlers. It's one of the first times you'll be encouraging real independence from your little one. Once your child can eat and drink independently (without leaving behind a huge mess), life gets a bit easier since you won't need to be personally involved in every meal! Sippy cups are typically parents' choice to help with the transition.

But . . . you knew there'd be a "but" . . . you want the right sippy cup. The delivery method is important when it comes to your child's dental and developmental health. According to our resident pediatric expert, Dr. Ari Brown (co-author of *Baby 411* and *Toddler 411*), spouted lids work just like bottles (your child will tilt his/her head back

to drink—see picture at right) so your child doesn't get to practice for a real cup.

Dentists also note that the flow of the liquid from a spouted cup is directed to the back of the top front teeth. This can easily lead to cavities. Hence, most dentists do NOT recommend using sippy cups with spouted lids.

Speech therapists also worry sippy cups with spouts could contribute to a lisping problem. The American Speech-Language-Hearing Association offers a detailed explanation of potential problems with spouted sippy cups. Their recommendation: straws, which baby can master by about nine months of age. They also recommend helping kids drink from an open top cup once they are around one year of age to help them master independent drinking. Most toddlers can drink from an open top cup by themselves by 18 months.

In light of all this expert advice, we recommend sippy cups with straws; we don't recommend spouted cups. Teaching your child to drink from a straw is a better strategy for dental health and will make the developmental transition to a lidless cup easier too.

The newest category of sippy cups are called "rimless trainers," which we also recommend. Our top pick is reviewed earlier in this section. From the side, these cups look like a regular cup with no lid. But when you look down from above, you'll see an insert that impedes the flow of liquid enough to help kids learn to drink from a lidless cup without pouring all of it on themselves. Some rimless trainers are self-sealing, while others slow down the flow rate.

Best Baby Bowls

Munchkin has won several of our test challenges in baby feeding utensils—and they topped the competition here as well. We liked **Munchkin's Stay Put bowls** ($8 for 3) for babies and toddlers best among the different suction bowls we tried. Yes, we gathered actual toddlers in high chairs and put these bowls to the test! We loved these easy-to-clean suction bowls, with bright colors and quick-release tabs. Dishwasher and microwave safe—but they can't be sterilized.

We also recommend the innovative **Bumkins Suction Silicone Baby Feeding Set** ($15). This silicone bowl and spoon works well, going from refrigerator to microwave . . . and even the oven! Great spoon and bowl, but we wish the suction was better.

Best Baby Spoon

For first-time feeders, our testers loved this utensil: **NumNum's Pre-Spoon GOOtensils** ($13). What is a pre-spoon? This clever utensil comes in both stage 1 (first-time feeders) and stage 2 (more experienced babies that have the hand-to-mouth motion down).

The first-stage spoon has cut-out grooves to hold food; and it doubles as a teether. The second-stage spoon holds more food and can be "preloaded" for a toddler who wants chunkier food. Caveat: these spoons better for thicker food. Thinner foods like rice cereal can easily fall out of the grooves.

The Best High Chairs

As soon as baby starts to eat solid food, you'll need this quintessential piece of baby furniture—the high chair. As par for the baby gear biz, you can spend $50 on a high chair . . . or $500. We'll break down what you really need and several crucial safety tips before we get to our picks!

7 Things No One Tells You About Buying A High Chair!

1 THERE ARE THREE TYPES OF HIGH CHAIRS: BASIC, MULTI-FUNCTION AND MODERN. Here's the run-down:

◆ *Basic* high chairs are sold in chain stores and aimed at parents on a budget or grandparents looking for a basic chair for occasional visits. These high chairs typically run from $30 to $100 and have few features. You won't find wheels, recline or adjustable height on budget chairs. Most budget chairs are foldable and come with a wipeable chair pad and single tray. Example: the **Cosco Simple Fold** (pictured) doesn't have any bells and whistles. It just folds and the tray adjusts. $30 at Walmart.

◆ *Multi-function* high chairs offer deluxe features and will morph into additional seating options as your child grows. Ranging in price from $100 to $250, multi-function chairs feature double trays, seat recline, adjustable height positions, foot rests, machine washable pads and wheels. More expensive chairs might have toys, designer fabrics and other upgrades. Multi-function means these chairs can often convert to toddler seats that attach to your dining room chair.

The **Graco Blossom** (pictured) accommodates infants, babies just starting to eat solids and toddlers. It also attaches to a regular dining chair. $123 on Amazon.

◆ Priced from $200 to $450, **modern high chairs** sell parents on an aesthetic. To borrow a term from fashion, these high chairs are "statement pieces." Seamless molded seats look futuristic with pops of bright colored pads. They may or may not have wheels, but some have pneumatic lift systems (like a barber's chair). Even though modern chairs are pricey, they oddly omit features seen in lower price models, like double trays, a compact fold, seat recline, etc.

2 **SURPRISE! THAT DISHWASHER-SAFE TRAY MAY NOT FIT IN YOUR DISHWASHER.** Most high chairs today come with a dishwasher-safe tray or tray insert that may claim to snap off and pop into the dishwasher for clean-up . . . but does it? In our reviews of high chairs, we'll note some models whose dishwasher-safe trays are too big to fit in an actual dishwasher. A word of advice: measure the bottom rack of your dishwasher and take that dimension with you when high chair shopping.

3 **THE X-FACTOR FOR ANY HIGH CHAIR: HOW EASY IS IT TO CLEAN?** So here's what a real baby looks like when eating:

Cute? Yes—but then you have to clean that spaghetti sauce from all those nooks and crannies of a high chair. Not fun.

Here's a tip some first-time parents miss: make sure the high chair you buy has a removable, washable seat cover OR a seat that easily sponges clean. In the latter category, chairs with vinyl trump those made of cloth. Vinyl can be wiped clean, while cloth typically has to be washed. This might be one of those first-time parent traps: seats with cloth covers sure look nicer than those made of vinyl. But the extra effort to machine wash a cloth cover is a pain . . . and some cloth covers can't be thrown in the dryer. That means waiting a day or more for a cover to line dry.

Watch out for seat pads that have ruffles or numerous crevices—these are food magnets and a bear to keep clean. What color cover should you get? Anything but white. Sure that fancy white leatherette high chair looks all shiny and new at the baby store, but it will forever be a cleaning nightmare once you start using it. Darker colors and patterns are better.

Of course, keeping a chair clean involves more than just the pad—look at the seat and tray itself. Avoid models with numerous crevices and cracks. Seamless seats and trays are best. FYI: Many high chair trays claim they are dishwasher safe, but have cracks that let water collect inside the tray. This can be a mold hazard, as it is hard to get the tray to properly dry.

4 **YOU DON'T HAVE TO BUY A HIGH CHAIR FOR QUITE A WHILE.** Although you may decide to register for a high chair during your pregnancy, you won't need one for at least four or five months after your baby is born. Why? Babies don't need high chairs until they start eating solid food.

Pediatricians don't recommend starting solids until at least four months of age. And if your baby isn't ready for solids till six months of age, that's still developmentally normal. If you don't have a lot of storage space, don't get a chair before you need it.

5 **ONE WORD: WHEELS!** If you have a small kitchen, you might not need a high chair with wheels, but if you plan to feed baby in the dining room and need to wash up in the kitchen, look for a chair with wheels. That way, you aren't tempted to walk away from your baby with the detachable tray, leaving them unattended. As you'll see in our Safety Alert section below, this can lead to kids escaping the harness and falling. Remember, though, that you want wheels that lock and unlock easily—they should move when you want them to but stay in one place when feeding baby.

6 **SAFETY STANDARDS FOR HIGH CHAIRS ARE VOLUNTARY.** Unlike with cribs and car seats, high chairs only have voluntary safety standards. In Safety Alerts below, we discuss some of the shortcomings of this voluntary system and what you as a parent can do to make your child safer in a high chair.

7 **MULTIPLE TRAYS ARE REALLY HELPFUL DURING CLEAN-UP.** We love high chair trays that come with a tray insert. That way you can clear up most of the mess quickly without releasing the main tray. You may still have to wipe down the main tray a bit, but most of the food will be on the insert.

Safety Alert: High Chairs

Here's the good news about high chair safety: the latest Consumer Product Safety Commission (CPSC) data shows that very few babies die in high chair accidents (a rate of one or less per year). Injuries, however, are another story. In 2015 (the most recent year statistics are available), the CPSC estimates that high chairs were the #4 cause on the list of injuries to children under five requiring an emergency room visit. That number: 11,100 high chair accidents.

In late 2015, the CPSC proposed new mandatory safety standards for high chairs. Currently, high chair safety standards are voluntary; this proposal would make standards mandatory. Within the report, the CPSC analyzed high chair injuries and made recommendations for mandatory rules based on that analysis. As you might guess, many injuries associated with high chairs were caused by falls. Thankfully, there is quite a lot you can do to prevent a fall in your kitchen or dining room:

◆ *Always use the harness.* We like five-point harnesses (like those in a car seat), rather than three-point (waist and crotch), so baby can't wiggle out and stand up. Never remove the tray without also removing your child. We know, it's easy to just pop off the tray and run it over to the sink for a minute, but kids are wily. They can wiggle out of a lot of straps and restraints if left to their own devices. Instead, consider wheeling or carrying (if you can) the high chair to the sink, then take off the tray.

high chairs

◆ *Passive restraints to avoid submarining under the tray.* Most high chair injuries occur when babies are not strapped into their chairs. Sadly, one to two deaths occur each year when babies "submarine" under the tray. To address these types of accidents, new high chairs now feature a "passive restraint" (a plastic post) under the tray to prevent this.

◆ *Some high chair makers attach this submarine protection to the tray; others have it attached to the seat.* We prefer posts that are attached to the seat. Why? If the post is on the tray and the tray is removed, there is a risk a child might be able to squirm out of the safety belts (which is all that would hold them in the chair). If it is attached to the chair, it's always there to help block an active baby. By the way, some wooden high chairs only seem to have a crotch strap—no plastic post. Again, not much is keeping baby safely in the chair. But let us reiterate: even if the high chair has a passive anti-submarine restraint, you STILL must strap in baby with the safety harness with EACH use. This prevents them from climbing out and falling.

◆ *Additional injuries occurred when chair frames or legs broke, seat supports failed and screws came loose* (also a potential choking hazard). Since these problems are caused by manufacturer defects, you may think there isn't much you can do to prevent them. However, we recommend parents carefully read and follow assembly instructions. Consider looking for unboxing videos online to supplement written instructions. And put a reminder in your phone to check screws and bolts once a month to be sure they haven't loosened. If you're considering a used high chair, check the CPSC's web site for any recalls of the chair you're considering and check for missing parts.

◆ *The report also noted some injuries (bruises and lacerations) occurred when children ran into pegs on the back of the chair,* which are used for hanging the tray when not in use. These are meant to be convenient storage, but often are projecting out from the back legs at just the right height for toddlers. If your chair comes with these pegs, we recommend removing them. Or folding the chair and putting it out of harm's way.

◆ Finally, the CPSC high chair report also assessed *high chairs in restaurants*, many of which do not adhere to the volunteer safety standards. For example, the report notes that restaurant high chairs often failed the anti-submarining test (babies can slide through the front openings or the sides and get their heads caught or fall right through to the floor). Stability was also a potential issue. The report was concerned that the narrow profile of many restaurant high chairs might lead to tipping and falling. We are also concerned that many restaurant chairs either don't have harnesses at all or only use three-point harnesses. There are hook-on chairs we recommend for parents who want to provide a safe seat for baby at a restaurant without using the restaurants high chair. See later in this chapter for suggestions.

The Best High Chairs. We break down our high chair recommendations into a few categories: Best High Chair (Overall), Best Modern High Chair, Best Urban/Space-Challenged High Chair, and Best High Chair for Grandma's House. Coming up next!

The Best High Chair: Compact Fold

If space is at a premium in your kitchen, a high chair that has a slim, compact fold is a must. You'd think that would be a standard feature, but surprisingly, no . . . some models don't fold at all!

It's the Catch 22 of high chairs. Most full-feature high chairs do NOT fold in a compact manner. And other bare bones high chairs do fold, but don't have the features most folks like.

For the best compact fold high chair, we'd give the nod to the **Graco Slim Snacker** ($60). It checks all the right boxes: full features yet compact fold. And a price that is easy on the wallet.

We loved this full-featured chair that quickly folds and stands. No assembly required, lightweight and 3-position recline. Drawback: No dishwasher-safe tray insert. And it can be difficult to clean.

Best Budget-Friendly High Chair

If bare bones is all you need, an IKEA high chair the fits the bill. The **IKEA Antilop** high chair costs all of $20 for a metal and plastic chair with anti-submarining bar molded into the seat and three-point safety belt. And yes, it includes a tray (but no seat pad).

IKEA has a couple of other high chair models, but the Antilop is the best rated by parents we interviewed. Yes, IKEA high chairs are clearly designed for older kids (no seat recline, for example) and don't have five-point safety belts which we prefer. That said, parents generally give the Antilop great reviews, noting it's really easy to clean. And it's hard to beat for 20 bucks.

Best Urban/Space-Challenged High Chair

Is space tight in your kitchen? The **Fisher-Price Space Saver** ($40-$50) lives up to its name—it's basically a high chair without the bulky base. You strap it to a regular chair.

The Space Saver features a full-size tray and three-position recline—plus it converts to a toddler booster. If you are short of space (think New York City apartment), this is a great choice.

Detractors point out that once you strap this thing to a chair, you can't push the chair under the table—hence defeating the space saving concept. We see that point, but still think this is a great solution for urban condos with little space to store a bulky high chair. Reader feedback on the Space Saver is very positive—we recommend it.

Best High Chair for Grandma's House

For grandma's house, a basic **Cosco Simple Fold** ($30-$50) should do the trick. No, it doesn't have the bells and whistle of $100+ chairs, but Grandma doesn't need all that. You get a seat with wipeable seat pad, double tray, 3-position tray adjust and slim fold. This chair doesn't recline, so you can't use it for kids under six months. No, the chair doesn't have wheels, but is easy to clean.

On pages (142-143), we have a chart that sums up our ratings for popular high chairs. Next up, let's look at the best portable high chairs (road trip!) and options for toddlers.

Best Hook-on Chair

The **Chicco Caddy** ($59) is our top pick as the best hook-on chair for travel and restaurants. We love the compact fold, three point harness and "quick grip" table clamps. The seat pad can be removed, although some parents note it can be difficult to remove the first few time, and it is machine washable.

Like most hook-on chairs, the Caddy only has a three-point harness. Because of this, some parents complain it's too easy for active kids to stand up even with the harness latched, so keep an eye on your child when using this or any other hook-chair.

In a recent update, Chicco debuted a revised version of the Caddy called the **Chicco Quick-Seat Hook-On Chair** ($70). The headline here is a new one-pull tightener feature that makes install quicker. But it is 50% more than the Caddy.

Similar but with more bells and whistles is the **Chicco 360 Hook On** ($90). The 360's seat rotates so you can more easily put your child in or take her out and comes with a tray. While parents like the rotating seat, some have complained this seat is harder to clean than the Caddy.

FYI: We don't recommend hook-on chairs as replacements for a high chair, although many parents with limited space choose a hook-on chair. Hook-on chairs are best when visiting friends and family or when eating at a restaurant. If you are looking for a full-feature high chair that can be attached to a dining room chair, consider the Fisher-Price Space Saver reviewed in our section earlier on high chairs.

Also Great: Inglesina Fast Table Chair

Although it's much more expensive than the Chicco Caddy, we think the **Inglesina Fast Table Chair with Tray** ($69), is an excellent second choice. It has a quick flat-fold for travel, a small storage pocket in the back and the cover is removable and hand-washable.

A neat trick: the carry bag is sewn to the bottom of the seat so you can never lose it. Parent feedback on this chair is excellent.

Best Toddler Travel High Chair

What's the best high chair for toddlers? Toddlers love their independence . . . so a high chair that lets them sit at the table like a big kid is a plus. And even if your child outgrows that baby high chair, they may still need a boost to sit in a regular chair. We tried out 9 high chair models with actual toddlers to find the best bets.

For the best travel toddler high chair, we recommend the **Chicco Pocket Snack Booster Seat** ($30). We liked this high chair's easy, compact fold—perfect for travel or just a day at Grandma's house.

The metal legs adjust this chair to three height positions, which is most helpful when you want to have your toddler pulled up to the table.

We should point out one caveat with chair: it is designed to ONLY be used when strapped to an adult-size chair (and that chair must be at least 14" wide, 14" deep and the back must be 12" high.)

The Chicco Pocket Snack Booster CANNOT be used by itself on the floor—it would tip over. The maker clearly points this out in the instructions and description of this chair . . . but some folks have missed that warning.

Best High Chair For Outdoors

The best portable high chair for outdoor adventure should have water resistant nylon fabric and feature a quick set up and fold. We think the **Summer Pop and Sit** ($35) portable booster is the best travel high chair for picnics, camping or other outdoor adventures A "life saver" is how our testers viewed this little gem, which is perfect to throw in the car for a road trip. Critics say it is hard to clean the nylon fabric, however.

HIGH CHAIRS

High chairs, compared

NAME	RATING	PRICE	TRAY HEIGHT	TRAY DEPTH	SUB?
BABY TREND SIT RIGHT	C+	$60-$125	8.5	8	SEAT
BLOOM FRESCO	D	$550-$680	10	8	SEAT
CHICCO POLLY	C+	$120-$230	7.5	7	TRAY
COSCO SIMPLE FOLD	C+	$65	*	*	SEAT
EVENFLO SYMMETRY	C	$50-70	*	*	SEAT
FISHER PRICE SPACE SAVER	A	$40-$50	7.5	5	SEAT
GRACO BLOSSOM	A	$124-$190	6	6	TRAY
GRACO EVERYSTEP	A	$130	*	*	TRAY
GRACO SLIM SNACKER	A	$60	*	*	TRAY
IKEA ANTILOP	C+	$20	*	*	SEAT
IKEA BLAMES	C+	$60	*	*	NONE
INGENUITY TRIO	B	$74	*	*	SEAT
INGLESINA GUSTO	B-	$150	5.5	8	TRAY
JOOVY NOOK	A-	$120	*	*	SEAT
NOMI HIGH CHAIR	B	$300-$520	*	*	SEAT
NUNA ZAZZ	B	$300	*	*	SEAT
MAXI COSI MINLA	B+	$220	*	*	TRAY
OXO TOT SPROUT	B-	$250	7	7	TRAY
PEREGO PRIMA PAPPA ZERO	C+	$200-$300	8.5	7	SEAT
PHIL & TEDS POPPY	C	$100-$150	*	*	TRAY
SAFETY 1ST ADAPTABLE	C+	$90	*	*	TRAY
SAFETY 1ST GROW & GO	C+	$75	*	*	TRAY
STOKKE CLIKK	B	$170	*	*	TRAY
STOKKE TRIPP TRAPP	A-	$200-$320	*	*	SEAT

KEY

TRAY HEIGHT: Distance from the seat to the top of the tray. Any measurement under 8″ is acceptable. Above 8″ is too tall.

DEPTH (tray to seat): Distance from the back of the seat to the tray. 5″ to 7″ is acceptable.

SUB?: Most high chairs have a special guard to prevent a child from submarining under the tray. Some models attach this to the chair; others to the tray. A better bet: those that attach to the seat. See discussion earlier in this chapter.

PAD	COMMENT
CLOTH	ONE-HAND TRAY RELEASE, FOLDS COMPACT FOR STORAGE
LEATHERETTE	SEAMLESS SEAT, AUTO HEIGHT, SEAT RECLINES
VINYL	HARD TO CLEAN, DIFFICULT TO ADJUST HARNESS
VINYL	LOWEST PRICE, GOOD FOR GRANDMA'S HOUSE
VINYL	COMPACT FOLD—BUT THE SEAT PAD IS NOT MACHINE WASHABLE
VINYL	ATTACHES TO CHAIR; GREAT FOR SMALL SPACES.
VINYL	CONVERTS TO TODDLER BOOSTER.
LEATHERETTE	MACHINE WASHABLE PAD, MORPHS INTO 7 USES (INCLUDING BOOSTER).
VINYL	COMPACT FOLD, BUT NO WHEELS. LARGE MESH STORAGE BASKET.
NONE	TRAY IS $5 EXTRA; BETTER FOR OLDER TODDLERS
NONE	NO HARNESS; BETTER FOR OLDER TODDLERS.
VINYL	TRANSITIONS FROM CHAIR TO BOOSTER
VINYL	EASY COMPACT FOLD; 4 HEIGHT POSITIONS
VINYL	LARGER TRAY, CAN FOLD WITH TRAY ATTACHED.
VINYL	FANCY BUT PRICEY, MORPHS FROM BABY BOUNCER TO TODDLER CHAIR
FOAM	"CRUMB FREE" DESIGN FOR EASY CLEANING.
CLOTH	REMOVABLE INFANT CUSHION, 6 MODES: CHAIR TO BOOSTER
VINYL	DOESN'T FOLD; WOOD HYBRID
VINYL	3 VERSIONS; MANY COLORS, HARD TO CLEAN
FOAM	SEAMLESS PAD, SMALL TRAY. HARD TO KEEP UNDER PAD AREA CLEAN
CLOTH	ULTRA COMPACT, STANDING FOLD
VINYL	COMPACT FOLD, WHEELS THAT LOCK, 6 HEIGHT POSITIONS.
VINYL	MID-CENTURY VIBE WITH WOOD LEGS, DISHWASHER SAFE TRAY.
CLOTH	BABY RAIL IS $70 EXTRA; NO TRAY

high chairs

PAD: Is the seat made of cloth or vinyl? We prefer vinyl for easier clean up. Cloth seats must be laundered and some can't be thrown in the drier (requiring a long wait for it to line dry). Of course, this feature isn't black and white—some vinyl seats have cloth edging/piping.

* Not applicable or not available. Some of these models were new as of press time, so we didn't have these specs yet.

Best Booster Seat For A Dining Table

Let's talk booster seats for toddlers at dinner time!

When it comes to buying a booster seat, you have two basic choices: tray or no tray.

The most popular kitchen boosters for toddlers are those without a tray. This type of booster helps boost a child up to the dining table, where they eat with the rest of the family.

Booster seats with trays are helpful if you have a younger child and you don't have room for a high chair. The tray is helpful for holding a bowl, etc.

Consider these tips when looking for a booster:

◆ *Is the booster dishwasher safe?* Yes, some models are designed to fit inside a dishwasher, simplifying cleanup.

◆ *Strap or no strap?* Some booster seats for the dining table have a safety strap to keep a toddler from falling out of the chair—however, these belts aren't foolproof. Regardless, if you're using a booster off the floor (attached to a kitchen chair) a strap may offer additional safety. Older kiddos may be fine without the strap.

◆ *Crevices can be a food magnet.* When it comes to toddlers and food, it's always surprising where the food ends up. The best booster seats are designed without cracks or crevices for food to hide!

After testing out several models and surveying our parent readers, here are our recommendations for the best booster seats for the dining table:

Best Booster Without Tray

Our top pick in this category is the **Prince Lionheart Soft Booster** ($36). Designed for kids three and up, the foam seat includes a rubberized, slip-resistant grip. It is a great option for kids who need a boost to reach the table comfortably. The soft foam padding is waterproof and cleans easily. This is a great booster to get you through the toddler years.

Best Modern Booster

Another good bet in the category of boosters without trays is the **OXO Tot Perch** booster seat ($40). It quickly collapses and has a carry handle for travel. Reader feedback on this one has been quite positive.

Best Booster With Tray

The **Fisher-Price Healthy Care Booster** ($27) seat is an affordable, yet feature-rich booster seat. With tray and height adjustability that folds and comes with a carry strap, it's a great option for parents to take out to dinner or to Grandma's house.

CHAPTER 7

Around the House: Play yards, Monitors, Bouncers, Safety

Inside this chapter

What's the best pacifier? Which baby monitor let's you stream your nursery online? What about the best tummy time mat? In this chapter, we explore everything for baby that's around the house. From bouncer seats to safety gates, play yards to swings, we've got recommendations. Finally, let's talk safety—we'll give you advice on affordable baby proofing.

The Best Pacifier

The best pacifier should mimic a human nipple, so as to not interfere with breastfeeding. They should also be easy to clean. Because pacifiers have been implicated in recent safety recalls, we look for pacifiers made by reputable brands that have a solid track record in this category.

Before we reveal our top pacifier pick, let's go over a few things to know about picking the best pacifier for your baby.

7 Things No One Tells You About Buying A Pacifier!

1 **WAIT TILL BREASTFEEDING IS WELL ESTABLISHED (AT LEAST FOUR TO SEVEN DAYS) BEFORE INTRODUCING A PACIFIER.** Lactation consultants tell us you don't want to confuse a newborn with a pacifier, so skip the pacifier for at least four days after birth while you try to establish good breastfeeding habits. If you've never breastfed before, you may not realize that it can be rather difficult at first. Breastfeeding may be a natural process, but it requires some skills on both your and your baby's part. So don't set yourself up for failure by confusing your baby with a pacifier at the outset. Don't worry, babies will still take that paci later.

2 **PACIFIERS CAN OFFER SOME PROTECTION AGAINST SIDS FOR THE FIRST SIX MONTHS TO ONE YEAR OF LIFE.** According to our in-house pediatrician and co-author of *Baby 411*, Dr. Ari Brown, pacifiers can greatly reduce the risk of Sudden Infant Death Syndrome (SIDS). A variety of studies, including a metadata study that looked at seven independent studies and results, have concluded that pacifiers can reduce the risk of SIDS "particularly when placed for sleep."

3 **GET RID OF PACIFIERS EARLY.** Pediatricians, the American Academy of Pediatrics and pediatric dentists all agree: *get rid of the pacifier by one year of age at the latest.* The risk for SIDS is greatest during the first six months of life, with the chances trailing off after a baby is one of year age. Why get rid of a pacifier after your baby turns one if your baby loves it? Let's talk about that next.

4 **SPEECH DELAYS AND ORTHODONTIC DAMAGE.** Your baby needs to develop language skills sooner than you think. Pacifier use after one year of age can cause speech delays. Although research on this subject is inconclusive, babies with pacifiers tend to grunt and point more to communicate—and some can miss speech or language developmental milestones, according to pediatricians we interviewed.

What about damage to teeth or your baby's jaw? Studies show pacifier use after age two can cause orthodontic problems. And that can mean a big orthodontist bill down the road. Bottom line: give up the pacifier BEFORE one year of age.

5 **EXTENDED USE OF PACIFIERS CAN LEAD TO EAR INFECTIONS.** According to Dr. Ari Brown, co-author of *Baby 411* and a practicing pediatrician: ". . . pacifiers are a known risk factor for ear infections." Our advice: use pacifiers at nap and bedtimes only for the first six months to a year. Give up the pacifier BEFORE your baby turns one.

6 **DON'T TURN THAT ORTHODONTIC PACI UPSIDE DOWN.** Orthodontic pacifiers like those made by NUK and MAM have an up side and a down side. Example: MAM pacifiers at right usually have pictures on their exterior button so you can see which way is up. Another clue: the tip of the nipple should point slightly upward to the top of baby's mouth.

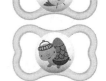

Don't allow your baby to use her orthodontic paci upside down, which leads baby to chew the pacifier. Then, when you're breastfeeding, he just might start chewing on you! Ouch! You can tell up from down by either the pattern on the pacifier or by the notch some paci's have on the top.

7 **IT'S EASIER TO BREAK A PACIFIER HABIT THAN A THUMB OR FINGER SUCKING HABIT.** Throughout this whole discussion, you may have been thinking: "I hope my baby just sucks his thumb instead of a pacifier. That's so much easier than worrying that the binky will fall out in the middle of the night."

Yes, but . . . you knew there was going to be a "but." Pediatric dentists note that getting rid of the paci is a lot easier than stopping thumb sucking. After all, baby has her thumb all the time. But a binky can be "lost" when you want to get rid of it.

Children who continue to use a pacifier or suck a thumb past two years of age risk serious damage to their teeth. Expensive orthodontia may be required, and in some severe cases, surgery.

Talk to your pediatrician if you have a child addicted to thumb or finger sucking for comfort and stress relief. They have tried and true methods to help your child stop without traumatizing her.

The Best Pacifier

After comparing and testing 17 baby pacifiers, we've picked the **Soothie by Philips Avent** ($8.49 for four) as our choice for overall best pacifier.

The best pacifier should mimic a human nipple, and hence, not interfere with breastfeeding. They should also be easy to clean. Because pacifiers have been implicated in recent safety recalls, we look for pacifiers made by reputable brands that have a solid track record in this category.

The Soothie hits all the right notes: it works well for newborns and young infants trying to establish breastfeeding as well as for older babies to provide some protection against SIDS (Sudden Infant Death Syndrome; see earlier for how pacifiers work to prevent SIDS).

Basically, pacifiers come in two types: one-piece construction with a straight nipple and three-piece construction with a molded orthodontic nipple. Soothies are the most popular one-piece option on the market, based on our surveys of readers and lactation consultants. Made of sturdy, hospital-grade silicone with no latex or BPA, you can sterilize Soothies or put them in the dishwasher.

Soothies are made by Philips Avent, which has a solid safety track record in this category. The brand has had no safety recalls for pacifiers in the past ten years.

Over 2000 U.S. hospitals hand out Soothies to parents of newborns. Our readers generally praise Soothies as excellent pacifiers, but a handful of parents said their babies did not like the Soothie's straight nipple. In those cases, these readers found orthodontic-style pacifiers by Nuk or MAM worked better for their babies.

Also Great: MAM pacifiers.

If Soothies aren't cutting it with your baby (yes, a minority of babies don't like them), consider an orthodontic pacifier like our runner up, **MAM Newborn Start**. These two-piece pacifiers include a BPA-free silicone nipple, plastic mouth guard with air circulation holes and a carry case. Price: $6 for a two pack.

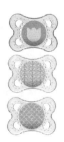

MAM's orthodontic nipple is best for older babies who have well established breast feeding habits (or are bottle feeders). FYI: MAM pacifiers can cause oral development issues if babies suck on them upside down, so make sure your baby has it in her mouth correctly.

MAM has a loyal following of parents who swear by these pacifiers. They like the small sized guard, light weight and multitude of cute colors and patterns. Many mentioned they love the glow in the dark version–they can find them in the middle of the night without turning on a light. One reader noted that her baby only wanted to suck on her finger to be soothed, but once he tried the MAM, she was freed from that duty.

Critics of MAM pacifiers say they are too small and rather expensive.

Despite these criticisms, we think MAM pacifiers are a great option for infants who are not breastfeeding and older babies with well established breastfeeding habits. Yes, they cost a bit more, but most parents say they're worth it.

Best Pacifier Clip

After comparing and testing nine different pacifier clips, we crown the **Babygoal Pacifier Clip** ($4.59) as the best pacifier clip. Babygoal's simple design and solid colors make this pacifier clip the best of the bunch. We liked the plastic clip and loop attachment, which is better than competitors' clips.

Best Bibs

Over the years, we've owned and tested hundreds of bibs for droolers, first-time solid-food eaters and "big kid" toddlers. In this round-up, we hand-tested for absorbency, washability, comfort and price. And our top pick for best bib overall is the **Bumkins SuperBib** ($13.49 for 3)–machine washable, durable and affordable. And cute!

For drool bibs, we recommend **YooFoss Baby Bibs Bandana Bib** ($14 for 8). These drool bibs won our testing with soft, 100% organic cotton fabric and photo-ready cute colors! Best feature: snaps, no velcro. Our testers loved that babies could NOT just rip off this bib, thanks to snaps in the back.

While standard bibs do a decent job at feeding, silicone bibs are excellent for their larger/wider pocket that catches more food. Our pick here is **Happy Healthy Parent Silicone**

Baby Bibs ($16 for 2). We loved these silicone bibs for their excellent design and adjustable button straps. Our testers loved the super light weight.

Best Humidifier

We always know when its wintertime here in Colorado—the furnace kicks in and everyone's skin dries out quicker than you can say Mojave Desert. Hence, humidifiers are a way of life here. But even if you live in a more humid climate, running a humidifier in your baby's room in the winter can keep throats, nasal passages and skin from drying out—and make everyone happier.

7 Things No One Tells You About Buying A Humidifier!

1 **THERE ARE TWO BASIC TYPES OF HUMIDIFIERS: EVAPORATIVE AND ULTRASONIC.** Evaporative humidifiers have a wick that soaks up water, then a fan blows the moisture out. These are often the least expensive type, but can be noisy . . . plus the filter must be replaced regularly.

Ultrasonic humidifiers use sound waves to disperse the moisture so there is no fan required. This makes ultrasonics much quieter than evaporative humidifiers. The downside, though, is sometimes they leave a coating of white dust in the room. And they can be more expensive

2 **HUMIDIFIERS ALSO COME IN WARM OR COLD MIST.** Warm mist humidifiers use a heating element to warm the water (cold mist do not). While that might sound appealing if you live in a cold climate, we do NOT recommend these humidifiers for baby's room. That's because warm mist humidifiers can overheat the room—and that's a risk factor for Sudden Infant Death Syndrome (SIDS). Also, the hot mist coming out of the humidifier can cause a scalding injury if touched by a wayward toddler.

Warm mist humidifiers require more cleaning and maintenance than cool mist ones. If you are tempted to buy a warm mist humidifier because your nursery is drafty, it would make more sense to buy a separate oil-filled space heater and a cool mist humidifier. That's because a space heater more efficiently heats the room than a warm mist humidifier. (Of course, there is still a safety problem with all space heaters—toddlers can burn themselves on any hot surface. The best long term solution is to have a HVAC specialist see if they can correct the heating/cooling issue in your baby's nursery).

3 **DON'T OVERSIZE THE HUMIDIFIER.** Humidifiers are rated by gallon output and most will tell you the size room they cover—match this to the size room your baby is in. You don't need a giant humidifier for most bedrooms.

4 **HUMIDIFIERS SHOULD BE CLEANED REGULARLY.** Humidifiers have detailed cleaning instructions—follow these! If not, you risk mold or mildew build-up in the unit or the shortening of the humidifier's lifespan.

humidifier

5 **CONSIDER AN ADJUSTABLE HUMIDISTAT.** A humidistat works like a thermostat, setting the humidity at a certain level and turning on or off the humidifier until it reaches that level. This is a nice feature, although it's not completely necessary.

6 **SKIP THE VAPORIZER.** A vaporizer is a humidifier that lets you disperse medication in your child's room. Generally, this is NOT recommended—that's because pediatricians rarely prescribe medication that needs to be vaporized these days.

7 **IF YOU'RE REMODELING, CONSIDER WHOLE HOUSE SOLUTIONS.** If you are planning to do any HVAC work on your home, consider installing a whole-house humidifier. These automatically kick in when your furnace runs (or can be controlled by a thermostat). Since they are permanently installed and plumbed to a water line, you never have to refill the humidifier. You do have to change the filter and do some maintenance, but that's typically just once a year. FYI: Honeywell makes a whole house steam humidifier which we use in our house—we'd recommend it.

The Best Humidifier (Cool Mist)

Yes, there is truth in advertising: **Crane's Adorable Ultrasonic Cool Mist Humidifier** is, well, adorable. But it actually works well, according to our readers.

Crane has 23 different animal shaped humidifiers as well as a train and Hello Kitty models. Priced at $40 to $50, parents praise the Crane humidifiers for the most part (quiet, easy to fill, easy to clean). But a few dissenters said it stopped working after a couple weeks, the output was too little for larger nurseries and they had problems with leaks. So . . . buy this humidifier from a store or website with an easy return policy just in case.

A few caveats to the Crane: it only has a one gallon tank, so it will require daily refilling. And we see some concerns it doesn't disperse the moisture well in a room—adding a small fan might help.

Best Bouncer Seat

Bouncers (also called activity seats) provide a comfy place for baby to hang out while you eat dinner, and the toy bar adds some mild amusement. The most common add-on to these products is a "Magic Fingers" vibration feature—the bouncer basically vibrates, simulating a car ride. Parents who have these bouncers tell us they'd rather have a kidney removed than give up their vibrating bouncer, as it appears the last line of defense in soothing a fussy baby, short of checking into a mental institution.

What features should you look for in a bouncer? Readers say a carrying handle is a big plus. Also: get a neutral fabric pattern, says another parent, since you'll probably be taking lots of photos of baby in this bouncer and neutral works better.

We break down our bouncer recommendations into three categories: Best Bouncer (Overall), Best Budget-Friendly Bouncer and Best Eco Bouncer.

Best Bouncer Seat (Overall)

After bouncing lots of babies in 15+ bouncer seats, we've chosen the **4Moms MamaRoo 4** as the best bouncer seat. If you are hoping for a gift in this category, this bouncer fits the bill, clocking in at a hefty $220 to $250.

MamaRoo's fans love the five unique motions (including car ride, ocean wave, etc.) as well as the built-in nature sounds and the relatively compact footprint. The most recent Mamaroo is Bluetooth-enabled so you control it with a smartphone app. One caveat: it only works to 25 lbs.

The Mamaroo is sold in two flavors—Classic (grey, black) and Plush (colored patterns). The Classic ($220) is a basic, canvas like fabric. The Plush ($250) has a softer, more velvet like cover. We've evaluated the feel of both versions and think the Classic is fine. FYI: an extra pad is $40.

4Moms also makes a scaled-down version of the MamaRoo called the RockARoo—we're not big fans of that model, which gets poor marks from our readers.

Best Budget-Friendly Bouncer

The **Fisher Price Infant to Toddler Rocker** ($42-$45) is an affordable bouncer that works up to 40 lbs. (hence the infant to toddler name). It is very lightweight, so it easily moves from room to room, but it doesn't collapse—so its use for travel is limited.

In infant mode, the seat reclines and a toy bar adds musical elements—of course, the key feature is that vibration, which is triggered by a button up front. In toddler mode, the chair sits more upright (and the toy bar is removed). Bottom line: at $25, this simple, affordable bouncer does the job.

Best Eco-Friendly Bouncer

If you want to take an eco-friendly approach to bouncers, the **Baby Bjorn Bouncer Bliss** is our top pick. No sounds, no lights, no batteries—the Bliss rocks when you move it.

Yes, it is pricey ($200), but you can use it up to 29 lbs. (most bouncers have 25 lb. weight limits). The Bliss has a three-position recline and collapses for travel/portability (it weighs just 7 lbs).

Readers love the Baby Bjorn's simplicity and design; critics say it is too pricey, as exemplified by the add-on wooden toy bar accessory for $50. We agree on that point, but think this bouncer is a good choice for those who want to go green.

The Best Play Yards

The portable play yard has been so popular in recent years that many parents consider it a necessity. Compared to rickety playpens of old, today's play yards fold compactly for portability and offer such handy features as bassinets, wheels and more. First, some shopping tips and then our recommendations.

7 Things No One Tells You About Buying a Play Yard

1 **DON'T BUY A SECOND-HAND PLAY YARD OR USE A HAND-ME-DOWN.** Many models have been the subject of recalls in recent years. Why? Those same features that make them convenient (the collapsibility to make the play yards "portable") worked too well in the past—some play yards collapsed with babies inside. Others had protruding rivets that caught some babies who wore pacifiers on a string (a BIG no-no, never have your baby wear a pacifier on a string). A slew of injuries and deaths have prompted the recall of ten million playpens over the years. Yes, you can search government recall lists (cpsc.gov) to see if that hand-me-down is recalled, but we'd skip the hassle and just buy new.

2 **GO FOR THE BASSINET FEATURE.** Some play yards feature bassinet inserts, which can be used for babies under three months of age (always check the weight guidelines). This is a handy feature that we recommend.

3 **SKIP THE "NEWBORN NAPPER."** Graco has added a newborn napper feature to some of its playpens. This is a separate sleep area designed to "cuddle your baby." You are supposed to use this napper before you use the bassinet feature. Our concern: the napper includes plush fabrics and a head pillow—we consider this an unsafe sleep environment. As we discussed in Chapter 2, Nursery, your baby should always be put down to sleep on his back on a *flat* surface with no soft bedding—the newborn napper is an *inclined* surface with the aforementioned pillow and plush fabrics on the side. Graco also makes a model (the Chadwick) that has non-removeable bumpers on the bassinet. We do not recommend this model play yard for the same reason we don't recommend you use bumpers in a crib.

4 **CHECK THE WEIGHT LIMITS.** Play yards have two weight limits: one for the bassinet and one for the entire play yard (without the bassinet). Graco and most other play yard versions have an overall weight limit of 30 lbs. and height limit of 35". The exception is the Arms Reach Co-Sleeper which tops out at 50 lbs. However, there is more variation in the weight limits for the bassinet attachments. Here are the weight limits for the bassinet attachments on various play yards:

Arms Reach Co-Sleeper	30 lbs.
Graco Pack N Play	15 lbs.
Chicco Lullaby	15 lbs.
Compass Aluminum	18 lbs.
Combi Play Yard	15 lbs.

5 **USEFUL FEATURES: STORAGE AND MORE STORAGE.** You can't have enough storage as a parent, so play yards with side-rail storage, compartments for diapers and the like are most welcome. We also like wheels for mobility and a canopy (if you plan to take the play yard outside or to the beach). If you want a play yard with canopy, look for those models that have "aluminized fabric" canopies—they reflect the sun's heat and UV rays to keep baby cooler.

6 **FEATURES THAT AREN'T WORTH IT: GIZMOS AND TOYS.** Play yard makers like to load up their products with gadgets, lullabies, toys, flashing lights and other bling. You don't need it.

7 **EVEN THOUGH ALL PLAY YARDS PITCH THEMSELVES AS PORTABLE, MOST AREN'T THAT EASY TO TRAVEL WITH.** Yes, most play yards claim they are portable—but the effort it takes to disassemble all the accessories makes it more likely that play pen will stay put. A better bet for portability: go for play yards that are specifically designed for travel. We recommend a travel crib in Chapter 2.

Up next, our recommendations for different types of play yards:

◆ Best Play Yard (Overall)   ◆ Best Play Yard For Travel
◆ Best Outdoor Play Yard   ◆ Best Extra-Large Play Yard
◆ Best Play Yard for Multiples

The Best Play Yard (Overall)

The **Graco Pack N Play On the Go** is our pick for best play yard overall. It's simple—bassinet, toy bar and wheels—but gets the job done. And the price? $55.

Graco is the market leader in this category—and given the value and features they offer, that's no surprise. The company offers a dozen models of playpens and each is well designed. Of course, if you want all the toys and gizmos, Graco has models with those features too—but you'll pay $100 to $200 for those versions. One caveat: skip the Graco models with "newborn nappers." As we explained earlier, we don't recommend these for safety reasons.

The Best Play Yard For Outdoors

Planning a beach outing? Soccer game? **Summer Infant Pop N' Play Portable Play Yard** ($73) is the best solution when you need a play yard for outdoors that sets up in seconds. Weighing just 12 lbs., the Pop N' Play has a water-resistant floor to keep kiddos dry in wet grass. Readers love the easy set up and overall design—it is about four feet wide and stands 26" tall. A separate $33 canopy that covers the entire play yard is handy at the beach or lake if you are in full sun.

The Best Play Yard for Multiples

Joovy's Room2 Portable Play Yard ($140) has ten square feet of area—twice the size of most standard playpens, giving multiples or toddlers more room to play. No, it doesn't include many other features you see in other playpens (no bassinet, diaper changing area, etc). However, it does what it does well—provide a large, safe area for babies to play. Readers love the easy set-up and heavy weight canvas fabric.

The Best Play Yard for Travel

Baby Bjorn Travel Crib Light is no bargain at $300 but it is super easy to set up and fold, based on our reader feedback. We like the light weight (13 lbs.) and the longevity (it can be used up to three years). For families who plan several road trips with baby, it is worth the investment.

The Best Extra Large Play Yard

Sure, playpens have been around for forever . . . but new to the market are extra large models that offer up to 27 square feet of play space. No, these playpens aren't for sleeping—but they are great to give baby more space to roam, while keeping them secure.

After evaluating a half dozen extra large playpens, we think **YOBEST's Extra Large Baby Playpen** ($170) is the best bet for most folks. Yes, this playpen boasts an impressive 27 square feet of

play space (it is 75" x 59" wide—yes that is more than six feet long by nearly five feet wide). To compare, consider the size of the most popular standard playpen (the Graco Pack 'N Play), which is 40" x 28.5"—basically half the size of the YOBEST.

Best Kids Indoor Climbers & Play Structure

For those rainy days, an indoor climber/play structure is a fun space for baby to hang out. This indoor corner climber (**SoftScape's Toddler Playtime Corner Climber,** $130) is a reader favorite—not only fun, but with a wipeable surface that is also very durable. We loved this structure's multiple configurations— great for climbing, sliding or just jumping around. Also nice: the polyurethane cover is durable AND easy to clean.

The Best Swings

Soothing a fussy baby has vexed many generations of parents—and the venerable baby swing has been there as a solution for decades.

One of the downsides of swings: they tend to take up a lot of floor space, which can be a challenge if you live in a smaller house or condo.

Fans of swings say they are worth their weight in gold for soothing baby, no matter how much floor space they use. Critics point out that not all babies like swings—so this might be a good product to pick up second hand if you come across one on Craigslist or a garage sale.

Swings have morphed over the years, as bouncers like the **4Mom's Mamaroo** (reviewed earlier) have taken on swing-like functions. Both bouncers and swings typically have 25 lb. weight limits, so there is no advantage of one over the other, except for space issues.

The Best Swing (Overall)

Fisher-Price has swings down to a science. The **Fisher-Price Snu-gabunny Cradle 'n Swing** ($128) allows for both side-to-side and front-back motion, three seat positions and a plush seat. There are six speeds, eight musical tunes and a two-position seat recline. FYI: Fisher Price makes many different versions of this swing in prices that range from $100 to $160—the difference is typically fashion.

Readers like the quiet motor and music tunes, which aren't as obnox-ious as other swings. A few dissenters say the swing broke after a short period of use (a month, for example)—however, Fisher-Price's customer service is responsive and solves issues.

We've also seen a few reports of defective swings that are dead on arrival or have loud motors that make a clicking sound. This appears to be a rare occurrence. To be safe, be sure to buy from a retailer with an easy return policy. And if you are buying this swing second-hand, be sure to test it before driving home (hint: take four fresh D-batteries with you to test it in case there is no power outlet handy).

Finally, we should note one final drawback: this swing takes a LARGE amount of floor space. At its widest point when set up, it takes up 37" of space!

The Best Portable Swing

Ingenuity Cozy Kingdom Portable Swing ($70) is a six-speed portable swing with removable head support. Even though this swing is portable, it lacks a carry handle (doh!). Comfort & Harmony is part of the Kids II brand empire. Since this swing folds away, it is a good bet for grandma's house.

Best Video Baby Monitor

For her first nine months, your baby is tethered to you via the umbilical cord. After that, it's the baby monitor that becomes your surrogate umbilical cord—enabling you to work in the garden, wander about the house, and do many things that other, childless human beings do, while still keeping tabs on a sleeping baby. Hence, this is a pretty important piece of equipment you'll use every day—a good one will make your life easier . . . and a bad one will be a never-ending source of irritation.

A quick safety tip for monitors: always keep the cord at least three feet away from your baby's crib. Cords from cameras/monitors are a strangulation hazard.

Major caveat to our recommendations: ANY baby monitor, even those that earn our highest ratings, can have problems with static, poor reception or interference. The best advice: keep your receipt and buy a monitor from a store with a good return policy. It might be trial and error to find one that works for you.

7 Things No One Tells You About Buying A Video Baby Monitor!

1 **THERE ARE THREE BASIC TYPES OF VIDEO MONITORS OUT THERE: FIXED, PTZ AND STREAMING.** Fixed monitors have a camera that is, well, fixed and is the most economical choice. PTZ stands for point/tilt/zoom, where a camera can move and tilt: some parents prefer PTZ monitors since they can scan a room for a wayward baby or toddler. Finally, streaming baby monitors can send a video signal over the internet, so grandparents and relatives can see the baby's nursery. Each type has its trade-offs—most streaming monitors are fixed. And most PTZ monitors can be pricey.

2 **SOME CAMERAS HAVE BETTER NIGHT VISION THAN OTHERS.** One of the key times you use a monitor is at night—or to see in a darkened room, while baby is sleeping. To help make visible pictures, cameras use night vision—basically a series of LED lights that bathe a nursery in infrared light. The goal isn't to have a super-crisp picture to see your baby's facial expressions. You just want to see if baby is sleeping. Or playing. Or standing up crying, etc. Of course, weak night vision that doesn't let you even see if your baby is sleeping or sitting up is a problem. And night vision is often limited in distance—you can't put the camera ten feet away from the crib and expect to see clearly in the dark.

3 BATTERY LIFE SUCKS FOR MOST VIDEO MONITORS. That's because portable video screens are power hogs. Expect to plug in the monitor for over-night monitoring— that's because most monitors only last two to four hours on battery power.

4 DON'T EXPECT HDTV-QUALITY PICTURES FROM MOST BABY MONITORS. Many video baby monitors have tiny screens (2.4″ to 3.5″) and low resolution pictures (640 x 280 pixels). This is a far cry from a HD camera, but remember the purpose of a monitor is to see what's going on in the nursery, not to count the freckles on your baby's cute little face (no matter how tempting).

5 VOICE-ON-EXCHANGE (VOX) MODE: GOOD OR EVIL? Vox is an optional setting on many monitors that only turns on the screen when baby makes a sound above a preset level. This is helpful to conserve battery.

Folks either love or hate VOX—fans love not having to hear every peep or squeak from baby. Critics say VOX mode can falsely trigger, awakening sleep-deprived parents when there isn't a problem in the nursery. Good news: monitors with VOX have a switch to toggle it off if you hate it.

6 THE Z IN PTZ CAMERAS STANDS FOR ZOOM. And some cameras offer this feature to let you zoom in on a particular area in the nursery. Be aware that most cameras have a digital zoom. This means the pixels in the camera are enlarged when you zoom. As a result, the picture becomes grainy. Hence, the zoom feature is less helpful than you'd think.

7 STREAMING: YES OR NO? The latest trend in baby monitors are those that can stream a picture online—so you can check baby while you are at work. Or a grandparent can see the nursery. This type of monitor can be tricky to set up, as it requires a secure connection to the internet. Depending on your internet router, these monitors can work fabulously . . . or not at all. Later in this chapter, we'll recommend a streaming baby monitor that is easy to set up.

In this next section, we recommend video baby monitors in two categories:

◆ Best Video Monitor, PTZ
◆ Best Video Monitor, Streaming
◆ Best Video Monitor With Two Cameras

Best Video Baby Monitor, PTZ

After researching and reviewing 16 different video monitor brands, we pick the **Infant Optics DXR-8** ($166) as the best video baby monitor.

The Infant Optics DXR-8 features a crisp (but not HD) 3.5" screen, two-way talk and pan/tilt/zoom.

This monitor also has interchangeable lenses (the normal and zoom lenses come in the box; wide angle is sold separately). The swappable lenses are unique and you might think, at first blush, what is the point? Why would you need to swap the normal angle lens with a zoom?

After playing around with this monitor for while, the most obvious answer is ease of installation. Depending on the configuration of your nursery, your only option may be to put the camera on a dresser across from the crib—then the normal lens might do. But if you mount the camera on a wall above the crib, the zoom lens might be better. (Always make sure cords are at least three feet from the crib).

Most folks repurpose a baby monitor later to monitor a toddler's room or play area—then the wide angle lens ($10, sold separately) might be the better bet. Of course, interchangeable lens means you might also lose the lenses (at least, that's what would happen to us)—but you can buy replacements from Infant Optics' web site.

Beyond the standard intercom and temperature sensor features (common on many monitors in this price point), we also liked the Infant Optics screen off, audio-only mode which is most useful during over-night hours. Infant Optics estimates the battery life at six hours (when the screen is turned on)—our research says that is relatively accurate. Obviously, it would make most sense to have the parent monitor plugged in (instead of using battery power) overnight, but the audio-only mode should get you through the night on a fully charged battery if you forget.

One nice feature: you can recharge the lithium-ion battery in the parent unit with any USB plug—computer, USB power cube, etc.

Need to monitor twins? Or quads? The Infant Optics DXR-8 lets you link up to four cameras to a single display, which will then cycle through the additional cameras every 12 seconds.

Night vision on the DXR-8 is impressive: here's how it looks compared to a Samsung monitor (see picture on next page). The DXR-8 (right) had an overall crisper and brighter picture when using night vision:

How's the range? The Infant Optics DXR-8 uses 2.4 Ghz technology—that provides secure transmission (the parent unit is paired with the camera) to prevent eavesdropping. The company claims a range of 700 feet line of sight. Real world tests indicate it works well in two or even three story homes, with few dropouts, say readers.

Flaws but not deal breakers. To Infant Optics credit, the company has tweaked the monitor over the years to address user complaints. Example: there used to be an audible beep when the monitor went into sleep mode or low battery—that obviously drove folks crazy at 2am. So Infant Optics enabled these beep alerts to be toggled off in the menu settings.

Here are the other key complaints:

No VOX. Voice-activation mode (VOX) turns on the video screen when a certain level of sound is detected. This is a relatively common feature on baby monitors today, but Infant Optics omits it. We should point out that the DXR-8 does have an audio-only night mode (described above) . . . but that means the audio is on all the time, not triggered by noise.

Somewhat bulky parent unit. Compared to the parent units of competitors like Summer or Project Nursery, the Infant Optics parent unit is kind of chunky. Here's what it looks like from behind (it ain't no iPhone).

Which brings us to flaw #2: notice the back of the parent unit has a stand but *no belt clip.* Hence carrying this unit around requires you to keep it in a pocket—and a large one at that.

No remaining battery life percentage indicator. Summer has this feature; Infant Optics just has an icon indicating battery life, but a percentage remaining would be more helpful.

Smallish screen, no HD. Competitors are busy rolling out five inch parent unit screens. And actual 720p HD resolution. By contrast the Infant Optics DXR-8 is old school at 640 x 480 resolution.

To address this drawback, Infant Optics recently came out with a PRO version of the DXR-8 that adds a 5″ screen and 720p HD resolution. But this model costs $200—we're not sure it is worth the extra expense. Most of our readers found the lower rez on the 3.5″ screen to be adequate enough to do the job. Plus there is the trade-off in battery life—the higher the resolution and bigger the screen, the less battery time you get.

Less than stellar audio. One thing Infant Optics could do is beef up the audio quality of the DXR-8. We found the sound to be kind of tinny, especially compared to Motorola's offerings. Again, most readers tell us the DXR-8 was adequate to do the job . . . but that is somewhat underwhelming for a $165 monitor. On the plus side, we found the video signal from the Infant

Optics unit to be less subject to drops compared to other monitors.

No online streaming. The Infant Optics DXR-8 only can send a signal to the parent unit—it can't stream video online to be viewed by a smartphone. Read our pick for the best streaming baby monitor below.

Also Recommended: Eufy BabyCare SpaceView Pro

The *Eufy SpaceView Pro* ($160) features excellent quality picture and large 5" parent unit. In a nutshell: very good ease of use. Less interference and longer range than competition. But no sound/light display and poor kickstand.

During our testing, we got 13 hours of battery life—that was tops in our testing. That means you can run this monitor on battery alone overnight. Few other monitors we tested could do that.

Best Video Baby Monitor, Streaming

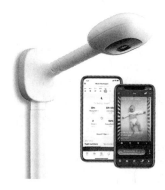

"Sleep analytics" is the new buzzword for video baby monitors and a couple of new baby monitors are leading the pack.

What is all the fuss about? Most video baby monitors are simple creatures—they just take video and transmit it to a parent unit. New cameras have fancy sensors and on-board processing that go beyond taking video—combined with cloud processing, they can tell you how well your baby slept at night, plus provide advice when you hit a sleep speed-bump.

If you think this sounds like AI in the nursery, you'd be right.

Leading this revolution are monitors like the *Nanit Plus* ($250). This HD monitor works on WiFi and has no parent unit—you have to use your own device to view the signal. The Nanit's app does more than just display a picture—you get detailed activity reports that tell you when baby fell asleep or woke. A dashboard tracks your baby's sleep over time, calculating "sleep efficiency" (amount of time your baby slept verus being awake, fed, etc.) See picture on next page.

When it comes to analytics, the Nanit's "Insights" (a separate subscription) provides more analysis and personalized sleep recommendations based your baby's age. This runs $200 a year, but as of this writing, Nanit gives a free year of Insights with any camera purchase.

So what's not to like about the Nanit? Well, for starters, for the analytics to work, the camera must be positioned directly above your baby's sleep space. A floor stand to accomplish this is an extra $80.

Despite all the whiz-bang tech, oddly, the Nanit does not let you change the camera's orientation. So you have to set it up in the correct orientation or you will miss a large part of your baby's sleep space.

Overall, we would recommend the Nanit. This is probably the future of baby monitors—albeit at a price.

All this innovation is encouraging—getting a baby to sleep has been an age-old dilemma, spawning an entire universe of books, videos and web sites. Heck, we even spend 40 pages in our *Baby 411* book on sleep advice (the most challenging part: adjusting your sleep expectations as baby transitions from newborn to a one-year-old).

So marrying all the latest research to actual baby sleep analytics is most promising.

On the dystopian side, you may wonder what these companies will do with all the data they are compiling on your baby and her sleep habits. While Nanit has a decent privacy policy, we wonder what all this data would be used for in the hands of a Google or Facebook.

Best Video Baby Monitor With Two Cameras

Got twins? Or need to monitor two spaces at once, say an older child and an newborn? A video monitor with two cameras may the be answer. After testing out several options, we liked the **Motorola MBP50-G2** ($161) best.

This monitor features a large-size 5″ parent unit and great overall picture quality. The split screen for viewing is most helpful. Unlike other fixed cameras, this one can pan, tilt and zoom around the nursery.

Another plus: this unit is expandable up to 4 cameras. There are also five pre-loaded lullabies (but you can't control the volume of this feature, which seems like an odd oversight).

What's not to like? At three hours, the battery life for this monitor is one of the shortest we tested. Now, most folks leave a monitor plugged in overnight so the battery isn't an issue. But if you plan to go cordless with this monitor for long stretches of time, this may not be the best choice.

Best Audio Baby Monitor

Sure, they are old school but for many parents, audio baby monitors are just the ticket. That's because even with no scientific training, you as a new parent will be able to discern your baby's cries (*I'm hungry!* sounds different from *I'm sick!*). No HD video picture necessary.

Bonus: audio monitors cost a fraction of video monitors. Here's our shopping advice.

7 Things No One Tells You About Buying An Audio Monitor!

1 HACKING ALERT: SOME AUDIO MONITORS ARE VULNERABLE TO EAVESDROPPING. You may have seen stories over the last few years about strangers being able to hack into baby monitors. Pretty creepy, we know. But remember this: an audio monitor is made up of a transmitter (the base unit in baby's room) and a receiver (kept in your room). Yes, you are basically putting a microphone in your baby's room. Anyone with another baby monitor on the same frequency could pick up conversations and sounds on your baby monitor.

The take home message: many baby monitors do not encrypt their transmission. Therefore the best advice is to remember that your house (or at least your baby's room) is bugged. If you want to protect your privacy, don't have any sensitive conversations within earshot of the baby monitor. You never know who might be listening. It is wise to turn OFF the baby monitor when baby isn't in the room.

So are there any monitors that are private? Until recently, the answer was no. But there is good news: several models feature "digital" (DECT) technology—their signals can't be intercepted, unlike older analog monitors. Both monitors we recommend use DECT.

2 BABY MONITORS EAT BATTERIES. Most baby monitors have the option of running on batteries or regular current (by plugging it into a wall outlet). Our advice: use the wall outlet as often as possible. Batteries don't last long—as little as eight to ten hours with continual use.

Another idea: you can buy another AC adapter for $10 or less—you can leave one AC adapter in your bedroom and have another one available in a different part of the house. (Warning: make sure you get the correct AC adapter for your monitor, in terms of voltage and polarity. Otherwise you can fry the monitor.

By the way, when shopping for an audio monitor, consider buying a model with a low battery indicator. Without that feature, your monitor could die with no warning (and you wondered why baby was so quiet!). Only a handful of monitors have low battery indicators. Both models we recommend on this page have low battery alerts.

3 INTERFERENCE ISSUES CAN HAMPER YOUR BABY MONITOR, thanks to all the gadgets in your house: WiFi routers, cell phones and other electronics.

Let's talk baby monitor frequencies and interference (geek alert: fun terms like megahertz will be used in the next paragraph).

Baby Monitor 101: the higher the frequency, the longer the range of the monitor. Basic baby monitors work on the 49 MHz frequency—these will work for a few hundred feet. Step up to a 900 MHz monitor and you can double the distance the monitor will work (some makers claim up to 1000 feet). Finally, there are baby monitors that work on the 2.4 GHz frequency, where you can pick up your baby in Brazil. Okay, not that far, but you get the idea. Of course, "range" estimates are just that—your real-life range will probably be much less than what's touted on the box.

Now here's the rub: Wi-Fi networks and cordless phones can often interfere with your baby monitor.

Wi-Fi routers work on the 2.4 GHz band—yep, the same frequency used by some baby audio monitors. FYI: Baby VIDEO monitors work on either the 900 MHz or 2.4 GHz frequencies and can have the same interference issues as audio monitors. Even if your router doesn't cause a problem, you neighbor's ten year old Linksys router may.

As we mentioned earlier, newer digital or DECT monitors, which work in the 1.9 GHz range, are a solution to many interference troubles. Since very few other electronics operate on this band, DECT monitors are virtually interference-free and work at even longer range than 2.4 GHz monitors. (Both of our recommended audio baby monitors are DECT).

So, to sum up, here is our advice: always keep the receipt. Baby monitors have one of the biggest complaint rates of all products we review.

We suspect all the electronic equipment in people's homes today (cell phones, Wi-Fi routers, large-screen TVs the size of a Sony Jumbotron), not to mention all the interference sources near your home (cell phone towers, etc.) must account for some of the problems folks have with baby monitors. Common complaints include static, lack of range, buzzing and worse—and those problems can happen with a baby monitor in any price range.

4 **OUT OF RANGE INDICATORS ARE HELPFUL.** If you plan to wander from the house and visit your garden, you may want to go for a monitor that warns you when you've strayed too far from its transmitter. Some models have a visual out of range indicator, while others beep at you. Of course, even if your monitor doesn't offer this feature, you'll probably realize when you're out of range—the background noise you hear in your home will disappear from the receiver.

5 **INTERCOMS ARE A NICE FEATURE TO CONSIDER.** More and more baby monitors are adding intercom features, enabling two-way talk between the transmitter and receiver.

Why is that helpful? Let's say you're breastfeeding your baby in the nursery. You're thirsty . . . or hungry or any of a hundred things. Wouldn't it be nice to buzz your partner to bring you a glass of water. Or perhaps your baby is alone in the room and awake, but you don't want to run in immediately to sooth her. You could talk to your baby on the intercom or sing a song, which might help her settle down.

6 **AUDIO BABY MONITORS ARE A SIGNIFICANT SAVINGS OVER VIDEO MONITORS.** At $50, an audio baby monitor is such a deal compared to a video monitor, which typically are $100+. And you don't have to see a picture of a crying baby to realize you'll need to check up on your child—you just need to hear it.

Video baby monitors are a gadget . . . fun, but not necessary for most folks. Think of video monitors as a pacifier for parents, especially nervous first-timers (we know, we were there too!). In most cases, however, a simple audio monitor will do the trick. Experienced parents will tell you that you don't need to see a picture of baby to know someone needs attention! You'll soon recognize your baby's cries just with the audio alone. Trust us.

7 **SKIP THE FRILLS.** You don't need a temperature gauge on your audio baby monitor— besides they aren't very accurate. A basic room thermometer/hygrometer (which monitors temp and humidity) costs $11 and will be far more accurate than your baby monitor. Just as you want a nursery at a comfortable temp (not too warm or too cool), you also should monitor humidity. The ideal range is about 40%.

Same goes for a nightlight—it isn't necessary to spend extra for a baby monitor with night light. Simple night lights with dawn to dusk sensors run $15 for four night lights, like the one pictured.

The Best Audio Baby Monitor

After researching and reviewing ten different baby audio monitor brands for quality (can you hear me now?) and durability, we pick the ***VTech Safe & Sound Digital Audio Monitor*** as the best audio baby monitor.

VTech's affordable Safe & Sound Digital Audio Monitor DM221 ($30 single, $40 double parent units) has 6.0 DECT technology for a secure, interference-free signal. This monitor is loaded with features (intercom, vibrating sound alert, rechargeable batteries with low battery alert and more). It is the best of the audio bunch, in our opinion. Range is rated to 1000 feet (your mileage may vary).

VTech is probably best-known for their cordless phones and interactive toys. In recents years, they entered the baby monitoring market with well-received audio and video models.

Parent feedback has been very positive—it's clear VTech's successful track record in cordless phones is a major help here with the technology. The few criticisms we heard from parents centered on the range being less than the stated 1000 feet (that's probably a given for most monitors, sorry to say).

VTech claims 18 hour battery life for this unit, which sounds like a stretch since most folks say it barely lasts a night. For night-time monitoring, we'd suggest leaving this unit plugged in, instead of running off batteries.

While we recommend this monitor, we should note we have received occasional reports from readers about defective VTech units. One reader said the quality of the monitor was excellent, but the battery on his unit would not hold a charge. Others report monitors that don't link properly. As with all monitors, we'd recommend purchasing this unit from a store or site that has a decent return policy just in case.

AROUND THE HOUSE

FYI: We'd get the double model even if you don't need two receivers—keep the extra one handy in case the first one gets damaged!

Also Great: VTech DM111

If you don't need two units, this simple model is a deal at $16: VTech's DM111. We liked this simple, no frills audio baby monitor— good clear audio, decent range and bright sound/light display. Could the battery last longer? Sure, but it works well enough.

Smart Baby Monitors: Not Ready for Prime Time

New "smart monitors" that watch your baby's vital signs have debuted to some fanfare in recent years. These wearables (socks, t-shirts, diaper sensors) monitor baby and are connected to smartphones. If baby's biometrics (pulse rate, respiration, blood oxygen, etc.) drop below a certain level, an alarm goes off on your smartphone.

So which one should you get? None. A 2017 review of these gadgets in the *Journal of the American Medical Association* found no scientific evidence they work.

"These devices are marketed aggressively to parents of healthy babies, promising peace of mind about their child's cardiorespiratory health," pediatrician Dr. Christopher P. Bonafide, with the Children's Hospital of Philadelphia, told the *Consumerist* web site. "But there is no evidence that these consumer infant physiological monitors are life-saving or even accurate, and these products may cause unnecessary fear, uncertainty and self-doubt in parents."

That's right—instead of giving parents piece of mind, smart monitors most likely cause a myriad of false alarms that make parenting even more stressful than it already is.

Bottom line: save your money and skip the smart monitors.

Safety: The Best Gates & More Safety Advice

Your baby's safety is Job #1 as a parent. So let's take a look at baby proofing your home.

7 Things No One Tells You About Buying A Safety Gate and Other Safety Tips!

1 **DON'T WAIT UNTIL YOUR BABY "ALMOST" DOES SOMETHING DANGEROUS BEFORE YOU BABY PROOF YOUR HOME.** Babies grow up so fast! In the blink of an eye your bundle of joy is calmly sitting in the middle of the living room sucking her fingers (or a toy, whatever). Next thing you know, she's scaling furniture and trying to make a run for it out an open door.

Of course, every baby is different, so let's talk typical milestones:

Rolls over: 2 to 4.5 months.

Stands holding onto something: 5 to 10 months.

Walks holding on to furniture (cruisers): 7.5 to 12.5 months.

Walks alone: 11 to 14.5 months

Yes, you read correctly: before you know it, your baby is standing, cruising and walking. And Murphy's Law of baby safety says your baby's attraction to anything is directly proportional to how dangerous it is.

So get down on your hands and knees and crawl through your home just like your baby will. Check for hazards like hanging lamp cords, blind cords, open electrical sockets, easy-to-climb items, anything you can think of that will attract babies. Then baby proof them all! See our top safety must haves later in this chapter.

2 **IF YOU'RE CONFUSED ABOUT WHICH TYPE OF SAFETY GATES YOU NEED, YOU'RE NOT ALONE.** Yes, there are several types of safety gates on the market. Pressure safety gates are the most common. These gates are sized slightly larger than a door or stair opening and then squeezed into the space using a spring to create pressure. The problem? They can be pushed over, especially by a large toddler or pet. This makes a pressure gate at the top of the stairs a no-no.

To solve the stair dilemma, we recommend hard-mounted gates at the top of staircases. These have a frame that is permanently attached to the walls or stair banisters with screws. Then there is a swinging gate with a parent-activated latch so you can get up or down the stairs.

Of course, one size doesn't fit all when it comes to safety gates. Options to consider are swinging openings on pressure gates, taller gates, wider gates or extensions for wide openings, and new fabrications such as wood and wood/metal combinations.

Yes, all the extras cost money; a basic wood or plastic pressure gate to seal off a dining room sells for as little as $20, while a hard mounted stair gate with stained wood and black metal spindles runs nearly $80. Extra wide gates can be over $100.

3 **DON'T OVERLOOK THE BOTTOM OF THE STAIRS.** That's right, you'll need a gate for the bottom of your stairs too. We recommend you place the bottom gate two steps up from the landing. Why? This way your baby can practice climbing stairs, with little chance of injury.

4 **MAKE SURE THE HARD-MOUNTED GATE HAS A STOP PIN FOR SAFETY.** A stop pin keeps the gate from swinging over open stairs. Our choice for best safety gate, the KidCo Safeway, has this.

5 **GATES ARE FOR MORE THAN STAIRS.** Gates and barriers are important to keep kids out of fireplaces, pet rooms and laundry rooms, to name a few. And don't forget window barriers. You can still have fresh air without worrying your baby will fall out the window if you use window guards. Don't worry—we'll give you recommendations for all this shortly.

6 **IF YOU'RE RENTING, STILL USE THE HARD MOUNTED GATES.** I know what you're thinking: my landlord is going to kill me if I attach a hard mounted gate on my stairs. We understand, but this is for your baby's safety. Patching walls and wood is actually simple; you can find great how-to-videos on YouTube.

7 Here are our top **11** safety must-haves for your home:

Top 11 Safety Must Haves

To sum up, here's our list of top safety items to have for your home (in no particular order).

◆ *Fire extinguishers* rated "ABC," for any type of fire.

◆ *Outlet covers.*

◆ *Baby monitor*—unless your house or apartment is very small, and you don't think it will be useful.

◆ *Smoke alarms.* The best smoke alarms have two systems for detecting fires—a photoelectric sensor for early detection of smoldering fires and a dual chamber ionization sensor for early detection of flaming fires. An example of this is the First Alert "Double Sensor" ($25 to $60). We'd recommend one smoke alarm for every bedroom, plus main hallways, basement and living rooms. And don't forget to replace the batteries twice a year. Both smoke alarms and carbon monoxide detectors can be found in warehouse clubs like Sam's and Costco at low prices or in Home Depot or Lowes home improvement stores.

◆ *Carbon monoxide detectors.* These special detectors sniff out dangerous carbon monoxide (CO) gas, which can result from a malfunctioning furnace. Put one CO detector in your baby's room and another in the main hallway of your home.

◆ *Cabinet and drawer locks.* For cabinets and drawers containing harmful cleaning supplies or utensils like knives, these are an essential investment. For playtime, designate at least one un-secured cabinet or drawer as "safe" and stock it with items safe for baby.

◆ *Spout cover for tub.*

◆ *Bath thermometer or anti-scald device.*

◆ *Toilet locks*—so your baby doesn't visit the Tidy Bowl Man. One of the best we've seen in years is KidCo's toilet lock ($18), an award-winning gizmo that does the trick. Check their web site at kidcoinc.com for a store that carries it.

◆ *Baby gates.* Recommendations are coming up next!

◆ *Furniture wall straps.* Since 2000, over 100 deaths have been caused by TV's and furniture tipping over onto kids. We recommend you anchor all your large furniture to the wall, especially shelves and dressers in baby's room. Once your child becomes a climber, she'll climb anything, so be prepared.

The Best Safety Gate for Stairs

After researching and reviewing over 20 safety gates, we pick the **KidCo Safeway Gate** ($43) as the best safety gate for hard mounting to the top of the stairs or anywhere you want to block baby's access.

The gate comes in a few different versions: straight ($43, available in black or white metal) as well as angled to fit all types of stairs. The angled version is a bit more expensive and comes in metal ($60, black or white).

These gates work on openings from 24 3/4" to 42.5". If you have an extra wide opening, KidCo also offers an extension for angled gates—you can buy a 9" extension for $25. The gate has one hand operation for adults plus quick release hardware if you

need to remove the barrier completely. One key quality feature: a stop pin that prevent the gate from swinging out over the stairs. Plus there is no bottom threshold to trip on (as with many pressure mount gates). The gate can also be easily removed if needed.

Reader feedback on this gate is very positive, with fans loving the ease of installation and small footprint (when open, it doesn't restrict the stairway).

The Best Pressure Safety Gate

While we prefer hard-mounted gates for areas like stairs, pressure mounts gates do have a purpose—they are best at blocking access to rooms that may have baby hazards (like a laundry room).

For this, we would recommend the **Regalo Easy Step Walk Thru Gate** pressure gate.

This gate has a one-hand opening for adults with an additional safety lock and fits in doorways between 29" and 39" wide. Made of steel, it comes in white and includes a 6" extension kit. For added strength, they include additional wall suction cups.

The Easy Step is priced at $40 for the 30" tall version. We judged the build and overall quality of Regalo's pressure gates to be the best on the market.

Other versions are available including an extra tall model (41"). Regalo also sells extensions of 4", 6", 12" and 24". While the gate is popular, some parents note it's easy to mis-install it, then wrongly conclude it's defective. Folks we interviewed recommend reading the directions carefully before trying to install it. Once they got the hang of the install, readers said they loved the gate.

Also Great: North States MyPet Paws 40" Portable Pet Gate

North States MyPet Paws 40" Portable Pet Gate ($20) is a super simple gate that works straight out of the box and is a snap to install. We liked the rubber bumpers that protect walls. Don't let the name fool you—this safety gate is great for both pets AND babies!

Best Play Yard Gate

This style of gate is designed to keep baby in, not out of an area. Set up in a hexagon (or octagon), play yard gates are best for babies who aren't walking but in the cute "sitting there and crawling phase." Once a baby can stand, they may be able to exert enough pressure to push over a play yard gate.

The North States Superyard XT Gate Play Yard is our pick as the best play yard gate. It is an expandable panel system (six, $70; or eight panels, $93) that is 26" high and provides a play area of 18.5 square feet. A two-panel extension kit ($30) provides even more area.

Some readers tell us they use this to protect large Christmas trees from toddlers. Yes, it is all plastic, but it is durable enough to corral babies who are crawling. A few parents say it is hard to open and close the gate (the hinges are tight), but overall, readers give this play yard solution a thumbs up.

Best Fireplace Hearth Gate

A fireplace is an obvious place baby doesn't need to visit— but how do you protect it? **KidCo's Auto Close HearthGate** ($180) is pricey but does the trick, in our testing. It is 29.95" tall and works on hearths six feet wide by two feet deep; extensions are available for bigger openings. The HearthGate also includes a walk-through gate that closes automatically.

Best Window Guard

An often over-looked area of baby proofing, window guards are important if you open windows for fresh air.

Here's the best window guard we found in our research: **Guardian Angel**. The company sells affordable metal window guards that fit just about any type of window ($90 for a four-bar gate that can extend from 35-58"). Guardian Angel window gates are hardware mounted.

Yes, these are a must for low windows your toddler can access or if you live in a high-rise condo building. Remember babies can climb furniture and access windows you think are safe—keep them locked or install a window guard.

Also Great: Super Stopper

Great for travel: the **Super Stopper** from Parent Units ($13) is a simple device that suctions on a window, preventing it from opening too far to let a toddler out. Perfect for grandma's house or that Airbnb rental.

The Best Baby Thermometer: Rectal

We know what you're thinking—really? Yes, the recommended way to take a baby's (under one year of age) temperature is with a rectal thermometer. Welcome to parenthood.

Let's consult our sister book, *Baby 411* for more on this:

"Most parents cringe just thinking about this task. Are you cringing? Don't. Babies really don't mind. It does not hurt or make them feel like you've invaded their space. In fact, it's a good trick to make them poop. But I digress.

"Rectal temperatures are the most accurate way to check a human's body temperature. And for infants under three months of age, one tenth of a degree will make the difference between whether you stay at home in your nice warm bed or head out for an evening of fun at your local emergency room.

"If you call the doctor at 2 am and tell her that your six week old has a fever, the first thing she will ask is, 'How did you take the temperature?' If you took it any way other than rectally, we make you get a rectal thermometer and call us back. Invest in one now—digital rectal thermometers cost $10 to $20.

"FYI: after one year of age, there is more flexibility about how to take your child's temperature. Trendy products on the market for toddler temperatures include a pacifier thermometer, ear thermometer, temporal artery scanners, and plastic skin stickers. Using an oral thermometer in the armpit is also okay. None of these are as accurate as a rectal temperature. But after a year of age, the actual degree of fever is much less important to making a management plan for your child. That is, a child with 101 or 103 is managed based on the other symptoms they have in addition to the fever."

So which one to get? After comparing and testing more than 15 differ-ent thermometers, we picked the **Vicks Baby Rectal Thermometer** ($12) as the best rectal thermometer for babies. It is easy to use and designed with a short probe to make sure it isn't inserted too far.

The Vicks Baby Rectal Thermometer is intended only for use as a rectal thermometer. It reads out the temp in only ten seconds, making it im-pressively fast. Readers tell us this thermometer is also very accurate when compared with a hospital-grade thermometer and it's affordable.

Best Baby Thermometer: Oral & Underarm

The **Vicks ComfortFlex Digital Thermometer** ($10) is both affordable and accurate. It takes oral, underarm and rectal temps.

In case you skipped this discussion earlier, we only recommend using oral or underarm thermometers *after* one year of age. Because fever in babies under one year can be significantly more dangerous than in babies over one, pediatricians prefer parents use a rectal thermometer for the most accurate reading.

After one year of age, any temperature (taken orally or underarm) of over 100° F should be considered a fever reported to your child's doctor.

Best Techie Baby Thermometer

If you'd like to your track your baby's temperature on a phone app, the **Kinsa Smart Thermometer** ($22) does just that—the thermometer connects via Bluetooth to your iOS or Android phone.

We found the Kinsa to be accurate and the app well designed. If your child has multiple illnesses (or you have more than one baby), the app helps keep track of all that, including medications. Accuracy on the Kinsa is excellent.

The latest version of the Kinsa thermometer now displays the temperature right on the device—an improvement over the previous version that required a wired connection to a smartphone.

Best Cabinet Locks

Baby proofing cabinets and drawers can be a challenge—there are a variety of places (bathrooms, kitchens) that need to be secured and different objects (dishwashers, for example) which can present unique problems.

So there isn't a one-size-fits-all solution for child safety locks. And sometimes, the simplest idea works the best. Example: **Adoric's Sliding Cabinet Locks** ($9) This basic locks (4-pack) keep little hands out of cabinets in kitchens and bathrooms, especially under sinks. This simple solution worked surprisingly well in our tests—our parent testers loved it. Caveat: only works on cabinets with pulls spaced no more than 5" apart.

Adhesive cabinet locks are another solution to keeping cabinets from prying little hands. You use adhesive to attach each end and then slide a button to open the latch. **Goodv Child Safety Cabinet Locks** ($15) worked well on dishwashers, ovens, toilet seats—more than just cabinets. Great for caregivers with arthritis. Caveat: installation can be frustrating.

thermometers

Best Baby Car Mirror

Safety experts agree: kids are safer when riding rear-facing in a car seat. And many states are now mandating longer use of rear-facing seats. That creates a new dilemma, however: how do you see what's going on back there?

To the rescue come baby car mirrors, small mirrors that are designed to give you a view of your rear-facing baby while driving. We tested a half dozen different baby car mirrors, checking to see which ones are most secure, easiest to view and install.

Before we recommend the best baby car mirror, a word on safety—these mirrors work well for seeing your baby in the backseat. In fact, perhaps they work too well! Some parents report the mirrors can be distracting, since as a parent you might be watching your baby instead of the road. Try to only look at these mirrors when your vehicle is stopped.

All these mirrors are made of shatterproof acrylic glass. The larger mirrors are convex in shape—that helps get a better view of the backseat. Some folks complain, however, that convex mirrors have a somewhat distorted view. This didn't bother us, but we can see the point of how a distorted view could be less than optimal.

Shynerk's Baby Car Mirror ($20, model SH-M-01) won the top honors in our testing. We found this mirror to be easiest to install and just the right size. Loved how it can swivel to show child in middle back seat.

If you've got an SUV and need a bigger mirror to see further back in the vehicle, there is a larger version of our top pick (Shynerk SH-M-02, $14.59) We loved how it can pivot to get just the right angle. Great for larger backseats.

For a budget-friendly baby car mirror, we think the **Jolly Jumper Driver's Baby Mirror** is a deal at $7. We love this super affordable mirror, which is easy to install. The Jollly Jumper may work better in smaller vehicles where you don't need keep an eye on a large backseat. But only one strap holds it in place, so it may fall down if not tightly secured.

CHAPTER 8

Car Seats: Picking the right child safety seat

Inside this chapter

What's the best car seat for your baby? What is the difference between an infant, convertible or booster seat? We'll discuss these answers, as well as detailed recommendations for each car seat type!

Let's talk child passenger safety—it's come a long way! Here's what car seat safety looked like in the 1960's:

Yes, that is basically a toddler with a pillow lying flat on an auto seat with a lap seat belt. What could go wrong?

Early car seats were just a way to corral babies from wandering around the vehicle—any straps/belts were minimal. While strollers have been around for centuries, it wasn't until 1978 that the first law was passed to mandate car seat use (trivia note: Tennessee was the first state to require usage).

Despite rapid advances in car seat technology, motor vehicle accidents still injure 97,000 kids under age 12 each year (National Center for Injury Prevention and Control, Centers for Disease Control and Prevention, 2018). And the government estimates 59% of car seats are not used correctly (NHTSA, 2018 study).

So our goal in this chapter is to help you pick out the best car seat to keep your new baby safe. A key point to remember: the best seat for your child is the one that correctly fits your child's weight and size—and can be correctly installed in your vehicle. Even the most expensive car seats ($500!) are dangerous if they aren't installed correctly . . . or are the wrong size for your baby.

Let's start at the beginning: infant car seats.

The Best Infant Car Seats

The Great Wall of Car Seats at your local baby mega-store sure looks intimidating. But don't fear, here is our car seat 101: there are three basic types of car seats: infant, convertible and booster. In this section, we're focusing on infant car seats.

7 Things No One Tells You About Buying an Infant Car Seat

1 **YOUR BABY MIGHT OUTGROW THAT INFANT SEAT LONG BEFORE THEY HIT THE WEIGHT LIMIT.** That's because infants grow so fast, they may out grow the seat by height long before weight. Bottom line: don't fret if you don't get the infant seat with the biggest weight limit—we generally recommend a seat with a 30 or 35 pound limit. A seat with a 22 lb. limit is also ok, if your newborn will be average in size at birth.

Even though your baby may outgrow their infant car seat early, that doesn't end rear-facing car seat use. The American Academy of Pediatrics recommends keeping your baby rear facing till two years of age (or as long as possible). While you can use a convertible car seat for both rear and forward facing installation, infant car seats are designed especially for babies and only babies. They often have features (newborn inserts and reclining bases) that fit small ones best. Which leads us to tip #2:

2 **THE SAFEST INFANT CAR SEAT IS THE ONE THAT FITS YOUR CAR AND YOUR BABY PLUS IS THE SIMPLEST TO INSTALL CORRECTLY.** Unfortunately, surveys reveal that as many as 59% of car seats are not used correctly. Either they are mis-installed or mis-adjusted. So a car seat that is EASY TO USE is safer than one that isn't, in our opinion. A key feature to look at: how easy is it to adjust and tighten the harness as baby grows? We tend to favor no rethread harnesses, enabling you to change the HEIGHT of the harness without rethreading the belts.

3 **CURVE BALL: STROLLER COMPATIBILITY.** Ever since the first "travel system" (stroller + infant car seat = travel system) debuted in the mid 90's, the calculus of an infant car seat purchase included this question: which strollers is that car seat compatible with? Sure, Brand X's infant car seats work with Brand X strollers. But then Brand Y strollers adds an adapter for Brand X infant car seat. And now things just got more complex.

Bottom line: some infant car seats are more cross compatible than others. The biggest infant car seat sellers, Graco and Chicco, probably have the most compatability. On the upper end, Maxi Cosi works with most upper-end strollers. (And Maxi Cosi uses the same adapters as Nuna and Cybex. Oy!).

Other infant car seats have much more limited compatibility. Example: the UPPAbaby Mesa infant seat works with the UPPAbaby Cruz and Vista strollers . . . and a couple of other strollers that have universal adapters (Thule, for example). But that is about it. So you better like the UPPAbaby stroller line if you are going with the UPPAbaby Mesa infant car seat.

4 **NECESSARY FEATURE: SIDE IMPACT PROTECTION.** Nearly one in four (24%) car crashes are side impact—and these can be deadly for children in the back seat. Of all child fatalities in car crashes, side impact crashes account for 32% of deaths. Protecting a child's head is crucial to surviving a side impact crash, as that is the area most vulnerable to injury.

FYI: First, understand that there is no federal safety standard for side impact protection. Seats are tested in FRONT crashes only. Some manufacturers test for side impact protection, but there is no way to verify claims that one seat outdoes another on side impact protection. The government has proposed a side impact test standard (way back in 2014), but as of this writing, there is no date yet for the start of such testing.

Of course, all infant seats provide some side impact protection—those that go the extra mile have extra cushions near the baby's head to distribute energy away. Some makers (Cybex) use a telescoping arm on the side of the car seat to add further protection. The good news is more seats on the market today feature side-impact protection.

Unfortunately, there is no current standard to *judge* these claims. Note: the safest place for your child's car seat is in the middle of the back seat. The middle of the back seat is farther away from a side impact collision than an outboard position and therefore safer. Picking a vehicle with rear-curtain air bags is also helpful—most newer model cars offer these type of air bags.

5 **NICE IF YOU CAN AFFORD IT: ANTI-REBOUND BARS.** Some of the more expensive infant car seats feature anti-rebound bars. As the name implies, this keeps the seat from rebounding and hitting the back of the vehicle seat in an accident. Anti-rebound bars aren't required in the U.S. and seats that don't have them still must meet minimum crash test standards. We'll probably see more of these bars in the future, but for now they are only seen in a handful of seats.

Is an anti-rebound bar a must? No—seats without them are still safe. The anti-rebound bar just adds an ADDITIONAL layer of safety. Examples of infant car seats with this feature include the Chicco KeyFit 35 and the Graco SnugRide SnugFit 35 DLX.

6 **ALSO NICE IF YOU CAN AFFORD IT: LOAD LEGS.** More common on European car seats than seen in North America, "load legs" are metal bars that extend from an infant car seat to the floor of the vehicle. In a collision, these legs absorb energy and keep an infant seat from rotating backwards.

As of this writing, only a handful of car seats have this feature. Examples: the Nuna Pipa and Pipa Lite, Clek Liing, Cybex Aton 2/M/Q and Cloud Q, Peg Perego Prima Viaggio 4-35 Nino, Maxi-Cosi Mico Max Plus

If you have a long commute and/or do a lot of highway driving, an infant seat with a load leg may make sense.

7 **NICE BUT NOT NECESSARY: PREMIUM LATCH CONNECTORS.** LATCH stands for Lower Anchors and Tethers for Children. LATCH is built into all vehicles manufactured since September 2002 and is a universal way to attach a car seat to a vehicle without using the vehicle belt. Note: LATCH isn't safer to use than the auto safety belt—it's just an alternative method.

Infant car seats come with two LATCH connectors, which attach to anchors in the seat back.

infant car seats

The least expensive infant car seats have basic LATCH connectors that are hooks (bottom). The more expensive options have "premium" LATCH connectors, which have push buttons (top). Some folks think push button versions are easier to attach to the anchor. Are they nice to have? Yes. Necessary? No. If you plan to frequently move your car seat between vehicles, premium LATCH may be worth it.

The Best Infant Car Seat (Overall)

After researching and reviewing 34 different infant car seats, we pick the ***Chicco KeyFit 35*** ($250) as the best infant car seat.

Crash protection for the Chicco KeyFit 35 is excellent, with added side impact protection and an anti-rebound bar making a difference.

The KeyFit gets high scores from our readers on ease of use—installation is a snap and adjusting the harness is easy. The seat also features EPS foam and a newborn insert.

The downsides? The seat is a bit pricey . . . and the canopy coverage is somewhat skimpy.

FYI: Chicco makes an astounding NINE different versions of the KeyFit. The flagship seat of the line (and the one we recommended in the previous edition of this book) was the KeyFit 30. However, the newer KeyFit 35 adds a few new features (anti-rebound bar, no-rethread harness, adjustable headrest and more leg room) that make it worth the upgrade.

Whichever version you choose, all Chicco KeyFits boast a nice list of features: a seat lined with EPS foam for improved side impact protection, thick seat padding, multi-position canopy and comfort grip handle.

Chicco hired a former Graco engineer (who worked on the SnugRide) to design the KeyFit and it shows in the details . . . the base has a "single-pull" LATCH adjustment, a spring-loaded, leveling foot to account for uneven back seats and even a smooth underside to keep from damaging your back seat upholstery.

As you'd expect from Chicco, the fashion of this seat has a hint of Italian flair and there is even a newborn insert to better fit smaller newborns and preemies.

Our readers have been very positive about the KeyFit's ease of use, lauding the no-twist, easy-to-adjust straps, the ability to leave the handle in the "up" position when driving (most seats require it to be lowered), and overall ease of installation.

Flaws but not deal breakers. Well, no seat is perfect. Here are our quibbles with the KeyFit 30:

◆ *The KeyFit carrier weighs 10.5 lbs., a tad heavier than other similar seats.* It takes two hands to release/rotate the handle on the seat.
◆ *The sunshade has its share of critics.* Some readers tell us they think it is too small and doesn't offer enough coverage (even with the extended visor that tucks away when not in use). It takes two hands to fully extend the canopy.
◆ *A few readers also report the fabric doesn't breathe, so the seat can get hot.* The recently released KeyFit 30 Zip Air with air mesh fabric appears to address that issue. If you live in a hot climate, this might be worth the extra $20.

The Chicco's stroller compatibility used to be an issue, but given the soaring sales of the KeyFit, more brands now offer adapters that fit the seat. Still, it might be wise to check to see if the stroller brand you want has a specific adapter for the KeyFit . . . a few smaller stroller brands still don't.

Also Great: Britax B-Safe Gen2 FlexFit+ Infant Car Seat

The **Britax B-Safe Gen2 FlexFit+** infant car seat is also a good pick, especially if you are a fan of Britax strollers (which, naturally, work with this infant seat without any additional adapters).

Yes, this seat is a splurge at $300—but if you are looking to spend some of the money you saved elsewhere in this book, this is a good investment.

We have recommended Britax infant seats for years, thanks to their safety track record and solid design.

The B-Safe Gen2 FlexFit+ is the 2021 revision of the B-Safe line and adds several new features. The big headline is a more roomy seat—that addresses a complaint that previous versions were too snug for larger babies.

Also new: one-hand harness buckle release—yes, it is now easier to remove baby from the seat, which is a nice new feature.

At this price, you get all the bells and whistles you'd expect: no rethread harness, excellent canopy and an adjustable base. And yes, there is a anti-rebound bar for additional safety.

Flaws but not deal breakers. All that safety goodness comes at a price. At $300, this seat is certainly among the more expensive ones out there (albeit less expensive than options like the Clek Liing).

Another negative: the carrier is heavy—slightly over 11 lbs.

One major consideration for this seat: stroller compatibility. If you are getting a Britax stroller, then the B-SAFE would be a no-brainer. As for compatibility with other strollers, well, that's going to be hit and miss (mostly miss). Fewer strollers are compatible with Britax's infant seat, compared with Graco and Chicco.

Best Budget-Friendly Infant Car Seat

The **Graco SnugRide SnugLock Extend2Fit 35** ($203) infant car seat is part of the best-selling SnugRide family that has earned high scores from our readers for ease of use and overall quality. Another major plus for the Snugride family: wide stroller compatibility, as most brands have Graco SnugRide adapters.

At this price, we think it is a great value for all its features. Most similar seats with anti-rebound bars and no-rethread harnesses are over $250. Add in the exclusive Extend2Fit extension panel that adds an additional 3 1/2 inches of legroom and you've got a winner.

The Extend2Fit also has SnugLock technology, which allows for a simpler, three-step install Graco calls "hassle free." We'd agree: this base, complete with four recline positions, was a snap to install in our hands-on inspection. It also has a newborn body pillow (supports babies as small as 4 lbs.), and a sunshade with better coverage than other seats we tested.

One caveat: the carrier for the Graco SnugRide SnugLock Extend2Fit 35 weighs in at a hefty 12.3 lbs. That puts it among the heavier infant carriers on the market.

Best Infant Car Seat For Urban Parents (and those with little space)

If you live in the urban core of a city, your criteria for an infant seat is probably different from those who live in the suburbs.

First, you may or may not have a car. That means your infant seat will have to be belted into an Uber/Lyft or taxi, requiring quick installation most likely without a base.

Urban parents are more likely to use their stroller to do everyday shopping, requiring an infant car seat to work natively with the stroller for the newborn months. (If you are a heavy user of mass transit, we'd suggest also looking at our baby carrier section on this site—it is easier to navigate stairs down to a subway with a carrier than a stroller/infant car seat).

So here's our pick: the **Cybex Aton 2 Sensorsafe** ($265).

The Cybex Aton 2 is the new improved version of the original with an anti-rebound load leg and added side impact protection. And it does all that at an astonishingly light weight of only 8.8 lbs.! (Other infant car seats can tip the scales at 11+ lbs. That may not sound like a lot, but if you are carrying an infant seat up or down stairs to a condo/apartment, you'll notice it).

The Aton 2 is also compatible with a wide range of strollers that work with the Maxi Cosi-type adapters. That's important because most upper-end strollers with additional weather protection favored by urban parents only offer Maxi Cosi adapters.

For urban parents who don't have a car but might be taking Uber or Lyft a lot, the Aton 2 is easy to belt in without a base. If you are lugging your baby around Manhattan or other urban area, it's a great, lightweight option.

The anti-rebound load leg on the base helps the Aton 2 with additional crash protection, as it protects the seat from rebounding in an accident.

Cybex makes several upgraded versions of the Aton (the Cloud Q and the M), but we think the basic Aton 2 is the best of the bunch.

infant car seats

CAR

INFANT SEATS

The following is a selection of better known infant car seats and how they compare on features:

Maker	Model	Price	Weight/ Height Limits	Side Impact	Load Leg	Anti-Rebound
Baby Jogger	City GO	$290-$350	35 lbs./32" *	◆		
Baby Trend	EZ Flex-Loc	$88-$115	30 lbs/30"			
Britax	B-Safe Gen2	$200	35 lbs./32"	◆		
	Endeavours	$200	35 lbs./32"	◆		◆
Chicco	KeyFit 30	$200	30 lbs./30"	◆		
	Fit2	$300-350	35 lbs./35"	◆		◆
Cybex	Aton 2 SensorSafe	$280	35 lbs./30"	◆	◆	
Evenflo	Embrace	$79	35 lbs./30"			
	LiteMax	$92	35 lbs./32"	◆		
GB	Asana35 DLX	$151	35 lbs./32"	◆	◆	
Graco	Snuglock Extend2Fit 35	$203	32 lbs./35"			◆
Maxi Cosi	Coral XP	$400	22 lbs./29"	◆	◆	
	Mico 30	$200	30 lbs./32"			
Nuna	Pipa	$320	32 lbs./32"	◆	◆	
	Pipa Lite LX	$400	32 lbs./32"	◆	◆	
Peg Perego	Primo Viaggio 4/35	$300	35 lbs./30"	◆		◆
	Primo Viaggio Nido	$300	35 lbs./32"	◆	◆	◆
Phil & Teds	Alpha	$200	35 lbs/32"			
Safety 1st	OnBoard 35 LT	$89-$99	35 lbs./32"	◆		
Simple Par.	Doona	$500	35 lbs./32"		◆	◆
Uppa Baby	Mesa	$300-$350	35 lbs./32"	◆		

KEY

SIDE IMPACT: Does the seat have side-impact protection?

FOAM TYPE: Does the seat have a EPS or EPP foam (or none at all)? This is for crash protection; EPP foam is softer (more comfortable) than EPS.

LOAD LEG.: Does the seat have a load leg for additional crash protection?

CARRIER WEIGHT: This is the weight of the carrier only (not the base).

BASE WIDTH	CARRIER WEIGHT	OUR RATING	PROS/CONS
17.5″	10.4 LBS.	B+	RE-BADGED GRACO SEAT, NO-RETHREAD HARNESS
16.4	9.4	D	PLACED LAST IN RECENT CRASH TESTING
17.5	9.8	A	ANTI-REBOUND BAR ON FLEXFIT+ VERSION
17.75	11.5	A	ANTI-REBOUND BAR, BUT PRICEY
17	9.4	A	BEST-SELLER, EASY INSTALL BUT SKIMPY CANOPY
17	11.3	A	TWO-STAGE BASE, ANTI-REBOUND BAR; PRICEY
15	8.8	A-	LIGHTWEIGHT, EASY INSTALL BUT PRICEY, SKIMPY CANOPY
18	7.0	D+	AFFORDABLE BUT NO SIDE IMPACT PROTECTION
17.75	8.7	B	LIGHTWEIGHT CARRIER BUT LARGE BASE
17.5	9.2	A-	HARD TO FIND, GOOD SAFETY, LIMITED STROLLER COMP.
15	12.3	A	EXCELLENT SAFETY BUT HEAVY, ANTI-REBOUND BAR
17.5	5.4	A-	INNOVATIVE SEAT WITHIN SEAT DESIGN
16	8.7	A-	LIGHTWEIGHT, GOOD STROLLER COMPATIBILITY
12.5	8.6	B-	$300 BUT LACKS NO RETHREAD HARNESS?
12.5	6.7	B-	LIGHTER WEIGHT BUT MUST BE INSTALLED WITH BASE
15.5	11.1	A	NO RETHREAD HARNESS, GREAT SAFETY BUT PRICEY
14.8	10.1	A-	GREAT SAFETY FEATURES, FULLY EXTENDED CANOPY, PRICEY
14.0	8.3	B	LIGHTWEIGHT BUT NO RETHREAD HARNESS, HARD TO FIND
15	9.0	B	AFFORDABLE, SIDE-IMPACT, POOR STROLLER COMPATIBILITY
15	15.5	B	MORPHS FROM CAR SEAT TO STROLLER; BUT $500?
14.25	10.5	B-	NO RETHREAD HARNESS BUT PRICEY, NO ANTI-REBOUND BAR

infant car seats

The Best Convertible Car Seat

Convertible car seats can be used for both infants and older children (most seats go up to 50 lbs., but many models top out at 65 lbs.)—infants ride rear facing; older kids over two years of age ride facing forward. Unlike infant seats, however, most convertibles do not have snap-in bases.

So, does it make more sense to buy one car seat (that is a convertible, which you will have to buy anyway) and just skip the infant car seat? There is considerable debate on this subject. Some safety advocates think convertible car seats are safer, pointing to crash test results that show convertible seats do a better job protecting babies than infant seats. That stands to reason since convertible seats are bigger (taller, wider) than infant car seats.

Others deride infant car seats for their overuse outside of a car (as a place for baby to nap), speculating that such babies are at risk for SIDS (Sudden Infant Death Syndrome, discussed in Chapter 2). That theory has been largely debunked, but there remain concerns about flat head syndrome (Positional Plagiocephaly) and neck tightness (Torticollis) when an infant seat is overused.

On the other side of the debate are advocates who say infant car seats fit newborns better—most are designed to accommodate a smaller body and baby travels in a semi-reclined position, which supports an infant's head and neck. Yes, some convertible seats recline—but the degree of recline can be affected by the angle of your vehicle's seat back.

Convenience is another issue for parents: an infant car seat is more than just a car seat—it's also an infant carrier when detached from its base. Big deal, you might say? Well, since newborns spend much of their time sleeping (and often fall asleep in the car), this is a big deal. By detaching the carrier from the auto base, you don't have to wake the baby when you leave the car. Use a convertible car seat, and you'll have to unbuckle the baby and move her into another type of carrier or stroller (and most likely wake her in the process).

Bottom line: there is no correct answer. Yes, you can skip the infant seat and go to a convertible from birth. But using an infant car seat correctly is just as safe, in our opinion.

Remember: babies should be REAR FACING until they reach two years of age, regardless of weight. If your child outgrows his infant car seat before one year of age, be sure to use a convertible seat in rear facing mode for as long as possible, given the seat's rear-facing weight/height limits.

7 Things No One Tells You About Buying A Convertible Car Seat!

1 **PRO TIP: HOW EASY IS IT TO REMOVE THE COVER FOR WASHING?** Yes, all car seats come out of the box looking fabulous. But any experienced parent will tell you how things can get ugly there in the back seat: spit up, juice spills and diaper blow outs. (Let's not visualize. Let's just move on). So then what? You have to remove the cover for cleaning.

That sounds simple, but the truth is some covers remove (and go back on) much easier than others. The best have zip-off or "easy remove" covers. Not so good: seats with multiple loops, snaps and other attachments.

Also: check to see if the cover is machine washable and dryable? Can you remove and wash the harness?

2 **SOME RECLINES ARE EASIER THAN OTHERS.** Most convertible seats recline for napping babies, but how EASY is it to recline? Remember that when a convertible seat is REAR-FACING, a lever on the front of the seat will be jammed up against the back seat.

3 **TWISTY STRAPS: THE PAIN THAT KEEPS ON GIVING.** Better quality car seats have thicker straps that don't twist. The result: it's easier to get a child in and out of a seat. Cheaper seats have cheaper webbing that can be a nightmare— "twisty straps" are a key reason why parents hate their car seats. Our top picks avoid the twisty strap issue.

4 **GIVE A SECOND LOOK AT THAT HARNESS BUCKLE.** For obvious safety reasons, the harness buckle (which holds the two shoulder straps in place) shouldn't be too easy to unclip. Only an adult should be able to do it. But each car seat brand takes a different approach to this critical piece of safety gear. When shopping, take a second to open and close the buckle yourself. Think about any caregivers who might be buckling in baby (grandparents may have less strength, etc).

Hint: "puzzle" or compound buckles can be particularly vexing! As implied by the name, a puzzle buckle must be put together in a particular order to latch—which can be darn near impossible with gloves on in the winter. These buckles tend to be seen more on lower-price seats.

5 **THE SUN IS NOT ALWAYS YOUR CAR SEAT'S FRIEND.** That plush, black velour car seat cover may look stunning out of the box, but when installed in a car that sits in the hot summer sun . . . you've got a recipe for Sweaty Baby Syndrome. If you have a choice between a dark color and one that is somewhat lighter, we'd go for the latter.

Another related issue: some car seats have exposed metal buckles and hardware. In the hot sun, these buckles can get toasty and possibly burn a child. Pro tip: look for a seat that has buckle clips or holders that keep metal out of direct sun.

6 **CONVERTIBLE DOES NOT NECESSARILY EQUAL PORTABLE.** Convertible car seats vary widely in weight, with some as low as 8 lbs. (Cosco Scenera Next) and others topping 34 lbs. (Clek Foonf, for example). Note that both seats pass federal crash test standard for safety.

While you shouldn't base your entire convertible car seat decision on weight, it may be an important factor for some parents. If you live an urban city center and don't own a car, then you'll need a lightweight seat when using Uber or a cab (see above for our convertible car seats for urban parents). If you see yourself moving a convertible seat between multiple vehicles on a frequent basis, buying a 30 lb.+ seat may have you cursing that decision for years.

7 **THERE IS NO CRASH TEST STANDARD FOR SIDE IMPACT PROTECTION—YET!** As you car seat shop, you'll see lots of seats promoting "side impact protection" with various headrests, cushions and gadgets. But remember this: as of this writing, there is NO federal side impact safety standard that car seat makers are required to pass.

Hence, we have little information to verify which seats are best at protecting children from side impact crashes. (Manufacturers do their own internal side impact crash testing, but aren't required to share those results with the public).

We should note that there is a PROPOSED side impact car seat safety standard that was published way back in 2014. But that rule isn't final yet as of press time and it isn't clear when that will take effect. Follow us on Facebook (facebook.com/babybargains) for the latest updates.

convertible car seats

Up next, our recommendations for convertible car seats. We will recommend seats in three categories: best convertible seat (overall), best budget-friendly convertible seat and best convertible seat for urban parents.

The Best Convertible Car Seat (Overall)

After researching and reviewing 50+ different convertible car seats, we pick the **Chicco NextFit Zip** ($300) the best convertible car seat. After successfully topping the infant car seat charts with their KeyFit infant seat, Chicco's NextFit launched back in 2013 as the brand's first effort in the convertible car seat market.

The seat features nine (!) recline positions, dual level indicators and a harness rated for 65 lbs. forward-facing (40 lbs. rear-facing). The NextFit has a small footprint (to work well with smaller cars) as well as an infant insert cushion.

The NextFit features "SuperCinch" LATCH technology, which makes it easier to tighten the LATCH belts. Also innovative: the seat's harness widens to accommodate larger toddlers. The no rethread harness is a major plus. And yes, the NextFit has side impact protection.

Feedback from our readers and online reviews have been quite positive—the Chicco NextFit earns overwhelmingly positive marks.

It's clear Chicco has done its homework with the NextFit: the seat is very easy to install, either with LATCH or vehicle belt. We like the harness adjuster and recline, which are as easy to use as any Britax seat. The attention to detail is obvious: note the storage compartment for the LATCH and tether straps; the fabric is also excellent quality and soft to the touch. Many parents say their kids prefer the Chicco NextFit to other convertibles when it comes to comfort.

So what's not to like? A few folks complained about the NextFit's deep side walls (which are there for side impact protection)—getting a squirmy toddler in and out of the seat can be a challenge, thanks to these walls. Seats like the Diono Radian are easier to use for toddlers, since they have lower side walls. So even though the NextFit expands to better fit toddlers, the deep side walls somewhat defeat the innovation when it comes to ease of use.

Also: the Chicco NextFit is quite heavy at 25 lbs. So this isn't the right seat if you plan to frequently move it from car to car.

The Chicco NextFit has been so successful, the company has come up with a series of spin-off versions. And we know, this can get confusing.

The version we like best is the NextFit Zip. The key upgrade is a "Zip & Wash" pad—which means you can easily zip off the cover to pop it in the washing machine. This is worth the $50 upgrade over the base model (called the NextFit Sport), in our opinion. Also added: Chicco's CupFolder.

Bottom line: the Chicco NextFit, in any version, is an excellent seat that earns our top rating. Installation is a snap and overall safety features are best in class.

Best Budget-Friendly Convertible Car Seat

For a decent, no-frills car seat, we recommend the **Cosco Scenera Next**. Yes, it lacks the whiz bang features of newer models, but this seat is the quiet, unsung hero of car seats. That's because it retails for $50 at Walmart—yes, you read that right: $50. This seat's low price makes the Scenera perfect for that little-used second car or Grandma's vehicle.

The Scenera is a basic, bare-bones convertible that is easy to install. With the prices of some car seats running $400+, it's nice to know you can find a decent seat for well under $100.

The Cosco Scenera has been around for many years. In a recent refresh, Cosco debuted an updated version of this seat called the Scenera Next, which works to 40 lbs. rear-facing and has a new narrow profile (17" wide). It is a Walmart exclusive. (Yes, the seat sometimes shows on Amazon, albeit at a higher price than Walmart).

Key features of the Scenera Next include:

◆ *Machine washable pad*—it's amazing more seats don't allow you to throw the pad in the washing machine. As any experienced parent will tell you, just about anything can happen in a car seat. Kudos to Cosco for this.

◆ *Comes fully assembled.* Five harness slots—the top one is only 13", however.

◆ *Lightweight.* This seat weighs about 7 lbs. You read that right! Compared to other seats that can tip the scales at nearly 30 lbs. empty, the Scenera Next is amazing and a good choice for travel.

convertible car seats

Consumer Reports gave this seat a "better" in crash protection in recent tests. As for ease of use, the Scenera earned just two stars from the NHTSA, with rear facing installation holding the seat's rating down. Nonetheless, we think this is a good, basic seat for secondary use.

Reader feedback on the Scenera Next is much the same as the Scenera—the same complaints about rear-facing installation and skimpy padding are outweighed by the light weight and the 40 lb. rear-facing limit.

Flaws but not deal breakers. Perhaps the biggest concern we have with the Cosco Scenera is the lack of side impact protection. We would suggest only using this seat in the middle position of a back seat—and it would best if your vehicle had rear curtain air bags.

While the Scenera Next garners mostly positive reviews (most parents finding it easy to install and use), there is one possible issue: in order to install the Scenera with the proper recline in rear-facing mode, you may have to use a rolled-up towel or pool noodle to get the proper angle. This depends in your vehicle (those with deep sloping back seats are more of an issue when installing the Scenera). Using these aids is perfectly safe, we should note.

Critics note the lack of padding or fancy fabric; the Scenera also lacks an infant insert, which means the smallest newborns may not fit well in the seat. And the top harness slot is only 13," so it is doubtful a kid will hit the 40 lb. weight limit before outgrowing this seat by height. But that's the trade-off for getting the price so low—again, we think this seat is best for that little-used second car or Grandma's car. Fans love the Scenera for airplane travel, where the seat's light weight is much appreciated.

A final negative: the Scenera shell edges can be rough. Without a seat protector (a thin towel will do), your car's upholstery may get scratched or damaged when using the Scenera.

Despite these flaws, we still think the Cosco Scenera Next is a good, basic seat for secondary use. Fans love the Scenera for airplane travel, where the seat's light weight is much appreciated.

Trend Watch: Seats with Naturally Flame-Retardant Covers?

One trend for car seats in the past couple of years are seats that use naturally flame-retardant fabrics. Often wool or wool blends, these car seat covers eschew fabrics that are treated with flame retardant chemicals (bromines, etc).

Ironically, it was the government that required car seat fabrics to be flame retardant—in case the seat catches fire after a crash. The wisdom behind this mandate can be debated, but car seat makers dutifully make their seat fabrics flame retardant by using various chemicals which themselves aren't exactly an eco-picnic.

Of course, you can also achieve flame retardancy by using a natural fabric like wool. UPPAbaby Mesa was the first to offer natural flame retardant covers, but only on a limited number of fashions. The Merino wool used is naturally flame retardant but comes at a price: about a $100 more than the standard fabric.

More brands have jumped on this trend in recent years: Britax has SafeWash, Chicco has ClearTex. You can get many popular car seats now in these fabrics, for an extra charge.

Clek's car seat fabrics are now "free of brominated and chlorinated flame retardants."

FYI: There is no scientific evidence that using a car seat with fabric that is treated with flame retardant chemicals is dangerous for your baby. However, we understand the concerns of parents about these chemicals and the desire to limit exposure of babies to chemical fire retardants.

Bottom line: if you prefer a car seat with fabric that is naturally flame-retardant without added chemicals, there are more choices on the market today.

convertible car seats

CONVERTIBLE SEATS

The following is a selection of popular convertible and all-in-one car seats and how they compare on features:

MAKER	MODEL	PRICE	WEIGHT LIMITS (IN LBS.) REAR	FORWARD	RATING
BABY TREND	PROTECT	$109	40 LBS.	65 LBS.	C
BRITAX	ADVOCATE	$350-$370	40	65	A-
	BOULEVARD CT	$325	40 LBS.	65 LBS.	A
	MARATHON CT	$280	40	65	A
CHICCO	NEXTFIT SPORT	$195	40	65	A
CLEK	FLLO	$380	50	65	B
	FOONF	$450	50	65	B
COSCO	APT 50	$60	40	50	B-
	SCENERA NEXT	$50	40	40	B+
CYBEX	SIRONA M	$310-$330	40	65	C+
DIONO	RADIAN 3RXT	$280	45	65/120	B-
EVENFLO	SYMPHONY	$180-250	40	65/110	B+
	TRIUMPH	$120-$150	40	65	C
GRACO	4EVER	$240-$280	40	65/120	A-
	EXTEND2FIT	$150	50	65	A-
	MILESTONE	$210	40	65/100	A-
	SLIMFIT	$180	40	65/100	A-
MAXI COSI	PRIA 85	$270	40	85	B+
	MAGELLAN XP	$350-400	40	65/120	A
NUNA	RAVA	$450	50	65	A-
PEG PEREGO	PRIMO VIAGGIO	$320-$350	45	70	A
SAFETY 1ST	CONTINUUM	$123	40	50/80	B
	GROW & GO EX	$140	40	65/100	A

Pros/Cons

Headrest pops off for better fit in smaller vehicles

Same as Boulevard, but added side impact protection

7 recline positions; Enhanced side impact protection

Basic side impact protection; no-rethread harness

No rethread harness; 9 recline positions. Fancier versions have zip-off covers

Lack of seat padding, Can't use until baby is 14 lbs.

Very Pricey, Bulky, lack of seat padding. Wool fabric on most expensive version

Affordable but no seat recline. Wide base. Disney version is same

Simple, affordable seat, great for air travel or grandparents

Feature rich, but can be difficult to install

Seat folds up; side impact protection; converts to booster

Easy to install with latch; smooth harness adjuster

No rethread harness but huge seat width

6 recline positions; side impact protect; no-rethread harness

One of the highest rear-facing limits on market

Like the 4ever but doesn't have backless booster mode

Narrower base allows better fit in smaller cars, easy to adjust

85 lb. harness limit is unique; machine washable pad; Max version adds infant insert

Adjustable torso side impact protection, 7 pos recline, machine washable cover

Side impact protection, extended rear-facing use to 50 lbs.

Side impact protection, adjustable headrest. Kinetic version adds anti-rebound bar

Converts to booster; machine wash/dry pad

QuickFit harness adjusts harness & headrest

convertible car seats

The Best All-in-One Car Seats

As the name implies, all-in-one car seats can be used from birth to booster seat age.

These seats have become increasingly popular in recent years, as more parents seek to extend rear-facing use to age 2, 3 and beyond. Instead of buying three seats, you could theoretically use an all-in-one seat from birth to booster age—one seat to rule them all.

More realistically, most parents we've surveyed are using all-in-one seats to replace convertible and booster seats (which means folks still buy a separate infant car seat for convenience sake).

All-in-one seats are not really a new thing—they trace their history to the late 90's when Cosco sold the Alpha Omega. That ill-fated seat had several major flaws (including a wretched booster mode). Good news: the current crop of all-in-one seats perform better than the Alpha Omegas of old.

The Best All-in-One Car Seat

After researching and reviewing 17 different all-in-one car seats, we pick the **Graco Trio Grow SnugLock LX 3-in-1** ($216) as the best all-in-one car seat on the market today.

The Graco Trio delivers on the all-in-one promise with an exceptionally well-designed seat that can be used rear-facing (4 to 40 lbs.), forward-facing with five point harness (22 to 65 lbs.) and then as a booster (high back, 40 to 100 lbs.) for older kiddos.

The stand-out features here include a harness that adjusts without rethreading, side impact protection, six recline positions and headrest with ten height adjustments. As for safety, the Trio scored at the top of the class in recent third-party crash tests.

The all-in-one car seat is the Fountain of Youth for car seat makers—the mythical seat that works from birth to college (ok, as a belt-positioning booster to 120 lbs., or when kids age out of booster seats and can correctly fit in a regular seat belt. That's usually around age ten or later).

Yet like Ponce De Leon, Graco's quest for the perfect all-in-one seat has been one of frustrating missteps—the brand's earlier attempts at all-in-one seats fell flat.

We've always been a bit skeptical of all-in-one car seats. As the saying goes, jack of all trades . . . but master of none. Many all-in-one car seats in the past had one or two great uses, but fell down when it came to a third. But there is good news: we finally have an all-in-one car seat we can recommend: Graco Trio.

Graco clearly has put a lot of thought into the Trio. Little touches like the harness that stores away in booster mode (you don't have to remove it from the seat) are very nice. The Trio is easy to fit in a vehicle in rear-facing mode. The steel reinforced frame and EPS-lined seat are pluses. You also get premium "push-on" LATCH connectors, which you would not expect at this price point.

Reader feedback and online reviews are very positive. Readers love how the fabric snaps off for cleaning—and yes, the cover is machine washable.

The Trio is easy to install and adjust.

Flaws but not deal breakers. What's not to love about the Graco Trio Grow SnugLock?

Well, this seat is rather bulky—it may be a tight fit in a small vehicle.

At nearly 22 lbs., the Trio is heavy . . . moving it from vehicle to vehicle would be a chore. If you are looking for a lighter weight car seat for carpooling, there are better choices out there.

Finally, let's talk about one unspoken flaw of all-in-one car seats—wear and tear on the fabric. Graco promises you can use the Trio until age ten or so. That's ten years worth of fabric use and abuse, starting with diaper blow-outs and continuing through toddler tummy troubles. Yes, you can clean the fabric . . . but we can imagine some kids reaching the point where they reject sitting in a "baby" seat that is stained/worn from years of use. Just sayin'.

Also Great: Graco Milestone

The Graco Milestone costs a bit less than the Trio ($202)—it is a previous generation seat that is still worthy of consideration. Basically, it is a scaled-down Trio, with fewer features.

Example: The Trio has six recline positions; the Milestone has four.

There are some other small differences as well—the Trio has two built-in cup holders. The Milestone has a single cup holder attached to the side of the seat.

Bottom line: the Graco Milestone is a good bet if you find it on sale (we've seen it on sale for as little as $150) or if the Trio is out of stock.

Best All-In-One Car Seat Splurge

Britax was late to the party in this category but their entry here—the **Britax One4Life** ($360 to $400)—is a winner.

The One4Life brings all of Britax's ease-of-use goodness (ClickTight installation) and safety features (SafeCell energy absorption) to a seat that can be used from birth to booster years (5 to 120 lbs).

As you might expect at this price level, you get all the bells and whistles—including Britax's Safe-Wash fabrics (no chemical flame retardants).

Feedback from our readers on this seat has been very positive (it is super easy to install), but we are a bit disappointed that there is no included anti-rebound bar—that's an extra $55 accessory. (Really?).

The Best Booster Car Seats

Welcome to the third and final stage of car seats: the booster. Your child needs a booster seat when he outgrows his convertible seat (assuming you didn't buy an all-in-one seat!). This happens when he exceeds the weight limit or when he is too tall for the harness (his shoulders are taller than the top slots in the seat). For most children, this happens around ages three to six (it varies depending on the convertible seat).

So what is a booster? This is one of the more confusing categories of car seats. Boosters started out as a way to boost a child to correctly sit in an auto safety belt.

In recent years, a new type of booster (harnessed boosters) blurred the lines between harnessed seats (like infant and convertible seats) and traditional belt-positioning boosters. These 3-in-1 or 4-in-1 seats morph as your child gets older: first in the harness, then with the auto safety belt and so on.

We'll discuss more about these different categories shortly.

A key point to remember: any child from 40 to 80 lbs. and less than 4'9" (generally, kids age four to eight) should be restrained in a booster seat. And in most states, booster seat use is mandated by law.

Our general rule: you should keep your child in a harnessed car seat as long as possible.

7 Things No One Tells You About Buying a Booster Car Seat!

1 BOOSTER SEATS COME IN FOUR DIFFERENT FLAVORS:

◆ *Harnessed boosters:* As discussed above, harnessed boosters morph from a forward-facing harnessed seat to a high-back belt-positioning booster (and in some case) to a backless booster.

With the five-point harness, boosters can generally be used up to 65, 80 or 90 lbs. Then the harness is removed, and the seat can be used as a belt-positioning booster, usually to 80 or 100 lbs.

Our top recommendation in this section is for a harnessed booster. The take-home message: we recommend a harnessed booster as the safest option to transport a toddler. Keep your child in the harness as long as possible (given seat weight/height limits).

◆ *High back boosters (HBB)*: Belt-positioning boosters come in two flavors: high back boosters and backless boosters. High back boosters have often been called "kid's captain's chairs," which they kind of resemble. They are designed to be simple, but provide vital safety features for children who've outgrown a harnessed seats.

These boosters properly position the lap belt on a child's strong hip bones, rather than letting it ride up on the soft internal organs. And they provide correct positioning of the shoulder belt, so the child can comfortably wear it and get critical upper body support.

The high back also protects the child's head from whiplash if there are no head restraints in the vehicle, and the high back may also give some side sleeping support. ALL of these boosters require a lap and shoulder belt. FYI: Some high back boosters convert into backless boosters for older kids.

◆ *Backless boosters:* These belt-positioning boosters work the same way as high back boosters—they just don't have a back.

Safety-wise, these can be a bit better than a high back booster, since the child sits against the vehicle seat. They do the same job positioning the lap belt, and usually include some sort of strap to adjust the shoulder belt. But they don't provide head support if you have low seat backs, and they don't give any side or sleeping support.

On the other hand, they are often popular with older kids, since they can be quite inconspicuous.

◆ *Special Needs Seats:* There are a few seats on the market now that don't really fit into any category. One is the Britax Traveler Plus, which is designed for special needs kids up to 105 lbs.

2 WHEN IS YOUR CHILD READY FOR THE AUTO SAFETY BELT? Some states allow children as young as six to legally ride in an auto safety belt (that is, booster seat use isn't required). But there is the law—and the law of physics. Numerous peer-reviewed safety studies show that continued booster seat use is the safest course . . . until a child can SAFELY use an auto safety belt. When is that?

When a child is over 4'9" and can sit with his or her back straight against the back seat cushion (with knees bent over the seat's edge), then he or she can go with just the auto's safety belt. Still have doubts? Try this Five-Step Test from Safety Belt Safe, USA:

- Does the child sit all the way back against the auto seat?
- Do the child's knees bend comfortably at the edge of the seat?
- Does the belt cross the shoulder between neck and arm?
- Is the lap belt as low as possible, touching the thighs?
- Can the child stay seated like this for the whole trip?

If you answered no to any of these questions, your child needs a booster seat, and will probably be more comfortable in one too.

3 USING A BOOSTER SEAT TOO SOON CAN BE DANGEROUS. You'll note that some harnessed boosters have starting weight limits as young as 20 lbs.—that could be as young as a six month aged baby! But remember this: all boosters are forward-facing. And the current recommendation by safety experts is to keep your child REAR-FACING until age 2 or longer. So even though you could use a forward-facing harnessed booster for a one year old, we wouldn't recommend it.

Also: don't abandon the harness too soon. Yes, you could switch to a belt-positioning booster as soon as four years (or 40 lbs.). Our advice: don't. Keep your child in that harness as long as you can (that's why our top recommended seats in this section have top harness limits of 80 and 90 lbs.).

4 YOUR CAR'S OWNER'S MANUAL IS AN IMPORTANT RESOURCE. Sure, you probably haven't look at it since you purchased the vehicle. But most auto manuals have detailed advice about car seat use. And that comes in especially handy when you start using a booster. That's because some boosters can use LATCH—but your vehicle may prohibit this use when the weight of your seat plus your child exceed a certain limit.

5 SITTING IN A BELT-POSITIONING BOOSTER REQUIRES MATURITY. Yes, we recommend using a harness as long as possible—but we are also the parents of two kids. And we remember the pleas from a toddler who didn't want to sit in a "baby seat" (that is, the harness). The challenge: to use a belt-positioning booster, a child must be mature enough to understand the iron clad rule: you NEVER wiggle out from under the belt when the car is in motion. Some kids are ready for this and others need more time in a harness!

6 ONLY USE CARDBOARD CUPS IN BOOSTER SEAT CUP HOLDERS. You'll note that many booster seats come with cup or juice box holders. These are a great convenience, but most car seat makers only recommend putting cardboard cups or juice boxes in these holders. Why? In a collision anything heavier than a cardboard juice box or cup can become a dangerous projectile.

7 THERE ISN'T ONE NATIONAL STANDARD FOR HOW LONG YOUR CHILD SHOULD BE IN A BOOSTER SEAT. Booster seat use is regulated on a state-by-state basis, at least when we're talking about how long kids must remain in a booster. Some states have an age limit, some a weight and/or height limit. If you're unsure about the rules in your state, check your state Department of Motor Vehicles' web site.

Best Booster Car Seat (Overall)

After researching and reviewing 51 different booster car seats, we pick the **Graco Nautilus Snuglock 3-in-1 Harness Booster** ($180-$192) as the best booster seat on the market today.

The Graco Nautilus works to 65 lbs. with the harness and 120 lbs. as a booster plus it can be used as a backless booster. The seat has enhanced side impact protection, an adjustable headrest and belt lock-offs, making it one of the most popular seats in this category.

Graco makes the best-selling harnessed booster seat on the market and it's easy to see why— the Nautilus works with a five-point harness to 65 lbs. and then converts to a high back booster (100 lbs.) and even a backless booster (120 lbs.) for older kids.

The harness is a big plus if you have a toddler who has outgrown his convertible seat, but wish to keep him in the harness for a while longer (the 65 lb. limit should fit most six year olds).

The Nautilus' other features include over molded armrests (with side storage), four-position recline and decent padding. The seat is lined with EPS foam.

So what is the Nautilus Elite's biggest selling point? The Nautilus Snuglock is competitively priced. As for reader feedback, the Graco Nautilus earns positive marks from readers for its overall ease of use. The IIHS ranks the Nautilus as a Best Bet when used in highback mode.

As always, Graco likes to make things confusing by coming up with a plethora of Nautilus models, usually to have something slightly different to sell various retailers. Bottom line: we like Graco Nautilus *SnugLock*, which was a recent refresh of the Nautilus that added "SnugLock," which enables quicker installation whether you use a safety belt or LATCH. Also included: Simple Safe Adjust, which makes it easier to adjust the harness and headrest as your child grows.

Cons but not deal breakers. The Graco Nautilus isn't perfect. Some readers tell us it is too snug to fit larger kids. The Nautilus also must be assembled, which includes several steps such as "Pull elastic loop on the seat pad through the vehicle belt guide on side of seat and attach to hook as shown. Repeat on other side." Compare that to Britax where the seat basically comes out of the box ready to use.

We're not saying the Nautilus is as fun to assemble as IKEA furniture, but we noted more than a few readers said assembling Graco boosters had them swearing like a pirate. So just a heads up.

booster car seats

Also Great: Chicco MyFit

The **Chicco MyFit** ($200) is the company's first foray into the har-
nessed combo booster category, previously dominated by the Britax
Frontier and Graco Nautilus seats. Like other harnessed boosters, this
seat is intended for toddlers in harness mode from 25 to 65 lbs. Then
the harness is removed and the seat is used with the car seat belt from
40 to 100 lbs.

We like the key features here: LATCH-compatible seat with a one-
pull harness tightener, no rethread harness, nine-position headrest and
four-position recline.

It also comes equipped with side impact protection, two "CupFolders" (folding cup holders)
and their LockSure seat belt installation.

Chicco makes three models of the MyFit: the basic ($200), the MyFit Zip ($250) with an extra zip
off cover and the Zip Air ($300). The Zip Air version has all the features of the Zip but adds an ad-
ditional; zip off cover and breathable backrest.

Our reader feedback on the Chicco MyFit has been quite positive. Ease of use (adjusting the
harness, etc.) is above average, in our hands-on testing. The upholstery is plush and comfy.

We found installation to be straight forward—we love Chicco's shoulder-belt lock-off, which is
easier to use than the competition. We noticed a few dissenting opinions on this from online reviewers, who found the high belt path and the need to thread the belt under the seat pad to be
somewhat vexing.

Chicco included its much-praised SuperCinch technology (this enables the seat to be installed
with one hand). But SuperCinch is only available on the Zip Air models.

Unlike other seats in this category, Chicco MyFit includes a bubble
level indicator (pictured) to help parents figure out if the seat is at the
correct angle even when it is reclined. That is a nice touch.

As for crash-testing, only *Consumer Reports* has tested this seat—it
scored a "better" in CR's three tier system: basic, better, best.

Cons but not deal breakers. The seat is rather heavy, so it may not
be the best solution for car pooling where you need to move it from
car to car.

Some children have complained about the non-removable chest pads under the chest clip.
They are rather stiff and can be uncomfortable. The bummer: you can't remove them, even to
clean them. The harness pads are required in harness mode.

Overall, this is a solid effort by Chicco in a new category for them. The price for the basic version
is comparable to our top recommendation, the Graco Nautilus Snuglock.

Best Budget-Friendly Booster Car Seat

What's the best harnessed booster for under $100? The ***Evenflo Maestro Sport*** is our pick—it has a five-point harness that can be used up to 50 lbs. After a child outgrows the harness, the Maestro becomes a belt-positioning booster up to 100 lbs. Best of all, the Maestro Sport is just $90.

The Maestro has performed better than Evenflo's other boosters, which are showing their age. The Insurance Institute for Highway Safety gives the seat a Best Bet rating and it earned four out of five stars for ease of use.

Reader feedback has been mostly positive. Fans cite the LATCH attachments, upfront harness adjustment and two crotch positions.

On the other hand, critics note the harness must be re-threaded when you need to change the height and you have to disassemble the seat to clean the pad.

Other parents criticized the effort needed to tighten the straps—it requires too much force, they say. But those are the trade-offs for the sub $100 price.

Bottom line: this is a better effort than Evenflo's other boosters and it is affordable . . . with harnessed boosters soaring to $300 and beyond, it's a pleasant surprise to find a seat that is both well designed and under $100.

booster car seats

Best Booster Car Seat For Urban Parents

You live in an urban city center and need to take Uber/Lyft or a taxi with a toddler that's outgrown a convertible seat. What's the best solution? We like the **The BumbleBum** ($30) an affordable, inflatable booster that is perfect for carpools or taxis. The Bumblebum's small size makes it perfect when you need to fit three toddlers in one back seat.

One caveat: this booster probably isn't the most comfortable for long commutes or road trips. Note to urban parents looking for a lightweight option for Uber and Lyft: The BumbleBum weighs just over one pound.

More Booster Seat Recommendations

We believe the safest place for your toddler and young child is in a harnessed booster seat, like the ones recommended earlier in this section.

Yes, there are two other booster seat types—belt-positioning high back boosters and backless boosters. These are for older children who've outgrown harnessed seats. (Note that our top recommended harnessed booster converts into a belt-positioning and backless booster).

So when would you need to purchase just a belt-positioning or backless booster? Well, let's assume you are in a minor car accident and decide to replace your first booster. But now your child is six years old and has outgrown the harness limit. Then you'd go for one of these seats.

Best Belt-Positioning Booster

The **Graco TurboBooster** ($50) is the best belt-positioning booster on the market today. It packs a good number of features into an affordable package: height-adjustable headrest, open belt loop design, armrests, back recline, cup holders and more. If you can afford the upgrade, the **Graco TurboBooster With Safety Surround** ($70 on Target.com) has additional side impact protection in the form of beefed up headrest and torso cushions.

Best Backless Booster

The best backless boosters on the market are the **Graco TurboBooster backless** ($20, pictured above) and the **Evenflo Big Kid** ($28). Both are affordable and easy to use boosters for older kids who don't need a high back booster.

The Graco backless option works from (roughly) ages four to ten (40 lbs. to 110 lbs.). Again, even though you could use this seat for kids as young as four, we'd suggest a harnessed seat until your child is beyond 80 lbs. or as long as possible.

How we picked recommended car seats

We evaluated car seats with hands on inspections, checking seats for ease of use (installation and adjusting the seat). We also gather significant reader feedback, tracking seats on quality and durability. Besides interviewing parents, we also talk with car seat "techs," certified child passenger safety technicians who install hundreds if not thousands of seats at safety check points nationwide.

We've been rating and reviewing car seats since 1994. During that time, we have also visited manufacturer facilities and watched car seat crash tests. While we don't personally crash test seats, we compare our reader feedback with crash tests done by organizations like the National Highway Traffic Safety Administration and *Consumer Reports*.

We also look at third-party evaluations of seats by groups like the Insurance Institute for Highway Safety (IIHS), which focuses on booster car seats.

Best Car Seat Protectors

Let's talk protective mats for vehicle seats. There's no escaping it: some car seats have sharp edges. When you tightly install these seats, they can sometimes damage your vehicle's interior—leaving dents or marks on the seat.

Even if your car seat doesn't have sharp edges, kids and cars can be a messy combo—muddy feet get seat backs dirty and juice boxes can spill. Protective mats help protect against the worst

booster car seats

dirt and grime.

So, it's simple—just get a protective mat, right? Well, no. As with any accessory you might use with a car seat, you should always consult your car seat maker's instruction manual first.

That's where things get tricky. Some car seat makers (Chicco, Cybex, Peg Perego) do not allow ANY mats to be used under their seats. Other car seat makers (Britax, Diono) only allow their own brand of mats. Good news: some popular seat makers like Graco actually give you the green light on vehicle seat protectors.

Before you purchase any of these mats, however, check your car seat's instruction manual to determine if the mat is allowed! While these recommendations were valid and correct as of publishing time, things can change.

So let's start with Graco—for these seats, we like ***Lusso Gear's Car Seat Protector*** ($25).

Yes, Graco allows most car seat protectors—and this one came out tops in our tests. Easy to install and affordable. We also liked how easy it is to clean. Downsides: it can slide on leather seats.

Got an UPPAbaby seat? Then we'd recommend ***Munchkin Brica Elite Seat Guardian Car Seat Protector*** ($30).

Approved for use by UPPAbaby, this protector impressed with how easy it is to clean and install. Grippy fabric prevents sliding. But it can leave marks on seat. And didn't work well in middle seats.

Finally, we should mention that some car seat makers make their own car seat protector mats.

The only seat protector Britax recommends is its own ***Britax Vehicle Seat Protector***—this pricey mat ($45) only protects the seat (not the seat back). Good news: it doesn't slide around. Bad news: its wide width makes it hard to use in the middle position.

If you own a Diono sea, the ***Diono Ultra Mat, Car Seat Protector*** ($22) is easy to install, grips well and easy to clean. But it can be slippy on leather seats.

CHAPTER 9

Strollers & Diaper Bags

Inside this chapter

W *here to begin? Strollers seem overwhelming—what do you really need? We'll give you the low down on finding the right stroller to match your lifestyle. Then check out our specific stroller picks, from a budget-friendly lightweight stroller to a fully-outfitted multi-function model. Finally, let's talk diaper bags—which are best?*

We like the British slang for strollers: pushchairs. That perfectly describes what we call strollers . . . baby chairs with wheels that you push. Simple!

Then you arrive at the baby superstore and look at the stroller section. "Section" doesn't quite describe it. It's Strollermageddon.

Travel systems, ultra-compact strollers, jogging models . . . wow. Prices from $30 up to $1900. And the brands! At last count, we figure there are *54* separate stroller brands sold in North America. With names you can't pronounce. Where to start?

That's why we are here. We've spent 25+ years researching, testing and writing about baby strollers. All the while not taking a single dime from the brands we review or recommend.

Before we get to our specific recommendations, let's start with some stroller basics. The goal is to match the right stroller to your lifestyle.

7 Things No One Tells You About Buying A Stroller

1 **WHAT'S YOUR STROLLER LIFESTYLE?** Before you fall you in love with a pricey stroller, ask yourself HOW you will be using a stroller. Yes, you.

Think of strollers as tools—the wrong tool for a job isn't going to help, no matter how shiny it is. It's the same for strollers.

Because we all live in different environs and want to go varied places, the key to stroller happiness is to understand how different stroller options fit your lifestyle. Hence, the perfect stroller for hiking in Colorado isn't the right one for a simple spin around a mall in Atlanta.

Climate plays another factor—in the Northeast, strollers have to be winterized to handle the cold and snow. Meanwhile, in Southern California, full canopies with extendable sunshades are helpful for shielding baby's eyes from late afternoon, low angle sunshine.

2 THE PERFECT STROLLER DOESN'T EXIST.

Your stroller needs will change over time. Babies/toddlers use strollers from birth to age four and sometimes beyond. The perfect stroller for a newborn isn't necessarily great for a toddler—although some strollers make a valiant effort at bridging the years.

And what if you add a second child in the mix?

The take-home message: no one stroller can meet all these needs. Most parents end up with more than one stroller. Let's review over the stroller landscape.

3 THERE ARE SIX TYPES OF STROLLERS ON THE MARKET...

THE 6 TYPES OF BABY STROLLERS

CHEAP, BARGAIN, INEXPENSIVE, EXPENSIVE, RIDICULOUSLY EXPENSIVE AND DAMN! THAT STROLLER COSTS MORE THAN MY FIRST CAR!

We kid. Actually, there are *seven* styles of strollers: umbrella/lightweight strollers, travel strollers, full-size strollers, multi-function strollers, jogging (or sport) strollers, all-terrain strollers and travel systems. Here's a quick look see:

◆ *Umbrella/lightweight strollers* are generally under 20 lbs. in weight. Some feature two handles and a long, narrow fold (like an umbrella; hence the name!). Most umbrellas strollers are very cheap ($30 to $50), although some upper end manufacturers have spruced them up to sell for $100 to $300 (UPPAbaby and Peg Perego have "luxury" umbrella strollers). Premium lightweight strollers boast features like extendible canopies, storage baskets, and high quality wheels. Because seat recline can be limited, many umbrella/lightweight strollers are designed for kids six months old and older.

◆ *Travel strollers* are lightweight strollers that are designed to fold up into a small suitcase that can fit in an airplane overhead bin. Best for frequent travellers, these strollers can be quite pricey.

◆ *Full-size strollers* used to be called carriages or prams. These strollers are more like a bed on wheels with a seat that reclines to nearly flat and can be enclosed like a bassinet for newborns. All that stroller goodness comes at a price: hefty weight, as much as 30 lbs. As a result, getting a full-size stroller in and out of the vehicle trunk can be a challenge. Entry level full-size strollers start at $200, but these can top $1000. In recent years, full-size strollers have fallen out of favor, replaced by . . .

◆ *Multi-function strollers* morph infant to toddler to a double stroller, with either an infant car seat adapter or bassinet accessory for newborns. A second seat accessory expands these strollers into doubles. Expect to pay $300 to $1000 for multi-function options (accessories like ride-on boards and second seats are almost always an additional cost). This stroller type has increased in popularity in recent years, as more parents have kids that are closer in age.

◆ *Jogging strollers* feature air-filled, bicycle-style tires and lightweight frames perfect for jogging or brisk walks on rough roads. The best strollers for running have a fixed front wheel for stability. Jogging stroller with lightweight aluminum frames usually run $300 and up although there are some cheaper, steel framed options on the market too.

◆ *All-terrain strollers* are eclipsing jogging strollers for all but the most devoted runner. In fact, they often look like joggers but have a swivel front wheel. Big tires take to hiking trails better than typical stroller wheels, but these strollers are bulky and heavy. And expensive: they can run more than $400 for popular brands. These strollers are also popular for the beach.

◆ *Travel systems* combine a stroller and infant car seat which snaps into the stroller. Typically sold at discount and big-box stores, travel systems are pitched to first-time parents and gift givers. Most feature basic infant car seats and full-size strollers at prices that range from $200 to $300. Travel systems have waned in popularity in recent years as more lightweight strollers have added infant car seat compatibility/adapters.

4 **BEWARE THESE COMMON STROLLER SAFETY HAZARDS.** Just because a stroller is on the shelves at the Baby Megastore doesn't mean it is safe. 12,000 babies each year are injured by strollers, according to the most recent government safety data.

Here are our top safety tips:

◆ *Never hang bags from the stroller handle.* Yes, it is tempting to hang that diaper bag or purse off your stroller handles. The danger: your stroller can tip backwards—and even if your child is in the five-point harness, injuries can still happen. Solution: put that purse in your stroller's storage basket. Or use a backpack diaper bag.

◆ **Don't leave your baby unattended** while sleeping in a stroller. Newborns, infants and toddlers all move around when they're sleeping. Injuries have occurred when babies creep down to the strap openings, so keep an eye on them. Take a baby out of a stroller and put them in a full-size crib for naps.

◆ **Don't trust your stroller's brakes.** The best stroller models have brakes on two wheels rather than one. But even if a stroller has the best brakes on the planet, never leave a stroller unattended on an incline with your baby inside.

◆ **Follow the weight limits.** Forty pounds is typically the maximum for most strollers.

◆ **Wait until baby is over one year of age before running with a stroller.** Pediatric experts tell us the neck muscles of infants under one year of age can't take the bumps of jogging or walking on rough terrain.

◆ **Fold and unfold your stroller away from your baby.** The opening/closing mechanisms of a stroller can be a pinching hazard, so don't open or close your stroller with baby nearby. Graco recalled over 5 million strollers back in 2014 for just such hazards.

5 THE SECRET TO A SMART STROLLER TEST DRIVE: ADD WEIGHT. Don't test drive that stroller empty. Take a backpack and put in about 20 lbs. worth of books. Stick that in the stroller seat and you'll see how that stroller actually steers/handles with a baby. And yes, practice folding and unfolding the stroller with the backpack in your arms!

6 WHAT STROLLER FEATURES REALLY MATTER . . . FOR BABIES. The Dreaded Wall of Strollers—more than one parent-to-be has been reduced to tears staring at a baby store's mind-boggling display of 37 stroller models. So let's break down what's REALLY important when stroller shopping for baby:

◆ **Reclining seat.** If you plan to use this stroller from birth, the seat must fully recline. That's because babies can't comfortably ride in a sitting position until around six months. And most newborns spend their time sleeping—seat recline is a necessity.

◆ **Extended canopy.** There are three types of stroller canopies: skimpy, extended and fully enclosing. Skimpy canopies only block the sun if it is directly overhead—great if you live at the equator. For everyone else, an extended canopy (also called an extended sunshade) are better at blocking all sun angles. Baby Jogger's canopies are a good example of extended canopies (pictured). The best canopies have multiple positions for flexibility. Fully enclosing canopies go a step fur-

ther—they completely block out the sun from a stroller. These are great, but unfortunately seen only on more expensive strollers.

FYI: If you live in an area with lots of mosquitos (we're looking at you, Florida), a bug net accessory is highly recommended.

◆ *All wheel suspension.* Stroller wheel suspension works like your car's shock absorbers, smoothing out life's little (and big) bumps.

7 WHAT STROLLER FEATURES REALLY MATTER . . . FOR PARENTS.

◆ *It's all about the storage.* Like napkins for toddlers, you can never have enough. We're not just talking about the size of the storage basket (but that helps). It's HOW you access the basket, especially if the seat is reclined. The best strollers add storage in areas you wouldn't think—on the hood, the back of the seat, a storage compartment with lid in a parent console for your phone and so on.

◆ *The right wheels.* Going for a nature walk on a dirt trail? Air-filled 12" rear tires are best. Navigating tight spaces at the Pikes Place Market in Seattle? Small 6" wheels enable tight turns.

◆ *Removable seat pad for washing.* Crushed-in cookies, spilt juice and the usual grime can make a stroller a mobile dirt-fest. Some models have removable seat cushions that are machine washable—other models let you remove all the fabric for washing.

◆ *Reversible seat.* When baby is young, you can have your child face you. Then when your toddler wants to see the world, the seat flips around.

◆ *The one-hand, flip flop friendly, standing fold.* The fewer the steps and hands you need to fold a stroller, the better. The best strollers have one-hand folds that stand when collapsed. If your stroller has a foot brake or release, make sure it is "flip flop friendly." Basically that means you can set and release a brake or folding mechanism *without* putting your toes underneath the lever and pushing up. Instead, you push *down* with your shoe/flip flop's sole. Voila! No messed up pedicure.

Flip Flop Friendly Brake

◆ *Height adjustable handle.* If you and your partner are two different statures, an adjustable handle is a must have.

Eco-friendly stroller certifications

There are three international organizations that test and certify textiles to meet environmental standards: OEKO-TEX, Global Organic Textile Standard (GOTS) and IVN Naturextil. All three of these certifications are optional—there is no legal standard for organic, non-allergenic, chemical free textiles in the U.S. Many of the stroller brands that are certified are European, with only a few U.S brands certified.

As of this writing, there is one eco-friendly certification on strollers sold in North America: OEKO-TEX. Here's some background:

OEKO-TEX is a German organization that offers "Standard 100 certification program for textiles at all steps in the manufacturing process. "Products marked with the label 'Confidence in textiles (Standard 100)' provide effective protection against allergenic substances, formaldehyde, heavy metals such as nickel or for example forbidden plasticizers (phthalates) in baby textiles," according to

OEKO-TEX's web site. OEKO-TEX offers a second certification called Green by OEKO-TEX, which means the "materials (were) tested for harmful substances," the product was "made in environmentally friendly facilities" and it was "made in safe and socially responsible workplaces."

We found only two stroller makers who are OEKO-TEX certified. At the time of this writing, all of BumbleRide and Nuna's stroller fabrics were OEKO-TEX certified—however, check their web sites for specific models' information.

Best Lightweight Strollers

Up next, we recommend lightweight strollers in several categories:

◆ Best Lightweight Stroller (Overall)
◆ Best Budget-Friendly Lightweight Stroller
◆ Best Lightweight Stroller For Urban Parents (Winter/Summer)
◆ Best High-Style Lightweight Stroller

Best Lightweight Stroller (Overall)

We waded through 74 lightweight strollers—folding, unfolding, buckling, un-buckling—until we found the very best lightweight stroller: the **Baby Jogger City Mini 2** ($250).

Lightweight strollers are the holy grail of the stroller market—enough convenience features (easy fold, cup holder) for parents and comfort (canopy, seat pad) for baby, but not too much to add unnecessary weight. We generally define "lightweight" as strollers under 20 lbs. empty. Our pick in this category is the Baby Jogger City Mini, an excellent tri-wheel stroller with over-sized canopy and fully reclining seat.

Baby Jogger's quick fold technology is amazing—you lift a strap in the middle of the stroller and zip! It's folded. An optional car seat adapter can turn a City Mini into a travel system if you wish. As a brand, Baby Jogger has a good reputation for quality. Now owned by Graco, Baby Jogger got its start by making (you guessed it) jogging strollers in the 80's. After going through a bankruptcy and ownership change in the early 2000's, the company pivoted to making easy-to-fold strollers in both the lightweight and multi-function markets.

The tri-wheel City Mini (single $250, 17.1 lbs.; double $500, 26.6 lbs.) is Baby Jogger's best-selling stroller, featuring a full recline and large canopy.

The secret sauce to the City Mini Series is the company's Quick-Fold technology: pull up on one strap and zip! The stroller collapses and folds. No complicated buttons or latches. No multi-step process. The Quick-Fold has super-sized Baby Jogger's sales in recent years and other stroller makers have rushed to copy it. Here's what City Mini looks like folded:

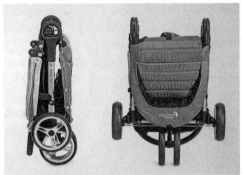

In a recent refresh of the City Mini (dubbed Mini 2), the stroller got an adjustable footrest (when raised, it provides front access to the storage basket), standing fold (yeah!) and included car seat adapters for Baby Jogger and Graco car seats. Those adapters used to be an extra $20.

Parent feedback on the City Mini has been quite positive. They praise the overall ease of use and features like the large canopy, which puts the canopies on other lightweight strollers to shame.

Finally, we should note that Baby Jogger sells car seat adapters as accessories for the City Mini that fit most major brands of car seats. This is one advantage the City Mini has over our other umbrella (lightweight) stroller picks—it can accommodate an infant car seat.

Baby Jogger also makes a raft of accessories for the City Mini: everything from weather shields to glider boards (for older toddlers to stand on), as well as a foot muff, cup holders and parent consoles. That's the advantage of going with a brand like Baby Jogger. Less expensive light-weight stroller brands typically have few (or no) accessories.

FYI: We should mention that Baby Jogger also has various spin-offs of the City Mini, including the *City Tour* (a four-wheeled version with more compact fold) and *City Mini GT* (with more rugged wheels).

strollers

Best Budget-Friendly Lightweight Stroller

Kolcraft's entry-level strollers are winners. Dollar for dollar, these are the best affordable strollers on the market. Compared to other low-end brands (Graco, Cosco), Kolcraft shines. The entry-level offering is the ***Kolcraft Cloud*** (9.5 lbs. pictured above at right), which comes in two versions. The basic Cloud umbrella stroller sold at Walmart for $27 is a simple umbrella stroller with cup holder, storage basket and extended canopy—a great deal!

The ***Kolcraft Cloud Plus*** adds a one-hand fold, multi-position seat recline and child snack tray for $63 (11.8 lbs., pictured above at left). There's even a ***Cloud Double*** side-by-side stroller for $80.

We like the affordable Cloud strollers—parents tell us they are a good value for the dollar, praising the simple fold and extended canopy (something often missing in the under $100 stroller market).

Best Lightweight Stroller for Urban Parents (Winter)

If you live in the city, you need a stroller that can navigate winter slush, snow and other non-weather city hazards (rough sidewalks). Our pick for these folks, the ***Baby Jogger City Mini GT 2*** ($360, 21.5 lbs.), is similar to the base City Mini but adds bigger, no-flat tires, as well as an adjustable handle bar with brake, a redesigned seat/canopy that provides more headroom, and an easier to access storage basket.

At 21.5 lbs., the City Mini GT 2 pushes the outer limits of what we consider lightweight. But that's the trade-off for the bigger wheels, which add about four pounds over the basic City Mini.

Also: Baby Jogger has a nice range of winter-fighting accessories, like a foot muff (for baby) and hand muff (for parents). Add in the weather shield and this stroller can battle whatever Mother Nature throws at you.

One caveat: the rear axle of the City Mini GT is about three inches off the ground. That means this stroller would struggle with deeper snow. If you regularly face deep snow, an all terrain stroller with higher ground clearance would be a better bet. We discuss these strollers later in this chapter.

Like its sibling stroller, the City Mini GT 2 got a recent refresh that added an adjustable footrest (when raised, it provides front access to the storage basket), standing fold (yeah!) and included car seat adapters for Baby Jogger and Graco car seats. Those adapters used to be an extra $20.

Best Lightweight Stroller Splurge

France may be famous for its wine and cheese . . . but strollers? Not so much. BabyZen 's designer, Jean-Michel Chaudeurge, hopes to change that with stylish strollers that aim to compete with that other European designer stroller megabrand, Bugaboo.

Chaudeurge worked at Fiat before joining his son Julien and launching various baby gear ventures (Chaudeurge's design credits also include the Beaba Babycook food processor). BabyZen has basically one model in the U.S.: the **BabyZen YOYO 2** (13.6 lbs) for $500.

A second version of the YOYO called the YOYO Complete runs $680 and includes a newborn bundle which includes a fully reclining seat that can be used from birth.

The YOYO claim to fame is its one-hand unfold and super compact folded form that will fit in an airline overhead bin.

When the YOYO first came out, it didn't make much of a splash. But BabyZen refreshed the stroller with a bigger basket, higher weight capacity, and padded carry strap. Yes it is very pricey, but they do throw in a rain protector and now the YOYO works with infant car seats (via car seat adapters sold separately). Too bad the cup holder is an extra $30.

In a recent revision (dubbed the YOYO 2), BabyZen added independent suspension in all four wheels. There was also a small change to the buckle system to make it more parent-friendly.

And yes, there is now a faux leather handlebar.

Yes, if you tried to justify this stroller for overall value, it would be a tough sell. But the design is the star here, with the white suspension wheels and the ability to morph from infant stroller to toddler stroller with a cushy padded seat.

What if you need a lightweight stroller that folds up compact for travel? That's our next topic!

Best Travel Stroller

Strollers specifically designed for travel have taken off in years, thanks to parents' desire to hit the road and new designs that fold up so compactly they can fit in an overhead airline bin.

In years past, most folks would rely on a cheap umbrella stroller, so named because they resemble an umbrella (long and skinny) when folded. The big problem: these strollers were routinely NOT allowed in overhead bins and thus became checked baggage or gate-checked. The result was often mangled strollers that were damaged or destroyed by malevolent baggage handlers.

The new era for travel strollers was kicked off by the 2015 launch of the GB Pockit ($165), a 10.5 lb. stroller that folded into the shape of small suitcase. It was the amazing fold that turned the Pockit into a social media sensation.

Too bad the Pockit as a stroller was such disappointment—from the joke of a canopy to the awkward two-hand fold to the horrible handling, the Pockit worked better on Facebook than in real life.

On the plus side, the Pockit's success at getting attention launched a travel stroller arms race, with several brands jumping into the "ultra-compact fold" category with better offerings. We count 11 travel stroller offerings today, with prices that range from $100 to $500.

We tried out several of the most popular travel strollers, checking to see how they performed in the real world (on planes, on city streets, etc.). We then surveyed the travel enthusiasts among our readers to find their favorites. Here is the one we liked best.

The Best Travel Stroller

The 13 lb. **Mountain Buggy Nano** ($165) is a dark horse in this category—especially since parent Mountain Buggy (part of the Phil & Ted's stroller group) is better known for its beefy SUV-like strollers.

The Nano, on the other hand, is a compact travel stroller that impressed us with its flexibility and overall quality . . . at a price that doesn't break the bank.

The star here is the quick fold. And we mean quick.

Ok, the fold requires two hands—but it is much easier than other travel stroller we tested. When folded, this seat scrunches up to 21″ x 12″ x 20″.

At 13 lbs., the Nano is easy to carry from its crossbar when folded. The 5″ wheels and tight turning radius make it easy to steer in tight places. Overall, we liked the stroller's handling and quality—note the little features like the brake that won't mess up a pedicure.

The reclining seat on the Nano is good for napping older babies, but the company still recommends babies should be six months or older to use this stroller. Cool feature: an extendable footrest to make naps cozier.

One final big plus: the Mountain Buggy is car seat compatible—it's universal adapter works with our top pick, the Chicco KeyFit 30. Competitors either have no car seat compatibility or they only work with pricey Maxi Cosi type seats (the Cybex Aton, etc). Even if you never use the car seat capability, the Nano can hold a baby/toddler up to 45 lbs.

Accessories like a rain shield and mesh cover for wind in a combo pack ($29.99) and a reversible liner for more padding or just a different look ($50) complete the Nano with extra travel flexibility.

Flaws but not deal breakers. The flip side of the small wheels is this—the Nano doesn't perform as well on varied terrain. Sure, smooth sidewalks and grass are no problem. But note: there is only rear-wheel suspension, so that makes for a bumpy ride when you take the Nano anywhere else but relatively smooth surfaces.

There is very little storage in the Nano and the basket only holds 11 lbs. worth of stuff—so anything besides a small diaper bag would be too much.

The Nano's smallish canopy comes in for a good amount of criticism. One reader noted it lacks a peek-a-boo window and the coverage it offers is minimal. Weirdly, when retracted, the canopy blocks the handlebar . . . so most folks use the canopy in the extended position, whether

strollers

they need it or not.

Bottom line: Well, no stroller is perfect. Despite these imperfections, we recommend the Mountain Buggy Nano as the Best Travel Stroller.

Up next, let's talk multi-function strollers, the Swiss Army knives of baby buggies.

Best Multi-Function Stroller for Kids Close in Age

If you plan to have two kids close in age, we'd suggest the **Baby Jogger City Select** ($330-$600, 28.1 lbs.). It can be configured 16 ways with an optional second seat, bassinet or car seat adapter (for Chicco, Peg Perego, Cybex, Maxi Cosi, Graco and Britax). The City Select is an excellent stroller with a quick fold.

Baby Jogger makes two versions of this stroller: a base model and the LUX.

As you might guess from the name, the LUX adds more plush fabrics (although we thought the fabric on the base model is fine).

But the LUX goes beyond just nicer fabrics. It actually folds about 30% smaller than the base model. And the LUX adds four more seat configurations, including a jump seat that can be used up to 45 lbs.

The wheels are also different: the base model has plastic front wheels, while the LUX has foam-filled wheels for both back and front. And the LUX has all wheel suspension, which the base model lacks.

At 28.4 lbs., the LUX is roughly the same weight as the original model.

One point to keep in mind: while Baby Jogger offers a raft of accessories for the City Select, some of the accessories aren't cross compatible. That is, the LUX cup holder and 2nd seat adapter don't work on the base model—and the base model's child tray doesn't work on the LUX. Confusing, we know.

Bottom line: the LUX model is probably worth the $100 to $150 upgrade, given all the extra features.

Overall, the Baby Jogger's City Select's quality is impressive—readers tell us they love it, especially when they have two babies close in age.

Best Budget-Friendly Multi-Function Stroller

Can you buy a multi-function stroller for under $500? The **Evenflo Pivot Xpand** ($323) hit all the right notes in our testing—at a price that is impressive.

And that price includes an infant car seat; a second seat is $107.

Evenflo doesn't often get praise from us for their strollers—low price usually means low quality. But we couldn't help but be intrigued with the new Evenflo Pivot Xpand Modular Travel System. Based off the Pivot, a single seat modular frame stroller, the Xpand adds new features including a surprisingly easy conversion to a double stroller . . . using no tools!

The biggest difference: the Pivot Xpand offers 22 different seating options to the Pivot's six options. And here's the amazing part: the adapters to add a second seat or car seat are built in to the stroller; they retract back when not in use!

That's a big deal, since most multi-position strollers require extra adapters as accessories to morph into double use—extra parts that are supposed to be stored somewhere when not in use.

The Pivot Xpand's other features include a toddler seat that converts to a lay-flat bassinet, a standing fold (with the toddler seat attached) and an expandable storage basket. The included car seat is the Evenflo SafeMax, which is a decent choice.

Reader feedback on this stroller has been quite positive. The stroller is easy to assemble.

Compared to ridiculously-priced multi-function strollers like the UPPAbaby Vista (which is pushing $1000), the Evenflo Pivot Xpand is a great budget-friendly solution.

Best All-Terrain Stroller

The crown for best all-terrain stroller goes to the **Thule Urban Glide 2** ($529, 25.3 lbs.).

We judged the Urban Glide 2 superior when it came to maneuverability and tracking (it has a turnable wheel that can be locked in two positions). The fold is also simple: flip open the secret compartment at the footrest, twist the release knob and voila! The stroller folds quickly.

As you'd expect in a premium all terrain stroller, the Thule Urban Glide also features a height-adjustable handle, robust wheel suspension and an extendable canopy with air mesh ventilation. Yes, there is a bassinet accessory as well.

One cool feature that the Thule has that the competition lacks: a covered storage basket. The zip-top cover keeps your items dry in case it is raining or there is mud on the trail—very nice!

A double version of the Urban Glide 2 is also available for $750.

A recent refresh of this stroller (the Urban Glide 2) included these improvements:

♦ *New integrated brake.* The Urban Glide 2 adds a brake that is integrated into the handle-bar—twist the blue portion and the stroller slows, which is helpful when going down a hill

♦ *Extended canopy.* Thule redesigned the Urban Glide 2's canopy to offer an extension with mesh ventilation in back (the new version still has the front sun visor too).

♦ *New accessories* including a bumper bar and rain cover as well as car seat adapters for the Maxi Cosi and Chicco infant car seats. The lack of these accessories was a major negative for the original Urban Glide.

♦ *Secure folding strap.* When folded, a new catch ensures the stroller stays folded.

The Thule Urban Glide has a silver frame—although there is one version with a jet black frame for an additional charge. Quite spiffy.

What we liked: Thule Urban Glide 2 vs. the competition. Unlike cheaper all-terrain strollers, the Thule Urban Glide 2 features 16" air-filled rear-wheels—this is key for trail hiking or snowy days. The rear-wheel suspension also helps smooth out bumps. These are features lacking, for example, on the Graco FastAction Fold Jogger.

Another key difference: the Thule has a 75 lb. weight capacity; the Graco is only 50. That's important because you often use an all-terrain stroller with older children on longer outings—and a 75 lb. weight capacity would work with kids up to age 7 or 8.

Finally, compared to the BOB Revolution, the Thule Urban Glide 2 has an easier, one-step fold, in our opinion.

What's not to like: downsides but not deal killers. At this price, the Thule Urban Glide 2 is at the top end of the all-terrain price range—and to make matters worse, items like a parent console, bumper bar or child snack tray are optional accessories. That will push the price of this stroller over $600.

While the fold on the Urban Glide 2 is quick, it is quite bulky when folded and will take up a good amount of trunk real estate. Yes, that's true for other all terrain strollers, however . . . to mitigate the bulkiness, the side wheels release for more compact storage.

We wish the Urban Glide 2 would stand when folded—instead, it folds down to the ground, which guarantees the fabric will get dirty/muddy too easily.

Unlike some competing strollers, the Thule Urban Glide 2 doesn't work out of the box with any infant car seats—you have to buy a separate adapter to use this stroller with an infant car seat. Graco Fastaction Fold Jogger, for example, works out of the box with most Graco infant car seats.

While we liked the reflective fabric on the Urban Glide 2, we thought Thule could have hidden the brake wires that are visible on the handle bar. Finally, the brake on the Urban Glide 2 is not flip-flop friendly—to release it, you have to push up from under the button, which will most likely mess up that pedicure.

Best Strollers for Running (and Power Walking)

Fixed-wheel jogging strollers with air-filled tires are best for folks who want to actually jog or run with a stroller—you can push them in a straight line. The disadvantage to these strollers: to turn them, you have to pick up the front wheel and move it. Hence, fixed wheel joggers aren't good for walking or shopping trips.

Another issue to consider: how young can your baby be and ride in a jogger? First, determine whether the seat reclines (not all models do). If it doesn't, wait until baby is at least six months old and can hold his or her head up. If you want to jog or run with the stroller, it might be best to wait until baby is at least a year old since all the jostling can be dangerous for a younger infant (their neck muscles can't handle the bumps). Ask your pediatrician for advice if you are unsure.

Another decision area: the frame. The cheapest strollers (under $200) have steel frames—they're strong but also heavy (and that could be a drawback for serious runners). The most expensive models ($300 to $400) have aluminum frames, which are the lightest in weight. Once again, if you plan casual walks, a steel frame is fine. Runners should go for aluminum.

Finally, remember the Trunk Rule. Any jogger is a lousy choice if you can't get it easily in your trunk. Check the DEPTH of the jogger when it is folded—compared this to your vehicle's trunk. Many joggers are rather bulky even when folded. One tip: quick release wheels help reduce the bulk, so check for that option.

So, which jogging stroller do we recommend? Let's break that down into two categories: power walking and serious runners. Note that our pick for serious runners has a fixed front wheel; if you want a stroller with a turnable front wheel (more suited to the mall or light duty outdoor activities), go for the power walking pick or see the best all-terrain stroller on the previous page.

One final caveat: air-filled tires give the smoothest ride—but they require maintenance. Yes, they can go flat . . . and you have to remember to put air in them when not used for a while! A bicycle tire tump and patch kit would be wise investments.

If that sounds like too much hassle, consider a stroller with foam-filled rubber tires—no flats! These are more common an all-terrain or multi-function strollers. The trade-off is weight: foam filled tires are often heavier than air-filled ones.

Best Stroller for Power Walking

Our pick for the best stroller for power walking is the ***Graco FastAction Fold Jogger*** ($180, 27 lbs.). It has a swivel front wheel that can be locked, plus a quick fold feature that earns kudos from readers. Add in a generous storage basket, parent console with cup holders plus an affordable price and you've got a great stroller for extended walking.

What's not to like? Well, this stroller is heavy—30% more than our pick for serious runners (below). When folded, the Graco FastAction Fold is quite large: 39"(!) in length, 23.6" in width and 15.3" in height. You might measure your vehicle's trunk before buying to make sure it will fit.

Despite this negative, we still think this is a great stroller for neighborhood walks.

Best Stroller for Serious Runners

For serious runners and joggers, our top pick for Best Jogging Stroller is the ***Thule Glide 2.0 Performance Jogging Stroller*** ($529, 21 lbs.). This model is a fixed wheel jogger with large 18" rear wheels and a 16" tire up front for a smooth glide. The lightweight 23.8 lb. frame and one-step fold make it the best option for folks who want to run with baby.

strollers

The Best Double Strollers

There are three types of double strollers that can transport two tikes: tandem models, side-by-side styles and sport strollers. Here's a quick 101 on double strollers.

A *tandem* stroller has a "front-back" configuration, where the younger child rides in back while the older child gets the view. These strollers are best for parents with a toddler and a new baby.

Side-by-side strollers, on the other hand, are best for parents of twins or babies close in age. In this case, there's never any competition for the front seat. The only downside: some of these strollers are so wide, they can't fit through narrow doorways or store aisles. (Hint: make sure the stroller is not wider than 30" to insure door compatibility). Another bummer: few side-by-side doubles have fully reclining seats, making them impractical for infants.

So, what to buy—a tandem or side by side? Our reader feedback shows parents are much happier with their side-by-side models than tandems. Why? The tandems can get darn near impossible to push when weighted down with two kids, due to their length-wise design. Yes, side by sides may not be able to fit through some narrow shopping aisles, but they seem to work better overall.

Finally, if you want to exercise with your stroller, look to the *sport* stroller category for the best options. Most of the strollers in this category are commonly referred to as jogging or running strollers although most parents don't actually run with them. We prefer to use the terms "sport" or "all-terrain."

Best Double Stroller (Overall)

After researching and rating 19 double strollers, we picked the **Contours Options Elite Tandem** as the best double stroller ($380).

The Contours Options Elite Tandem is one of the best tandem stroller options on the market. It can take two infant seats (or one infant seat, one toddler seat) with an universal car seat adapter (an extra $30 accessory) and has a standing fold.

Contours (owned by Kolcraft) is the exception to the rule that you need a successful infant car seat to succeed in the stroller market—despite the lack of any travel systems, Contours has survived, thanks to an emphasis on under-served market segments (namely double strollers).

Contours is a mid-price line with upgraded features and fabrics while their sister stroller line, Kolcraft makes entry-level models under their own name.

The Options Elite tandem stroller (32 lbs.) has rubber coated rear wheels, side storage basket access and seat back storage. The Elite also has an extendable canopy with mesh air vent.

But here's where the rubber hits the road: the Elite has seven different configurations with seats that can reverse or mix one (or two) infant car seats and a seat. The Options features a standing fold, reclining seats, adjustable footrests and decent-size canopies. For an extra $30, Contours offers an universal carseat adapter, or model-specific adapters for major brands.

What do parents say about the Contours Options Elite Tandem stroller? The comments are overwhelmingly positive. Parents especially like the versatility of the seat arrangements. Plus you can use almost any popular infant seat on the stroller. Others noted the stroller was easy to maneuver, often a problem with other cheaper tandem strollers.

Flaws but not deal breakers. The Contours Options Elite tandem is an excellent double stroller with one big disadvantage: weight. At 34 lbs., the Elite is not only heavy but bulky when folded (it can easily eat up the entire trunk in a vehicle). While fans loved the multiple configurations and overall ease of use, the lack of a parent console (save one skimpy cup holder) is a bummer.

To remedy this, we'd suggest a universal parent console like this one pictured at right from Baby Jogger for $26.

Best Budget-Friendly Double Stroller

Our pick for best budget-friendly double stroller is the **_Joovy Caboose Stand-on Tandem_** ($140-$150, 26 lbs.).

This stroller really isn't a double stroller with two seats, but a "stand-on tandem"—the younger child sits in front while the older child stands in back (there is also a jump seat for the older child to sit on). This is a better solution when you have an older toddler who doesn't want to ride all the time in a stroller . . . but still gets tired and needs a place to sit on long outings.

Bonus: this stroller also includes a universal infant car seat adapter. At $140 to $150, this stroller is a very good value—since most doubles are $200+.

Readers generally love this stroller, but a few critics note the wheels are designed for smooth surfaces, not rough or broken sidewalks. We'd agree—this isn't an all-terrain stroller.

Best Side-by-Side Double Stroller

Our top choice for best side-by-side stroller is the **_Chicco Echo Twin_** ($180). Based on the popular Chicco Mini Bravo, the Echo Twin is a two-handled umbrella style stroller with rear wheel suspension, full recline, padded five-point harness, and a cup holder. Other features include adjustable leg rest and compact fold.

We also liked the independent four-position recline on both seats.

A nice feature for parents of twins (or two kids close together in age): it fits easily into a trunk without eating up too much space.

The Echo Twin has individually adjustable canopies that have zip-off rear flaps, which allow for additional airflow. The seats have a one-hand recline and they can be adjusted individually. Another plus: the recline here is a full recline, so babies as young as six months will be comfortable napping in this stroller.

The double wheels have both suspension (for a smoother ride) and swivel locks in front as well as a rear wheel brake.

Overall, readers tell us they love this stroller, especially for its compact size when folded.

Flaws but not deal breakers. While the Chicco Echo Twin has mostly positive reviews, some parents (even those who love it) complain that the stroller is heavy. At 30 lbs., it's not a piece of cake to lift into your trunk, but that's true of almost every double stroller on the market today.

Others note it can be too wide (33.5") to fit through doors and the canopies are rather small. Another disadvantage: there is no parent console, only a parent cup holder. And there isn't even a cup holder for the kids!

Also Great: Joovy Scooter X2 Double Stroller

The ***Joovy ScooterX2*** ($237) is a lightweight side-by-side twin stroller with an elliptical frame. It also features a deep (but not full) seat recline. Like all Joovy strollers, the Scooter X2 features an oversized canopy and large storage basket.

There are even two cup holders/storage pockets on the back of each seat. In a recent refresh, the ScooterX2 gained larger wheels (7″ front, 9″ rear), new graphite frame and improved fold.

Best Sport Double Stroller

The **Thule Urban Glide 2.0 Double Jogging Stroller** is the double version of the popular Urban Glide 2.0. It has the same front swivel wheel, height-adjustable handle, robust wheel suspension and an extendable canopy with air mesh ventilation.

One cool feature that the Thule has that the competition lacks: a covered storage basket. The zip-top cover keeps your items dry in case it is raining or there is mud on the trail—very nice!

In a previous version of this review, we picked the BOB Revolution FLEX Duallie Jogging Stroller as the best double stroller. While the BOB still has it strong points, the newer Thule Urban Glide 2.0 Double Jogging stroller has a much easier, one step fold. The BOB requires two steps.

Another difference between the Revolution and the Urban Glide 2.0: the twist action hand break. We think this is easier to use than the lever on the Revolution. The Revolution costs $40 less than the Thule double, however.

Thanks to quick release wheels, the Thule Urban Glide 2.0 Double folds down into a relatively narrow space (30.7" x 34.2" x 16.1"). Even so, that takes up a good amount of trunk space, especially in a smaller vehicle. Still this compares favorably with the Revolution, whose fold is a few inches more bulky (34.5" by 34.5").

In the past year, Thule upgraded the Urban Glide 2.0—the double version shares these same improvements:

◆ **Extended canopy.** Thule redesigned the Urban Glide 2's canopy to offer an extension with mesh ventilation in back (the new version still has the front sun visor).

◆ **New accessories** including a bumper bar ($30) and rain cover ($40) as well as car seat adapters for the Maxi Cosi and Chicco infant car seats ($60 each). The lack of these accessories was a major negative for the original Urban Glide.

The Best Stroller Wagons

The stroller wagon is the platypus of kid transportation—part utility wagon, part baby stroller. Great for outdoor adventures—think the zoo, soccer games or the beach—stroller wagons are super helpful . . . and can be rather pricey. We tested the top seven stroller wagons on the market today before picking these best bets. We judged on overall quality, utility and affordability.

Best Overall Stroller Wagon

Best known for its less expensive strollers, Evenflo jumped into the stroller wagon category with this affordable entry: the **Pivot Explore All-Terrain Stroller Wagon** ($284). The key feature here we liked: the handle flips so you can push or pull from either side of the stroller wagon. That was impressive in our testing.

Stroller wagons are great for outdoor adventures: the zoo, picnics, hikes, etc. One place you can't take them, unfortunately, is Disney. The parks banned stroller wagons recently.

We loved the Pivot's reversible handle, generous storage and all-terrain wheels . Dual canopies are excellent, but critics note it is heavy and the fold could be easier.

Best Splurge Stroller Wagon

Pricey yet beloved wagon, the **Keenz Stroller Wagon** ($520) is a parent favorite and an excellent splurge-worthy choice. We tested the latest model and liked the double five-point safety harnesses with height adjustments, one-step brake and height adjustable handles—one on either side of the stroller so you can pull or push.

We really liked this model with its numerous included accessories. Pricey, but great for beach outings. Fun canopy and height adjustable handles, but it is smallish.

Best Stroller Wagon 2+ Kids

Most stroller wagons are designed for one or two toddlers—so, what to do if you have to transport three or four kiddos? We'd suggest the **WonderFold** wagon ($550), which has seating for four with two five-point safety harnesses. We liked the elevated seats that let kids see over the sides of the wagon. The foam EVA 10" rear wheels and 8" front wheels do a good job on gravel or sand, so this wagon would be great for the beach or hikes.

We really liked this wagon: one-step fold, huge capacity and mesh side panels are the stars here. Love the removable fabric for washing. But it is heavy and bulky when folded.

Best Budget-Friendly Stroller Wagon

Stroller wagons are a great concept, but the high price of popular models puts it out of reach for many folks. Good news: when we tested several options, we found one that is both affordable and functional: **WagonBuddy's Push and Pull Handle** stroller wagon ($188). No, it isn't as fancy as other models on the market . . . but it gets the job done if you want to do the occasional zoo outing.

This model is best for outdoor adventures on paved surfaces (zoo, etc). We liked the full canopy and easy assembly. But the fold is a touch difficult. Capacity: 120 lbs.

Best Stroller Wagon If You Hit The Lottery

If there are no budget constraints on your stroller wagon purchase, we'd give a serious look at the **Veer Cruiser** ($600)—this is the stroller wagon hybrid that kicked off the craze to start with! It's basically the Cadillac of stroller wagons.

Yes, the Veer is crazy pricey but an amazing stroller wagon that has a plethora of great accessories. Contoured seats, snack tray and quality construction are high points.

The Best Diaper Bags

We consider ourselves experts at diaper bags—we got five of them as gifts. While you don't need five, this important piece of luggage may feel like an extra appendage after your baby's first year. And diaper bags are for more than just holding diapers—many include compartments for baby bottles, clothes, and changing pads. With that in mind, let's take a look at what separates great diaper bags from the rest of the pack. In addition, we'll give you our list of eight items for a well-stocked diaper bag.

7 Things No One Tells You About Buying A Diaper Bag

1 THE SHEAR NUMBERS OF DIAPER BAGS CAN SEEM OVERWHELMING. Yes, it seems like there is a separate diaper bag available for each of the four million moms that will give birth this year. So how do you know which one is best?

Here's our checklist: the best diaper bags are made of tear-resistant fabric and loaded with all sorts of useful pockets. Contrast that with low quality brands that lack many pockets and are made of cheap, thin vinyl—after a couple of uses, they start to split and crack. Yes, high quality diaper bags will cost more ($50 to $150 versus $30 to $45), but you'll be much happier in the long run.

Another item on our checklist: diapers bags that don't look like diaper bags. A well-made diaper bag that doesn't look like a diaper bag will make a great piece of carry-on luggage later in life.

2 YOU MAY NOT NEED TO BUY A DIAPER BAG AFTER ALL. Many folks have a favorite bag or backpack that can double as a diaper bag. Besides the obvious (wipes and diapers), put in a large zip-lock bag as a holder for dirty/wet items. Add a couple of receiving blankets (as changing pads) plus the key items listed in tip #3, and you have a complete diaper bag. You can buy many items found in a diaper bag (such as a changing pad) a la carte at most baby stores.

3 DRUM ROLL! HERE ARE OUR EIGHT ESSENTIAL ITEMS FOR YOUR DIAPER BAG.

◆ *Extra diapers*. Put a dozen in the big bag, two or three in the small one. Why so many? Babies can go through quite a few in a very short time. Of course, when baby gets older (say over a year), you can cut back on the number of diapers you need for a trip. Another wise tip: put whole packages of diapers and wipes in your car(s). We did this after we forgot our diaper bag one too many times and needed an emergency diaper. (The only bummer: here in Colorado, the wipes we keep in the car sometimes freeze in the winter!

◆ *Travel-size wipes package.* A good idea: a plastic Tupperware container that holds a small stack of wipes. Some wipe makers sell travel packs that are allegedly "re-sealable" to retain moisture; we found that they aren't. And they are expensive. For example, a Huggies travel pack of 16 wipes is $2. That works out to 12¢ per wipe compared to 2¢ per wipe if you buy a Huggies refill box of 624 wipes.

◆ *Blanket and change of clothes.* Despite the reams of scientists who work on diapers, they still aren't leak-proof–plan for it. A change of clothes is most useful for babies under six months of age, when leaks are more common. After that point, this becomes less necessary

◆ *Hat or cap.* We like the foreign legion-type hats that have flaps to cover your baby's neck and ears (about $10 to $20). Warmer caps are helpful to chase away a chill, since the head is where babies lose the most heat.

◆ *Baby toiletries.* Babies can't take much direct exposure to sunlight–sunscreen (30 SPF or higher) is a good bet for all infants. Besides sunscreen, other optional accessories include bottles of lotion and diaper rash cream. The best bet: buy these in small travel or trial sizes. Don't forget insect repellent as well. This can be applied to infants two months of age and older.

◆ *Don't forget some toys.* We like compact rattles, board books, teethers, etc.

◆ *Snacks.* When baby starts to eat solid foods, having a few snacks in the diaper bag (a bottle of water, crackers, a small box of cereal) is a smart move. But don't bring them in plastic bags. Instead bring reusable plastic containers. Plastic bags are a suffocation hazard and should be kept far away from babies and toddlers.

◆ *Your stuff.* Be careful putting your wallet into the diaper bag—we advise against it. We left our diaper bag behind one too many times before we learned this lesson. Put your name and phone number in the bag in case it is lost.

4 IF THE BUDGET ALLOWS, GET TWO DIAPER BAGS. Buy one that is a full-size, all-option big hummer for longer trips (or overnight stays) and the other that is a mini-bag for a short hop to dinner or shopping. Here's what each should have:

◆ *The full-size bag:* This needs a waterproof changing pad that folds up, waterproof pouch or pocket for wet clothes, a couple compartments for diapers, blankets/clothes, etc. Super-deluxe brands have bottle compartments with Thinsulate to keep bottles warm or cold. Another plus: outside pockets for books and small toys. A zippered outside pocket is good for change or your sunglasses. A cell phone pocket is also a plus.

◆ *The small bag:* This has enough room for a couple diapers, travel wipe package, keys, wallet and cell phone. Some models have a bottle pocket and room for one change of clothes.

5 IF MONEY IS TIGHT, JUST GO FOR THE SMALL BAG. To be honest, the full-size bag is often just a security blanket for first-time parents—some think they need to lug around every possible item in case of a diaper catastrophe. But, in the real world, you'll quickly discover schlepping that big full-size bag everywhere isn't practical. While a big bag is nice for overnight or long trips, we'll bet you will be using the small bag much more often.

6 **FABRIC IS IMPORTANT.** Look for fabric that is easy to wipe clean or throw in the wash. (Sorry, stash away those expensive totes from your pre-baby years for some future day). Smooshed up crackers, wet clothes, and spit up are facts of life. So stick with easy clean fabric. And consider a diaper bag with a bright colored interior lining. Black linings make it hard to see items, but bright colors like red make it much easier.

7 **BE SAFE: DON'T HANG YOUR DIAPER BAG ON THE BACK OF YOUR STROLLER.** While you may see lots of parents hanging their diaper bags on the handles of their strollers, we generally don't recommend this. Kids can get injured when they are climbing out of the stroller and it flips up because the heavy diaper bag pulls down the back of the stroller.

Some diaper bags come with special stroller clips. If you're considering using those clips, try them without the baby in the stroller. Since every stroller is different, you'll want to confirm that the stroller won't tip with a bag hanging on the handlebars. And some stroller makers also make a matching bag that will work with their stroller. If you're determined to hang your bag on the stroller, buying a bag from the stroller maker may be the safer way to go.

Our diaper bag picks are divided into the following categories:

◆ The Best Diaper Bag (Overall)
◆ The Best Budget-Friendly Diaper Bag
◆ The Best Designer Diaper Bag

The Best Diaper Bag (Overall)

The **Hap-Tim Multi-Function Diaper Bag Backpack** offers an impressive, affordable diaper backpack option. With 13 pockets (one insulated outside bottle pocket), padded shoulder straps, a stay-open top zipper (like an old fashioned doctor's bag) and stylish fabric, the Hap-Tim sells for a reasonable $38.

Parents like the many pockets, the light grey or dark grey heathered fabrics and roomy interior. The downsides are that it takes two hands to open and close the main compartment, the straps have been known to come unstitched and the side wipes pocket is not as easy to use as on other bags we tried. However, if your budget is closer to $50 than $100 for diaper bag, the Hap-Tim is a good choice.

Best Lightweight Backpack Diaper Bag

Skip Hop makes one of the lightest weight backpack diaper bags—the **Skip Hop Riverside Ultra Light Backpack** weighs just 8 oz. With a total of eight pockets (two side insulated bottle pockets), an extra wide opening and cushioned changing pad, this water resistant pack can hold a lot of stuff. The $35 price is a good deal.

Best Budget-Friendly Diaper Bag

At first, you might think a diaper bag that costs under $50 isn't really that cheap. After all, you can find plenty of options in that price range. But those cheaper options usually only include a diaper changing pad. The **SoHo diaper bag** ($37) has *seven* pieces: the large main bag, zippered mini purse, insulated bottle bag, Grips stroller attachments, two accessory cases and changing pad. The diaper bag itself has several outside pockets and a zip closure on top. Score!

Best Tote Diaper Bag

Yes, backpack diaper bags seem to have taken over, but if you prefer a tote style? Our top pick is the ***Skip Hop Duo Signature*** ($50-$70), which comes in a plethora of colors and patterns and is reasonably priced.

The Duo is Skip Hop's largest bag with eleven pockets including a cell phone pocket, magnetic closures instead of zippers and their cool Shuttle Clips, which allow you to clip it to a stroller. Yes, it has a shoulder strap too and changing pad, plus it comes in eleven colors and patterns.

Some parents say the bag holds less than they expected and the magnetic closures don't work as well if you stuff the bag really full. Those complaints aside, Skip Hop is a great option if you are looking for a full-size diaper bag with a bit more style.

The Duo also comes in other versions (example: Special Edition) with fancier fabrics and only nine pockets. FYI: Prices for the Duo Signature bag can vary by fabric—we've seen some versions on sale for as little as $40.

Also Great: Ju-Ju-Be Hobo Be

This bag gets raves from readers. Most of Ju-Ju-Be designs are pricey, but folks think the ***Ju-Ju-Be Hobo Be*** is worth it. This messenger style bag comes with five zippered pockets, three main pockets, antimicrobial treated inner fabric, Teflon-treated outer fabric, a changing pad, and memory foam padded strap. A wide variety of colors and styles are available.

Like Skip Hop's Duo, the prices for the Ju-Ju-Be- Hobo Be range widely ($70-$115), depending on the fabric.

Best Breast Pump Bag

If you only received the basic breast pump motor and collection set from your insurance company, Ju-Ju-Be makes two aftermarket breast pump bags to store and carry your pump: the **Ju-Ju-Be Be Supplied** ($95, pictured above) and the **Be Pumped** ($135).

Both options have a dedicated giant pocket insulated for sound so you can keep it in the bag and muffle the sound of some of the louder pumps out there. The Be Supplied is the basic model with four pockets and a detachable messenger strap. It's also treated with teflon and has luggage feet to protect surfaces.

In the larger Be Pumped, they've added additional pockets like a cell phone pocket, four mesh pockets and two zippered pockets and a changing/staging pad. Also included is a wet bag, mini bottle cooler and organizer bag ($50 if you buy them separately).

We love Ju-Ju-Be's light colored linings and special fabric treatments to inhibit bacteria, mold and mildew. The bags come in just a couple fabrics for each style, and they aren't the cheapest options on the market, but they have great features nonetheless. We highly recommend them.

Top 7 Essentials for Your Diaper Bag

"Be prepared" is the mantra for seasoned parents who dare venture out of a house with a baby or toddler—and a diaper bag is the key defense against chaos. But what to carry?

As a seasoned parent who's seen more than my share of diaper blowouts, a well-equipped diaper bag needs to carry a wide arsenal of not-so-obvious tools beyond diapers and wipes. Here are our Top 7 Essentials for Your Diaper Bag:

1 **ZIPPERED WATERPROOF POUCHES!** *Bantoye 10 Pcs A4 Zipper File Bags, Zippered Waterproof PVC Pouch Plastic Zip Document Filing Folder ($11)*

Diaper bags can quickly become a jumbled mess: these water-proof zippered pouches keep things in order.

They are perfect for storing personal or baby items—give each color a specific purpose (blue for binkies, etc). Pro tip: keep ALL liquids in your diaper bag inside bags like this, even if you think the lid is on tight! Consider getting a mix of sizes— these bags are roughly 9" x 13", perfect to hold soiled clothes or cloth diapers.

You might also buy some smaller pencil case-size bags like these to hold items like pacifiers or keys.

2 SUN HAT. *i play. Brim Sun Protection Hat | All-day UPF 50+ sun protection for head, neck, & eyes. ($10.50-$21.50)*

Whether you have a summer or winter baby, a sun hat is a must for outings for both sun protection . . . and cute pictures.

It's always the item you're most likely to forget: a sun hat for baby or toddler. Throw this into a diaper bag for those days at the park, strolls around a lake and other outings where the sun may be a bit too strong for the little one. We liked this one by i play, which also has a variety of different styles and a zillion colors.

3 USB POWER BANK. *Anker PowerCore 10000 PD Redux ($40)*
Mommy (and daddy) brain is real. When a sleep-deprived you steps out for the day with an uncharged phone (or worse, a forgotten charging cord) this will be your savior.

Not everything in the diaper bag is for baby—a portable USB Power Bank like the Anker PowerCore 10000 will provide an emergency jolt of juice for your dying cell phone. In fact, it has enough juice to charge even the largest smartphones three times. Charge it up, toss in your diaper bag and forget it . . . until the low battery warning flashes.

4 EXTRA SOCKS. *Trumpette Unisex-Baby Perfect Little Dozen Milestone Baby Socks ($27 for six)*

Babies and socks are like opposite poles of a magnet—socks tend to disappear faster than ice cream on a hot day. A pair or two of extra socks in the diaper bag is a must.

Yes, a diaper bag can never have enough extra socks—and Trumpette is one of our favorites. Sure, they are a bit pricier than other basic socks, but Trumpette socks are super soft and actually designed to stay ON your baby or toddler's feet with a dab of spandex! No kidding. These are a reader favorite.

5 DIAPER RASH CREAM. *Balmex Complete Protection Diaper Rash Cream w/Zinc Oxide, 4 Ounce ($7)*

After testing 13 over-the-counter diaper rash remedies on actual baby butts and consulting with pediatricians who fight the diaper rash battle every day, we picked Balmex Diaper Rash Cream as the best diaper rash cream.

A travel-size tube of Balmex is a must for your diaper bag—as any experienced parent knows, a baby with diaper rash is going to make everyone unhappy.

Parents tell us they like the creamy texture; it's not as sticky as many other zinc oxide diaper rash cream—and we would agree with this after road-testing several diaper rash creams ourselves. The scent isn't bad either.

6 WATER BOTTLE. *Hydro Flask Double Wall Vacuum Insulated Stainless Steel Leak Proof Sports Water Bottle, Standard Mouth with BPA Free Flex Cap ($30)*

Hydration is key—and this insulated stainless steel water bottle is our favorite.

If you are breastfeeding, hydration is important! And if you're formula feeding, this bottle can keep warm water ready to mix with formula (pro tip: don't mix until you are ready to feed baby).

Sure, you can buy a cheap water bottle for less than this top pick—but do you want your water to stay cold for a full day outing with baby? Yes, you do. And if you prefer caffeine-infused hydration, the Hydro Flask will keep it hot for half a day. And, yes, we independently tested a Hydro Flask to confirm those claims!

Hint: pick a bright color to find it in a full diaper bag.

7 STAIN REMOVER. *Tide to Go Instant Stain Remover Liquid Pen, 3 Count ($7)*

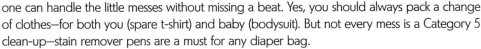

Spit-up happens—on both your clothes and baby. No, this won't handle a diaper blow-out, but we love Tide To Go pens to handle the little messes.

Comedian Dennis Miller once said "You can have kids . . . or nice things." Stains are a fact of life when it comes to being a parent. As an experienced mom, you'll learn that stain remover pens like this one can handle the little messes without missing a beat. Yes, you should always pack a change of clothes—for both you (spare t-shirt) and baby (bodysuit). But not every mess is a Category 5 clean-up—stain remover pens are a must for any diaper bag.

diaper bags

CHAPTER 10

Baby Carriers

Inside this chapter

S ure, baby wearing has been around for centuries, but a recent renaissance has sent the sales of baby carriers soaring. We've been fans of baby wearing since the 90's (before it was cool). So take a tour with us of the different types of carriers—we've got tips, advice and recommendations.

Baby wearing fans seem to divide into two camps: those that want to wear their babies for their first year, and those who are fans of extended baby wearing into toddlerhood.

As a result, we have basic carriers that work up to 25 lbs. that are designed for babies up to 18 months. And newer carriers that now work up to 45 lbs. (for the curious, that is the weight of an average five-year old).

Just to make it more confusing, it seems like there are 437 different carrier makes and models on the market, from simple slings to fancy backpacks. And we've noticed over the years that every single one of those models has a parent who's a big fan.

How to find the right carrier for you? That advice is up next.

7 Things No One Tells You About Buying A Baby Carrier

1 WAIT! THERE ARE **THAT** MANY DIFFERENT TYPES OF CARRIERS?

Do you want a soft structured carrier? For infants or extended use? What about slings? What the heck is a Mei Tai? A rum-based drink from Hawaii?

Ok, let's take a deep breath. Carriers come in a variety of types. Let's review:

◆ **Front carriers** (aka Soft Structured Carriers) are the most well-known and popular of all the carrier types. The 800-pound gorilla in this category is the Baby Bjorn, which is Sweden's most successful export since ABBA.

Front carriers basically are designed like a fabric pouch worn on your chest with straps connecting at the shoulders and waist with buckles or snaps. These type of carriers are made for infants up to around 30 lbs. although some hybrids like the Boba 4G can carry older kids up to 45 lbs. Nowadays, soft structured carriers are more flexible, allowing baby to be carried on your back and hip as well as in front.

◆ A sub category of front carriers is the *mei ta (also referred to as meh dai)*, or *Asian carrier*. Inspired by carriers used in Asia (particularly China), mei tais have an unstructured body and are tied on rather than buckled. This allows for infinite adjustment.

◆ *Slings* and *pouches* (which are unstructured carriers) have been around forever. These carriers are basically pockets of fabric that can be adjusted with a ring or velcro. Babies can recline in slings or sit upright once they're old enough. Most slings and pouches are only rated up to 35 lbs., so they are more appropriate for infants.

◆ *Wrap around carriers* are one long piece of cloth that is twisted and folded to create a pouch for baby. Typically the fabric has some stretch to it. This type of carrier has the steepest learning curve for parents. Most designs are intended for smaller, younger babies up to 35 lbs.

◆ *Backpack or frame carriers* are designed for hiking with lightweight aluminum frames, high quality waterproof fabrics and ergonomically designed straps. Many include sunshades, lots of storage and adjustable seating as baby grows.

2 **THINK ABOUT HOW LONG YOU ENVISION USING A CARRIER.** The most common baby carriers (Baby Bjorn Original, for example) are designed for use up 25 lbs. The average boy would reach this weight around 18 months (girls a few months after that). Other carriers aim for extended use, up to 30 or even 45 lbs. (that's a three, four or even five year old!).

Of course there is no right or wrong answer—it's your call.

If you only envision using a carrier in baby's first year—then focus on carriers that have the 25 lb. limits. If extended baby wearing is something you'd like to try, look at brands with higher weight limits, like ERGObaby, Boba, Beco and so on.

3 **JUST BECAUSE YOU LOVE A CARRIER DOESN'T MEAN YOUR BABY WILL.** That's right—some babies can be darn right fussy about carriers. Your baby may love carrier A but hate style B, so hang on to your receipt (or buy from a source with a good return policy). Every baby is different, so a carrier that works for your sister-in-law may induce screaming fits from your baby. Some moms actually buy a couple types of carriers to see what works, then return the ones that don't.

4 **BABY WEARING LOOKS SIMPLE, BUT BE AWARE OF THESE KEY SAFETY PRECAUTIONS.** Back in 2010, the Consumer Product Safety Commission issued these baby wearing tips:

◆ Premature infants and those with low birth weight (under 7 lbs., including twins or infants with breathing issues such as a cold) should not be placed in a sling.

◆ Make sure the infant's face is not covered and can be seen at all times regardless of the type of carrier you're using.

◆ Frequently check on your baby to make sure he is breathing.

Check the graphic to see how to correctly and incorrectly wear your baby:

Right	Wrong	Wrong	Wrong	Wrong
Chin up; Face visible; Nose and mouth free	Baby's face is covered	Baby is too low	Baby is hunched with chin touching chest	Baby's face is pressed tight against wearer

5 **SOME CARRIERS HAVE A STEEP LEARNING CURVE.** An example: wrap around carriers. These long pieces of fabric need to be wrapped surprisingly tight to keep baby in the proper position and support a parent's back. This can take some practice.

Even some soft structured carriers have lots of buckles, Velcro and adjustments that can get complicated.

Yes, slings are the easiest carrier to use, but still may require a little practice. Make sure you read the directions, watch instructional videos online and practice before you try your carrier with an actual baby. The first few times, you may want to have a second person handy to help you get all the adjustments correct.

6 **CHEAP CARRIERS COME WITH A HIDDEN COST.** Yes, there are $15 baby carriers at discount stores. What's the difference between this and our recommended carriers, which run about $150-$200?

A sad truth about carriers: a cheap carrier is no bargain if it hurts your back or is uncomfortably hot. And sadly, those $15 carriers score low on parent happiness, according to the many interviews we've done over the years with parents.

When purchasing a carrier, investing more money buys comfort and ease of use. For example, the fabric is softer when you spend more and the padding is thicker. Often hook and loop closures are industrial strength (Velcro vs. Aplix, for example) with more pricey carriers.

Deluxe slings may come with padded side rails and more expensive back pack carriers may have toddler stirrups to help older kids sit up comfortably.

7 **OPTIONAL ACCESSORIES ARE OFTEN WORTH THE PRICE.** Drool bibs that attach to the carrier, sunshades for backpack carriers, extra long straps to fit a taller spouse—all worthy extras! One of our faves: teething pads for the ERGObaby carriers. Love 'em.

carriers

Organic fabric certifications

Several eco-friendly baby carriers tout various organic fabric certifications. Here's a quick 101 on what these mean.

There are three international organizations that test and certify textiles. These are OEKO-TEX, Global Organic Textile Standard (GOTS) and Textile Exchange (OCS). All three of these certifications are optional—there is no legal standard for organic, non-allergenic, chemical free textiles in the U.S. Many of the companies that are certified are European, with only a few U.S. brands certified. Here's a bit about each of the three organizations.

◆ *OEKO-TEX* is a German organization that offers a Standard 100 certification program for textiles at all steps in the manufacturing process. Here's what the label means:

"Products marked with the label 'Confidence in textiles (Standard 100)' provide effective protection against allergenic substances, formaldehyde, heavy metals such as nickel or, for example, forbidden plasticizers (phthalates) in baby textiles."

OEKO-TEX offers a second certification called Green by OEKO-TEX, which means the "materials (were) tested for harmful substances," the product was "made in environmentally friendly facilities" and it was "made in safe and socially responsible workplaces."

◆ *GOTS (Global Organic Textile Standard)* certifies textiles as organic. To meet their qualifications, "only textile products that contain a minimum of 70% organic fibers can become GOTS certified. All chemical inputs such as dyestuffs and auxiliaries used must meet certain environmental and toxicological criteria. The choice of accessories is limited in accordance with ecological aspects as well. A functional waste water treatment plant is mandatory for any wet-processing unit involved and all processors must comply with minimum social criteria." Basically, beyond using organic materials, companies must also be socially responsible to their workers and the community.

◆ *Textile Exchange (OCS).* Previously referred to as the Organic Exchange (OE) Standard, the international Textile Exchange certifies textiles according to their Organic Content Standard (OCS). They verify the steps in the supply chain to make certain the materials used in end products like diapers are sustainably sourced/grown, processed and manufactured.

There are only a few carrier manufacturers we can find with one of these international certifications. These companies typically sell both conventionally grown textiles as well as organic, so you'll need to refer to specific organic styles to get certified textiles:

Baby K'Tan (GOTS)   Beco (GOTS)
Boba (OEKO-TEX and GOTS) Ergobaby (OEKO-TEX)
Moby (OCS)   Mountain Buggy (OEKO-TEX)
Tula (OEKO-TEX)

Carrier brands that claim to use organic textiles (for at least some styes) but do not have any info on certifications posted online: Lillebaby, and Stokke.

How We Picked A Winner

We evaluate carriers with in-depth inspections, checking models for overall quality and ease of use—for example, checking the ease of adjustment between smaller moms and taller dads, as well as detailed looks at fabric, fasteners and construction.

We also gather significant reader feedback (this book has over 1 million copies in print), tracking carriers on quality and durability. Besides interviewing parents, we regularly talk with retailers to see which brands are most trustworthy and other key quality metrics.

The reliability of carrier manufacturers is another key factor—we meet with key company executives at least once a year. Since we've been doing this since 1994, we have developed detailed profiles of major carrier brands that help guide our recommendations.

The Best Baby Carrier (Overall)

ERGObaby's Ergo Omni 360° ($130-$180) is our top pick for best front carrier. Compared to its many rivals, the Ergo Omni 360° has best-in-class quality, construction and safety. As the name implies, the Omni 360° is a front carrier that allows you to face baby out as well as in, plus piggy back or on the hip.

ERGObaby debuted their first front carrier in 2002. Designer Karin Frost wasn't satisfied with carrier options when she had her first child, so she created a soft-structured carrier with multiple positions. First sewn in Hawaii, the original ERGO design worked in three positions: front carry facing inward, back carry and hip carry. ERGO refined the concept over the years, culminating with the Omni 360°, which adds that fourth position of forward facing out. Here's an overview:

The Omni 360° is made with a structured bucket seat that keeps babies legs and hips in the correct position (no dangling legs). It comes with a wide waist belt, which can be worn high when baby is little and adjusted down to carry the weight of older babies and toddlers. A plus: the Omni 360° can be used with infants as small as 7 lbs. without a special infant insert. Older versions of the 360° required a separate insert ($25 extra).

New in the past year, ERGObaby released a variation on this carrier, the Omni 360° in "cool air mesh." This version swaps the buttons that narrow the seat with sliders for an easier, one-handed adjustment. The mesh version comes in four colors and runs $175.00.

The ERGObaby Omni 360°'s weight range is 7 to 45 lbs. The forward facing out carry is recommended for babies six months old and older. The straps on the Omni 360° can be used in the traditional H position or crossed in the back for a more custom fit.

Feedback on the Omni 360° from parents has been mostly positive. Ease of use is excellent say readers. Critics of this carrier say the hood is too small and doesn't store away. A few complain that the back latch is uncomfortable and hard to buckle (when used in the H-strap configuration). Despite these minor concerns, the ERGObaby Omni 360° is an excellent carrier that wins our overall pick for best carrier.

Also Great: Cat Bird Baby Pikkolo

Runner up for best carrier is the **Pikkolo** ($99) from Cat Bird Baby. This carrier is a mash-up of a front carrier and a mei tai with buckles instead of long ties. It's also more flexible than most other front carriers—it can be used in front facing both in and out, on the back and as a hip carrier. FYI: This carrier is only sold on Cat Bird Baby's web site.

Also Great: Boba 4G Carrier

The recently revised **Boba 4GS Carrier** ($105-$120) now includes an infant insert so it can be used with babies as little as 7 lbs.

Other features we love include a removable sleeping hood included with a pocket. Also great: a removable foot rests for toddlers, a purse holder strap, smartphone pocket and a sliding chest strap.

Readers love this carrier—it is worth a look if you want a soft-structured front carrier.

The Best Sling Carrier

After comparing and testing more than ten different types of baby slings, we chose the **Maya Wrap Lightly Padded Ring Sling** ($80) as the best sling carrier.

Maya Wrap has consistently been a favorite of our readers, who love its flexibility and comfort. Helpful instructional videos are available on their web site. The rings are made of ¼″ anodized aluminum, the fabrics are 100% cotton hand-loomed and are only made of one layer of fabric. As a result, the Maya Wrap sling carrier is quite lightweight and breathable. It comes in four sizes with nearly 20 fabric options.

Two versions are offered: the Lightly Padded ($80) and the ComfortFit ($90). The difference? The Lightly Padded version has padding on the shoulder while the ComfortFit has no padding. One advantage to the ComfortFit—the shoulder fabric can be adjusted while the padded shoulder cannot. Parents seem to prefer the Lightly Padded, and, oddly, the ComfortFit is more expensive.

Reader feedback on the Maya Wrap sling carrier is positive, although some parents complain about the long piece of fabric that hangs from the rings when the sling is being used. If you want to avoid a lot of extra fabric, you can size down your wrap so the hanging fabric is shorter. Another complaint: it can be painful to use with older babies or for long periods of time. We judged these issues to be minor and recommend the Maya Wrap as our top pick for sling carriers.

Also Great: Moby Sling

A reader favorite, the **Moby Sling** ($50) is a good bet for beginners. This ring sling features thick fabric and easy adjustments. Folks love the sturdy fabric, which is still breathable. Still we know some folks are intimidated by ring slings, but there is good news: quite a few YouTube videos provide helpful tips and advice on this sling.

Best Wrap Carrier

We road-tested 13 different wrap baby carriers before crowning the winner: the **Baby Wrap Carrier by KeaBabies** ($25) is our choice for best wrap carrier thanks to overall comfort and front and back carrying flexibility.

KeaBabies gets its name from a New Zealand Alpine Parrot called a Kea, hence the parrot logo on the carrier's box.

KeaBabies Wrap Carrier is made from a blended fabric of 95% cotton, 5% spandex. The claim: it has "just the right stretch" to secure your baby and still give you excellent back support. One size fits all and the company notes that bigger moms and dads can tie the waist straps in back rather than bringing them around to the front.

After evaluating more than a dozen wrap carriers that can top $100, the KeaBabies' Wrap Carrier wins not only in comfort but also affordability. At only $19.86, this is the least expensive wrap on the market. This affordable price makes it easy to take a chance on trying a wrap carrier since your investment is minimal.

The real star here is the fabric—it's both soft, yet stretchy. Compared to other wrap carriers we tested, the KeaBabies' Wrap Carrier hits that sweet spot—stretchy enough to fit baby snugly, but not too stretchy.

What's not to like? Well, like all wrap carriers, there is a bit of a learning curve to the KeaBabies' Wrap Carrier. Fortunately, that's what YouTube is for! And the company has detailed instructions online as well.

Another small negative: KeaBabies doesn't disclose where the carrier is made or the origin of the fabric. We can guess the answers (China and China), but it would be nice if they were a bit more transparent. Another concern: there is a minimum weight (7 lbs.) but not a maximum weight.

Bottom line: the Baby Wrap Carrier by KeaBabies is an excellent carrier that tops the competition in comfort and flexibility. At under $20, it is a steal.

Best Backpack Carrier

Love to hike? A frame carrier is the best option for hikers—these carriers have more support for parents and comfort features for babies than typical baby carriers.

After comparing and testing nearly a dozen backpack carriers, we picked the **Deuter Kid Comfort Pro** ($340) as our choice for best backpack carrier.

Features include a contoured hip belt, zipped compartment under the seat, 5-point harness, side entry, large mesh storage pockets, and breathable seat cushions. Best feature: a sun canopy that rolls out when needed and tucks away when not.

This backpack carrier hits all the right notes: adjustability, storage and great safety features.

There's even a smaller daypack that separates from the main unit for shorter day hikes.

Reader feedback on this carrier is excellent. Yes, it is pricey—but for serious hikers, this is the best bet in our opinion.

carriers

CHAPTER 11

ODDS & ENDS

Odds & Ends: Maternity Pillows, Tummy Time Mats, etc.

Inside this chapter

A *maternity pillow is one of those purchases that looks nutty—until you need one. And for a good night's sleep, these pillows are a life-saver. We'll cover the best ones here, plus look at tummy-time mats and baby sunglasses.*

The Best Maternity Pillow

As you get later in your pregnancy, sleep can become tricky. A maternity pillow can be worth its weight in gold. Here's a look at the best maternity pillows, starting off with some shopping tips you might not have thought about!

7 Things No One Tells You About Buying A Maternity Pillow

1 **DIFFERENT KINDS OF PILLOWS CAN HELP YOU SLEEP, BUT SOME AREN'T LABELED "MATERNITY PILLOWS".** If this is your first pregnancy, you may be wondering why do I need this at all? In a nutshell, obstetricians recommend pregnant moms STOP sleeping on their backs at about 20 weeks. As our resident OB expert, Michele Hakakha notes in the book *Expecting 411*, "This prevents your big ol' uterus from putting pressure on your major blood vessels (the aorta and vena cava). It's best to lie on your left side for optimal blood circulation but the right side is okay."

So that means you'll be sleeping on your side—but as your baby grows, so does the difficulty of getting a good night's sleep. To the rescue comes the maternity pillow.

FYI: some of these pillows are specifically designed for pregnancy while others are touted as solutions for a multitude of ailments, some of which can occur during pregnancy.

For example, on the inexpensive end of the spectrum is the **knee pillow**. This type of pillow is usually the cheapest at about $15 to $20—basically, it is a foam block that is placed between the knees during sleep. This can help with back, leg and knee pain as well as sciatica (official definition from the Mayo Clinic: pain that radiates

maternity pillow

along the path of your sciatic nerve . . . from your lower back through your hips and buttocks and down each leg). Yes, all symptoms you may experience in pregnancy.

Next is the ***pregnancy wedge pillow***. Just what it sounds like, this option is usually made of memory foam (with a cover), which can be wedged:

- under your tummy (to bring you pregnant belly up to a comfortable level),
- behind your back (to keep back sleepers from rolling onto their backs),
- between the knees,
- under your head (elevating your head if you're suffering from heartburn and reflux).

Prices range widely from $12 to $40 and wedges will also vary in height and shape.

Full-length body pillows look similar to a super long rectangular pillow or a body-length tube. Basically, you can snuggle up to a body pillow in front of you, or use it behind your back to avoid rolling over. These retail for $20 to $200 depending on the type of fill.

C-Shaped pillows are sewn into a c-shaped tube. The bottom curl is tucked between your knees while the top curve is used as a pillow for your head and you can "hug" the top end to your chest. No need for an additional head pillow when you have a c-shaped pillow. You'll find C-shaped pillows for between $30 and $70.

Finally, there are ***U-shaped pillows***, used by straddling one side of the U. The top connected section functions as the pillow for your head. (FYI: Some people reverse the pillow and prop their feet on the U while using their regular pillow at the open top). This type of pillow basically engulfs you on both sides of your body. Because it's bigger than the other types of pillows we mentioned, U-shaped pillows can be pricey: $40 to $100.

2 MATERNITY PILLOWS CAN BE NOISY. . . AND HOT . . . AND FLAT. The fill used in maternity pillows can vary widely. Here are the most common types:

- *Styrofoam balls*, similar to those used in bean bags, rustle rather loudly. If you're a light sleeper, this is one fill you might want to stay away from.
- *Polyester fiberfill is very quiet*, but depending on the amount and quantity, can lose its fluffiness or be uncomfortably hot.
- *Plastic microbeads* (smaller than those Styrofoam balls) offer good support but aren't available in most maternity pillow, just tube-shaped body pillows.
- *Memory foam* seems to be everywhere these days. . . and yes, there are maternity pillows that utilize this kind of fill. But if you are hot and sweaty at night (darn those hormones!), solid memory foam will be probably too hot. Most manufacturers use shredded foam to allow for more airflow and hence a cooler experience.
- Finally, a few pillows may be filled with *natural ingredients* (not always organic, however). For example, we found body pillows with wool filling covered in organic cotton (example:

Holy Lamb Organic Body Pillow, $155). Others have feather filling, kapok (a fiber from the Ceiba tree; example: Sleeping Bean Body Pillow, $70), cotton and spelt husks (aka: buckwheat). As you might guess, pillows filled with these alternatives sell for higher prices than standard fill.

3 **THE PILLOWCASE MAY BE, UH, A CHALLENGE TO CHANGE.** Yep, our veterinarian told us this one. He grew to hate the maternity pillow his wife used because he had to put the case back on after washing—as it turns out, not a simple task. The easiest cases have zippers (and may be worth the extra money), but they're rare. Most are just slip on and considering the unique shapes of these pillows, you can imagine the effort to slip a case over them.

4 **YOU MAY NOT EVEN NEED ONE.** The general rule of thumb of maternity pillows: first pregnancies maybe but later pregnancies probably yes. Few moms get really huge in their first pregnancies (those carrying multiples are the exception), so even if you need a little something, the solution might just be a wedge or knee pillow.

But when moms are in their second and third pregnancies, they show sooner and get bigger. It's like when you wear a pair of jean that just came out of the dryer and they're tight, then if you wear them again later (without washing), they're looser. The ligaments and muscles "remember" being pregnant during subsequent pregnancies and stretch out a bit more. That's when a maternity pillow may be a necessity.

5 **YOUR BED SIZE MAY RULE OUT CERTAIN PILLOW.** Many of the U-shaped maternity pillows are 35 to 36 inches wide. A queen size mattress is 60 inches wide. So your pillow will potentially take up more than half the bed. Imagine adding in a dog or cat and a partner. Will you all fit? If sleeping quarters are tight, choose a body pillow or wedge versus a U or C-shaped maternity pillow.

6 **ONE SIZE DOES NOT FIT ALL.** Petite moms may need a smaller size maternity pillow. Good news if you're under 5'4": some maternity pillows come in petite sizes. Compare sizing info before purchasing.

7 **MOST PREGNANT MOMS SEEM TO PREFER THEIR OWN PILLOW WHEN USING A BODY PILLOW.** What we mean is some moms-to-be don't find that body pillows have enough support for the head and neck. If you are very picky about the pillow under your head/neck, consider a U-shaped pillow. You can position it with the opening at your head and easily continue using your regular pillow.

How We Picked A Winner

We evaluate maternity pillow with both personal testing, and testing among friends, family and our readers. We also poll our readers online (our book has over one million copies in print), tracking maternity pillows on quality and durability.

The Best Maternity Pillow (Overall)

After comparing and testing more than 20 different types of maternity pillows, we picked the **PharMeDoc Pregnancy Pillow with Jersey Cover** ($48) as the best maternity pillow.

Like most C-shaped pillows, the PharMeDoc Pregnancy Pillow with Jersey Cover cradles your head, goes under your belly and extends between your legs to support your hips. The fill is a polyfill blend. The best part, according to our testers: the 100% cotton jersey knit cover. This removable, washable cover is super soft with double stitched seams for extra strength.

Additional woven cotton covers are available separately on the company's web site. After your baby is born, you can use the PharMeDoc as either a breastfeeding pillow or toddler pillow.

While most of our readers give the PharMeDoc high marks, a few complained that their pillow covers weren't easy to put back on after cleaning, which unfortunately is a problem with many maternity pillows we looked at.

Another issue: after several months the filling may shift or compact. Again, this is a common complaint with body pillows. The soft, comfy cover outweighs these concerns, in our opinion.

The Best Maternity Pillow (Wedge)

If you're looking for a little bit of lift under your pregnant belly, but not much more, a foam wedge may be all you need. You can also use it behind your back if you worry about rolling onto your back at night (back sleeping is not recommended for pregnant women after 20 weeks) or between your knees. Good news: this is one of the cheapest option for pregnancy support.

Our top recommended wedge is the **Boppy Pregnancy Wedge** for only $16. Made of firm foam (but not memory foam), the Boppy comes with a 100% pima cotton zip off cover that is machine washable. The wedge is sized fairly small and portable for traveling.

The Boppy gets great reviews from our parents—they loved the size and portability. But almost everyone notes it has a strong smell when first taken out of the package. We recommend you let it air out for at least a day or two when you get it.

The Best Maternity Pillow (Knee Pillow)

Made of memory foam and sculpted to fit comfortably between the knees, knee pillows help with sciatic nerve and back pain by properly aligning the hips, knees and spine. Before you spend $40 or $50 on a full body maternity pillow, this might be an affordable place to start. At $20, our top pick, the **Modvel Orthopedic Knee Pillow** has impressive support and a quilted cover that can be removed for washing. I've used it personally and can say it is worth the money!

While some readers thought the pillow was too small and compressed too easily, others thought it did a good job of staying place at night and keeping its shape. Bottom line: this knee pillow is a good bet.

The Best Maternity Pillow for Petites

The **Leachco Snoogle Mini Compact Side Sleeper** is a winner for petite moms. And it works well in a smaller bed (queen) or for a bed full of pets, kids and your partner. At $50, it's a good value. The biggest issue with the Snoogle Mini: the cover. It's darn difficult to get on and off for cleaning.

The Best Maternity Pillow If Carrying Twins

Moms of twins we've interviewed unanimously recommend U-shaped maternity pillows. Yes, as a mom of twins-to-be, you probably realize you'll be packing on extra pounds—and that translates into more sleeping issues. Mothers of twins should expect to gain between 37 and 54 lbs. during their pregnancies (singletons only add 25 to 30 lbs.). That extra weight puts more pressure on ligaments, muscles and bones leading to more pain and discomfort.

Our top recommended U-shaped pillow is **Queen Rose Full Body Pillow U-Shaped Pregnancy Pillow** ($65-$70). This pillow cradles the whole body supporting both the back and the belly. While most fans love the soft cover, a few found it too hot. And this is a LARGE pillow and may only work in king-size beds.

maternity pillow

The Best Tummy Time Mats

Ask your mom or dad, do they remember tummy time? Bet the answer will be "Huh? What's that?" Yep, tummy time is a relatively new concept in the world of parenting.

In 1994, the American Academy of Pediatrics and various child health advocates joined together on a campaign to combat Sudden Infant Death Syndrome. The campaign, called the Back to Sleep Campaign, centered around placing all infants to sleep on their backs as well as several other recommendations.

The good news: the campaign has been so successful, it has cut SIDS deaths in half (SIDS research continues to look at other factors and one day hopes to cut it down to no deaths). The less good news: sleeping exclusively on the back can lead some babies to suffer "positional plagiocephaly" or, as it is more commonly known, flat head syndrome. Babies with severe positional plagiocephaly need expensive treatment including helmets to correct head shape.

There are some things you can do to avoid or lessen prevent this, among them practicing "tummy time" with your baby. Tummy time is just a cute moniker for the practice of encouraging your baby to spend time on her tummy playing, stretching and strengthening back and neck muscles.

Here are our tips for successful tummy time:

◆ Start with a few minutes at a time during waking hours every time you do a diaper change.
◆ For babies under two months of age, aim for one to two minutes of tummy time about eight times a day.
◆ For older babies (older than two months), gradually increase tummy time . . . you can stop when your baby tells you that's enough.

What if your baby hates tummy time? Well, exercise is hard work (don't we adults know that!) and it's the same for babies. You can get down there on the floor with him so it isn't so lonely. And, of course, there are products that can help make tummy time more fun.

That's why we're here to help you with our recommendations for the Best Tummy Time Mats! We tested 23 play mats and pillows with actual real-life kiddos. The following are our top five picks in no particular order for best tummy time mats. Some of these are exclusively for tummy time, while others have multiple functions.

Best Tummy Time Mat #1:
Infantino Pond Pals Twist and Fold Activity Gym and Play Mat

The **Infantino Twist and Fold Mat** scored high among our testers thanks to a handy little crescent-shaped pillow in one corner to help prop up your baby during tummy time. We liked the bright and cheerful patterns and the mat itself is sized just right (18′ x 24″). Compared to other tummy time mats, the Infantino is also well priced at $40. Not the cheapest, but not the most expensive.

The Twist and Fold has four arches and comes with multiple loops to connect toys. In our tests, we loved the detachable toys with their large eyes and different textures. The mirror is a nice addition as well. The whole mat folds down by twisting the plastic handle at the top. It folds up into a long tubular shape (you wrap the mat around it).

Our readers note the mat is easy to clean, portable and easy to assemble. Adaptability is another plus: you can use it as a tummy time mat (babies can bat at the toys or look in the mirror) and older babies will use it as a play space with the detachable toys. The biggest complaint: the twist and fold action to fold it up is not as easy as it should be. Our testers noted the arches needed to be pushed down slightly while twisting.

That caveat aside, the Infantino Twist and Fold Mat is an excellent tummy time mat.

Best Tummy Time Mat #2:
Tiny Love Gymini Super Deluxe Lights and Music Play Mat

Tiny Love has been making Gymini play gyms for at least 20 years and it shows. Among the variety of options Gymini offers in this category, we like the **Tiny Love Gymini Super Deluxe Lights and Music** ($60) as a best bet for tummy time mats.

It includes an interactive music and lights controller in the corner baby can swat to start a string of lights, classical music, or nursery rhymes. The arches have a mirror and loops for toys in the shape of various animals.

In our tests, we found the Gymini arches and mat to be easy to fold up and snap together for transport. The mat is machine washable but take care to remove the music box and mirror first.

Our testers were pleased overall with the Gymini. They like the many different textures and sounds on the mat and the attachable toys. Many readers praised the music and nursery rhymes as well—baby can activate the music and lights if she hits the flowers on the mat, for example. On the other hand, some parents noted the music box sounded distorted and it quickly burns through AA batteries.

Because of the music and lights feature, this mat is pretty expensive at $60. Yes, this is also a play mat for older babies for extended use . . . but this option is at the top of the price range for most folks. Despite that, given the features and overall quality, we recommend the Tiny Love Gymini Super Deluxe Lights and Music.

Best Tummy Time Mat #3:
Fisher-Price Rainforest Music & Lights Deluxe Gym

Fisher-Price's Rainforest Music & Lights Deluxe Gym ($60) has a lot of similarities to the Gymini reviewed earlier. It comes with a music/light show feature that is responsive to baby's movement.

Fisher-Price has an interesting feature for this tummy time mat: baby can trigger the music/lights for a short period of time . . or parents can set the music box (cleverly disguised as a toucan) to play for 20 minutes of music or sounds.

Our testers like the four detachable toys, mirror and sensory play mat. By kicking or swatting at the arches, babies can trigger the lights and sounds. Or the toucan can be removed and taken with you anywhere you want to go.

Testers enthusiastically praised this tummy time mat. Fisher-Price's quality is a cut above other brands in this category, from the fabric feel to the sound/lights implementation.

Kids seem to love the Toucan music feature the most, although one parent noted that the location at the top of the crossbars means baby can't see the lights that well. A handful of online reviewers, however, noted that the toucan was defective on their models and needed to be replace/returned. Check carefully that your toucan works properly as soon as you get the mat.

If music is a must on your tummy time mat shopping list, the Fisher-Price Rainforest Music & Lights Deluxe Gym is an excellent choice.

Best Tummy Time Mat #4:
Tiny Love Tummy Time Under The Sea Playmat

The **Tiny Love Under the Sea Tummy Time playmat** is for the minimalist parent who just wants to concentrate on tummy time with baby without sound and light gizmos. At only $40, this entry is one of the more affordable tummy time mats we tested, yet scored high in our tests.

First, we like the large booster pillow attached to the mat. Our tester parents said it seemed more comfortable for baby than the smaller pillows on other competitor mats. The googly eyes of the crab were cute and really drew baby's attention.

The Tiny Love Under the Sea Tummy Time playmat comes with a stand alone mirror and a teether toy which connects to the pillow. The pillow doesn't velcro to the mat, so you can place it anywhere you want.

There is no light and music option here, just the basics. And a few dissenting testers complained that the padding was non-existent. They recommend the mat be used on carpeting or extra padding, not on a hardwood or tile floor—and we see that point.

Overall, we will recommend the Tiny Love Under the Seat Tummy Time playmat. Our testers liked the bright colors and singled out the pillow for special praise—the crab design and eyeballs are quite clever.

Best Tummy Time Mat #5: Lovevery Play Mat

If your budget allows and you'd like a more eco-friendly option, we'd recommend the **Lovevery Play Mat**. It's definitely deluxe so you'll need lots of space; it has wooden folding legs if you want to minimize plastic and it comes with 24 play activities. Price: $140.

Yes, that's quite spendy—but you get wooden toys, organic cotton teethers and toys, mirrors and more. One of our readers summed it up this way:

"I was struggling to find a play mat that catered to actual time spent on the tummy. A lot of the options out there focus on what's hanging from the top—but the point of tummy time is to be prone facing! Most mats don't include much stimulation when facing down—except for the Play Gym by Lovevery.

"It's much more expensive, but it focuses on keeping baby entertained while on their stomach, with lots of different options. The colors are more muted so it's a nice reprieve from the bright baby toys, but baby seems to love it. "

The Play Mat is also machine washable but consider hand washing. Some parents noted it frayed in the wash even when following washing directions. It's also really big (you could even use it for twins), so it may not work in a smaller house or apartment. Despite those cons, parents who parted with the $140 loved it.

Best Baby and Toddler Sunglasses

Back in 2011, the American Academy of Pediatrics issued a policy statement warning about UV exposure and babies/toddlers. The basic recommendation was to wear sunglasses when out in the sun (along with wearing sunscreen, having babies under six months of age avoid direct sun exposure, etc.).

When it comes to picking the best sunglasses for babies and toddlers, we look for shatter resistant polycarbonate lenses that block 100% of ultraviolet rays. Lenses should be gray or "very, very dark gray" (credit: Lego Batman).

To test the contenders, we purchased a variety of baby/toddler sunglasses and checked for warped lenses and flexible frames. The best designs are elongated (wraparound) to avoid seeping sunlight from the sides. Here are few more tips when shopping for baby sunglasses:

sunglasses

7 Things No One Tells You About Buying a Baby & Toddler Sunglasses!

1 **SUNGLASSES SHOULD BE RATED UV 400 TO BLOCK 100% OF UV LIGHT.** Look for a tag on the sunglasses calling out the UV blockage rating. Sometimes you might see a label stating the lenses are rated UV400. This is the same as a 100% rating.

2 **ALL BABY AND KID SUNGLASS LENSES ARE MADE OF PLASTIC, BUT NOT ALL PLASTIC IS CREATED EQUAL.** The best lenses are polycarbonate (for durability and shatter resistance) with a scratch resistant coating.

3 **AVOID COLORED LENSES.** Gray and dark gray are your best choice, not because gray helps with the glare. Rather, colored lenses (it is common to see yellow lenses online) can distort the natural colors your baby sees. Gray lenses allow baby to see the natural world in living color.

4 **BECAUSE BABIES' EYES ARE STILL DEVELOPING, DON'T OVER USE SUNGLASSES.** Sunglasses make it hard for kids to see contrast, so only use them in full sun.

5 **MAKE SURE THE FIT IS SNUG BUT DOESN'T FORCE THE LENSES TOO CLOSE TO THE EYELASHES AND EYES.** Babies may try to remove sunglasses, so versions with adjustable Velcro straps may be a best bet. Toddlers, however, will want "grown up" looking glasses, so they may not be excited by the straps.

6 **WHEN TRYING SUNGLASSES ON YOUR CHILD, DO IT OUTSIDE SO SHE CAN SEE THE DIFFERENCE.** This will keep her interested in wearing them. Model good behavior yourself: always wear your sunglasses outside. And take lots of pictures of kids with sunglasses on, praising them for wearing them. If you make it a habit today, your child will grow up with healthier eyes.

7 **SUNGLASSES AREN'T JUST FOR SUMMER.** That's right, winter can be just as hard on the eyes. Take it from folks who know what a Colorado winter looks like, snow reflects up to 80% of the sun's rays—reflected glare from snow can be intense.

The Best Sunglasses: Baby

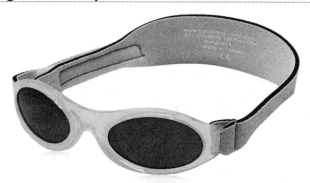

After researching, reviewing and testing a dozen baby and toddler sunglasses, we pick the **Baby Banz Adventure BANZ** ($17) as the best sunglasses for babies.

Baby Banz sunglasses come with all the sun protection you need from a pair of sunglasses, plus a baby-friendly hook and look strap to keep them secure. The strap is made from comfy neoprene while the frame and lenses are polycarbonate and shatter resistant. Baby Banz offers a one year replacement guarantee on the lenses, frame and strap.

Our tests and reader feedback concur: Baby Banz Adventure BANZ are the winner here.

Baby Banz Adventure BANZ checked all the right boxes. We loved Baby Banz's breathable neoprene strap which keep the glasses on even when baby tries to remove them (a gripe from many parents). The strap also adjusts with velcro, so it can accommodate different head sizes and growth. Included with the Adventure BANZ are an embedded rubber nose and brow piece to make the frames more comfortable.

Baby Banz are well priced. They also make a Toddler Kids' Adventure BANZ (size 2-5) for $17, and a polarized version for $22. Polarized lenses aren't a necessity in our opinion, just a nice option. Polarized lenses are great at cutting glare, so they may be good for a water environment, say at the beach.

Another plus, Adventure BANZ come in around twenty colors and styles.

Flaws but not deal breakers. The Adventure BANZ sunglasses aren't perfect. In our tests, a few parents complained that the lenses are too close to baby's eyes. But the biggest issue appears to be the sizing. There are two options: 0-2 years and 2-5 years. The bulk of complaints we see from our testers and online reviewers are folks who picked the wrong size—it's confusing because the product description online doesn't clearly delineate the baby versus toddler sizes. The toddler size is called Kid's Adventure BANZ while the baby version is just called BANZ. Only by looking at the description can you tell if it is for 0-2 or 2-5.

Also: a few people with very small babies noted the baby version was still too big for their babies. One parent solved the problem by sewing it to be smaller.

Overall, once they had the right size, parents were very happy with the quality of Adventure BANZ by Baby Banz. There are a few different styles from this company, but we liked the wrap-around styling of the Adventure BANZ best.

sunglasses

Also Great: Tuga Baby/Toddler UV 400 Sunglasses

Tuga Baby/Toddler UV 400 Sunglasses ($15-$20, recommended age: 0-5 years) are a good runner-up. We liked the interchangeable neoprene straps that fit a child from newborn up to five years of age. For a very reasonable price, you also get a carrying case and shatterproof polycarbonate lenses. While our testers praised Tuga sunglasses for the most part, there were some complaints about frames cracking or lenses that sat too close to baby's eyes, causing irritation.

Best Sunglasses: Toddlers

In our tests, ***Kushies Toddler Sunglasses*** ($10, recommended age: one year and older) hit all the right notes. Priced affordably, the glasses offer 100% UV protection, scratch and shatter resistant polycarbonate lenses, and rubber frames. It's the flexible rubber frames that are the home run here. Testers noted that their toddlers couldn't break the frames! (FYI: We don't recommend Kushies infant sunglasses because they don't have a strap.)

Best Balance Bikes

Balance bikes are pedal-free bikes that teach kids how to balance on two wheels. Baby balance bikes have an extra set of wheels to provide more stability for the youngest riders.

Let's talk safety before we discuss the best baby balance bikes. Make sure you follow the age and weight guidelines for balance bikes—some of these picks are recommended for use as young as 10 months, others are 12 months.

Also remember that although balance bike makers say these bikes can be used indoors or outside, we would recommend only outdoor use. Why? When used indoors, a baby on a balance bike can easily run into objects that might tumble over on them. This is why we don't recommend baby walkers: too many injuries. Any device with wheels must be carefully supervised by an adult at all times—and outside, there is less of a chance of that kind of accident.

Best Balance Bike For 1 Year Old

After testing several baby balance bikes, we ended up crowning **Ancaixin's** baby balance bike ($59) as the best of the best.

With use from 10 to 24 months and a 50 lb. capacity, this bike had the right combination of fun and ease of use.

We loved the cushioned seat, light weight and no-tools assembly of this bike! Foam wheels mean no flat tires and there are six colors to choose from. But you can't change the seat height.

Best Budget-Friendly Balance Bike

Our testers loved how fun this bike was—the **Retrospec Cricket** ($40) And the price is easier on the wallet. No, the seat or handlebars aren't adjustable. And it fits smaller kids better than bigger ones.

balance bikes

Best Baby-to-Toddler Balance Bike

Balance bikes for babies are cute, but if the seat doesn't adjust, they won't grow with your child—and hence a baby will quickly outgrow it. This choice, the ***allobebe Baby Balance Bike*** ($60) allows longer use thanks to its adjustability.

This bike is easy to assemble and has additional safety features—the handlebar doesn't allow tight turns, for example. But seat isn't very padded.

CHAPTER 12

Pregnancy Gear

Let's talk the best gear for pregnancy. What about those belly bands? Do they work? We'll review the best bets. Then we'll take a look at things to soothe an upset tummy—pregnancy candy and tea. Finally, we'll discuss pregnancy journals, announcements and more.

Best Belly Band for Pregnancy

What are the best belly bands for pregnancy? We asked a panel of pregnant women to try out 10 of the most popular belly bands. Which offered the most support? Easiest to put on? Most comfortable? Here are the winners.

Best For First-Timer Moms

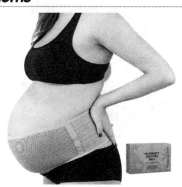

When it comes to belly bands for pregnancy, one size does not fit all. That's what we've learned over the years, reviewing these products and talking with our readers about what works.

For first-time pregnancies, a smaller belly band will work for most folks (unless you are having twins). In this category, we tried out 10 different options before deciding **KeaBabies belly band** ($19) is the best bet.

We loved the good support and stretch fabric, with two sizes available. The KeaBabies band also can be used postpartum. Critics note it can be seen under clothes, so it may not work well in a professional setting.

Best Light Support Band

For postpartum (or earlier in a pregnancy), you may only need a belly band with light support. After testing several options, we think **Rheane's** seamless belly band ($14) is the best bet—and easy on the wallet.

Great for postpartum or light support early in pregnancy, this band's soft fabric is quite comfy. A silicone band keeps it in place, but critics note it can stretch out over time.

Best Custom-Fit Belly Band

Most of the belly bands for pregnancy we tested are one size fits all. If only the world was so simple!

The truth is first time moms need a different band than second-time moms, who tend to get bigger earlier/overall. And moms-to-be of twins? Forget about that one-size fits all!

We tried out several belts that came in different sizes before deciding that the **NeoTech Care Pregnancy Support Maternity Belt** ($27) is the best bet here.

Fantastic support! We liked the multiple sizes available for this band, which is easy to put on. But it isn't quite as breathable as others and may slide around.

Best Pregnancy Pops Candy

Morning sickness, the struggle is real—can we get an amen?

We took 20 of the most popular ones on the market today and asked a panel of pregnant women which ones they liked best. We ranked them on quality, flavor and value.

Here are the ones we'd recommend.

Best Peppermint-Flavored Pregnancy Pops Candy. Peppermint is one of those flavors that many pregnant women find pleasing, according to our interviews with expectant mothers over the last 10 years. We liked ***Tummydrop's Natural Peppermints*** ($12) as the best bet here, based on our testing and feedback from readers.

These were our favorite peppermint drops—organic ingredients, low in sugar and made in an allergen-free factory. Soothing, but not long lasting and a bit pricey.

Best Sour Pregnancy Pops Candy. Do you prefer sour to sweet? We liked ***Three Lollies Value Preggie Pop Drops*** ($13) best in that group—no GMO's, gluten-free and made in the USA. Note: these drops are sweetened with corn syrup.

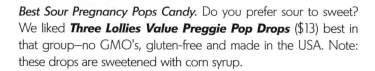

Best Organic Pregnancy Pops Candy. Ginger drops is another favorite of expectant mothers—and we agree. They are quite pleasing. We tried out several different ginger candies before deciding ***Pink Stork*** ($13) was the best bet. Our tester panel liked the taste and the natural/organic ingredients.

Pink Stork's naturally flavored ginger/raspberry drops have no preservatives, artificial colors, soy, or dairy.

Best Alternative to Candy For Pregnancy. If pregnancy drops and candy aren't your thing, this band may be worth a try. After comparing and testing a raft of different bands, we thought ***Sea-Band Anti-Nausea Acupressure Wristband*** ($8.29) was the best in terms of quality and value.

This band is an good alternative to drops or candy—especially if you don't like ginger or peppermint. Washable, reusable and easy on the wallet.

Best Pregnancy Tea

What are the best pregnancy teas? We asked a panel of expectant mothers to try out a dozen different teas for pregnancy. Which ones tasted the best? Were most soothing? Best flavor?

Best Citrus Pregnancy Tea. After testing a dozen different teas for pregnancy, we think **Earth Mama's Organic Tea** ($4.74 for 15 count) is the best citrus-y flavored tea. It won kudos for flavor, which is a blend of chamomile, lemon, oatstraw, orange peel and red raspberry leaf.

We liked the smooth flavor with notes of lemon, raspberry and orange. Also great: this tea has no GMO's.

Best Raspberry Pregnancy Tea. We tried out several raspberry pregnancy teas before deciding **Traditional Medicinals Organic Pregnancy Tea** ($26 for 6 count) had the best flavor profile. There is a hint of spearmint, which we found soothing. But it is rather pricey!

Best Sweet Pregnancy Tea. If you prefer sweet tea, we'd recommend **Pink Stork Labor Prep Tea** ($13 for 30 count). We tried out several sweet pregnancy floral teas and this was a clear winner. It had the best flavor, with a touch of sweetness. FYI: An unsweetened version also available.

Best Pregnancy Journals

Tracking your pregnancy via a journal is great way to preserve memories. What are the best journals for pregnancy? We rounded up a dozen of the more popular journals and had our readers who are expecting give them a whirl. Here's the ones they liked the best.

Best Pregnancy Journal Overall. After looking at a dozen pregnancy journals and having pregnant moms use them for a month, we think **Pearhead's My Pregnancy Journal** ($14.49) is the best overall. Split into seven sections, this journal prompts you to record thoughts by trimester and other milestones. Spiral bound. Cute design.

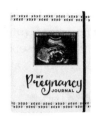

Best Pregnancy Journal Month by Month. **Expecting You — A Keepsake Pregnancy Journal** ($13.46) tracks pregnancy month by month. We liked the overall design, with a ribbon marker and gender-neutral graphics. Also nice: color illustrations. Critics wish it was organized by week instead of month.

Best Budget-Friendly Pregnancy Journal. This full color, paperback journal (**The First-Time Mom's Pregnancy Journal**, $10) is divided by trimesters with pages for each week of pregnancy. You'd think that would be standard for pregnancy journals, but most others we tried out were organized by month or trimester. We preferred this journal's week by week format. And it is easy on the wallet!

We liked the checklists, space for photos and writing prompts in this paperback-style journal. Full color and nicely illustrated! Critics wish it was spiral bound.

Best Pregnancy Announcements

Looking for a creative way to announce your pregnancy? We rounded up 20 different pregnancy announcements in order find the best bets. Which was cutest? Most clever? Handmade? Here are the ones we'd recommend! FYI: All of these are sold on Amazon.

Best Scratch Off Pregnancy Announcement. **5 Pregnancy Announcement Scratch off Cards**. ($13) Yes, these are pregnancy announcements disguised as lottery tickets!

Yet everyone is a winner—scratch off the dollar signs to find three pictures in a row, then scratch off the prize box! Surprise! "We're having a baby!"

Best Dog Photo Prop/Pregnancy Announcement. Add your due date to this cute chalkboard announcement, hang around your dog's neck and poof! Instagram gold! $6, from **Pearhead Pet Keepsake**. (Cute dog not included—you're on your own to supply that!).

Best Handmade Pregnancy Announcement. Yes, this is a real quail egg—inside is the pregnancy announcement along with confetti! Includes gift box tied with ribbon. Very original! **The Surprise! Quail Egg Pregnancy Announcement** runs $17 each. Hint: you might want to open this outside, as the confetti goes everywhere!

CHAPTER 13

What Does it All Mean?

How much money can you save if you follow all the tips and suggestions in this book? Let's take a look at the average cost of having a baby from the introduction and compare it with our Baby Bargains budget.

Your Baby's First Year

ITEM	AVERAGE	BABY BARGAINS BUDGET
Crib, mattress, dresser, rocker	$1680	$1433
Bedding / Decor	$350	$222
Baby Clothes	$665	$301
Disposable Diapers	$910	$400
Maternity/Nursing Clothes	$1420	$550
Nursery items, high chair, toys	$575	$225
Baby Food/Formula	$1160	$350
Stroller, Car Seats, Carrier	$800	$490
Miscellaneous	$570	$500
TOTAL	$8130	$4323
TOTAL SAVINGS:		***$3807***

WOW! You just saved over $3800! We hope the savings makes it worth the price of this book. We'd love to hear from you on how much you saved with our book—feel free to email, write or call us. See the "How to Reach Us" page at the back of this book.

What does it all mean?

At this point, we usually have something pithy to say as we end the book. But, as parents of two boys, we're just too tired. We're going to bed, so feel free to make up your own ending.

And thanks for reading *Baby Bargains*.

APPENDIX A

Registry Cheat Sheets

Time is tight—we know. So to help juice your baby registry, here are the Baby Bargains Registry Cheat Sheets.

These sample registries follow our recommendations for each chapter of this book. Enjoy!

Good

Item	Baby Bargains recommends	Price
Crib	IKEA Sniglar	$79
Mattress	Safety 1st Heavenly Dreams	$63
Dresser	IKEA Hemnes Double Dresser	$249
Changing pad	Summer Infant Contoured Changing Pad	$20
Glider Rocker	IKEA POÄNG rocking chair	$149
Bedding	Aden + Anais cotton sheets (4)	$60
Wearable blanket	Halo SleepSack	$22
Breast pump	Medela Swing mini-electric	$142
Bottles	Dr. Brown's Original Bottle Newborn Kit	$30
High Chair	Fisher-Price Space Saver	$50
Bathtub	First Years Sure Comfort Deluxe Tub	$20
Potty seat	IKEA LILLA potty	$5
Audio monitor*	VTech Safe & Sound Digital Audio Monitor	$30
Video Monitor	Infant Optics DXR-8	$166
Play Yard/Bassinet	Graco Pack N Play On the Go	$67
Bouncer	Fisher-Price Infant to Toddler Rocker	$38
Humidifier	Crane Adorable Ultrasonic Cool Mist	$38
Swing	Fisher Price Cradle 'n Swing	$121
Safety gate	KidCo Safeway Gates (2)	$86
Thermometer	Vicks Baby Rectal Thermometer	$12
Infant Car Seat	Graco SnugRide SnugLock Extend2Fit 35	$203
Convertible Seat	Cosco Scenera Next	$50
Stroller	Kolcraft Cloud Plus	$66
Diaper Bag	SoHo diaper bag	$37
Carrier	Maya Wrap Lightly Padded Ring Sling	$80
Clothing	Wait until after showers; see Chapter 4	
	TOTAL	**$1883**

registry cheat sheets

Better

Item	Baby Bargains recommends	Price
Crib	Graco Benton	$160
Mattress	Naturepedic Organic Cotton Lightweight	$259
Dresser	DaVinci Jayden 6-Drawer Double	$399
Changing pad	Summer Infant Contoured Changing Pad	$20
Glider Rocker	DaVinci Olive Upholstered Swivel	$329
Bedding	Aiden + Anais sheets (4)	$60
Wearable blanket	Halo SleepSack	$22
Breast pump	Spectra Baby USA S1 Plus	$200
Bottles	Dr. Brown's Original Bottle Newborn Kit	$30
High Chair	Joovy Nook	$120
Bathtub	First Years Sure Comfort Deluxe Tub	$20
Potty seat	Nuby My Real Potty Training Toilet	$30
Audio monitor*	VTech Safe & Sound Digital Audio Monitor	$30
Video Monitor	Infant Optics DXR-8	$166
Play Yard/Bassinet	Graco Pack N Play On the Go	$67
Bouncer	Fisher Price Infant to Toddler Rocker	$38
Humidifier	Crane Adorable Ultrasonic Cool Mist	$40
Swing	Fisher Price Cradle 'n Swing	$121
Safety gate	KidCo Safeway Gates (2)	$86
Thermometer	Vicks Baby Rectal Thermometer	$12
Infant Car Seat	Britax B-Safe Gen2 FlexFit+	$300
Convertible Seat	Chicco NextFit Sport	$250
Stroller	Baby Jogger City Mini 2	$250
Diaper Bag	Ju-Ju-Be Hobo Be	$70
Carrier	Ergo Baby Omni 360°	$130
Clothing	Wait until after showers; Chapter 4	
TOTAL		**$3209**

Audio monitor is optional—you can get either audio or video. You most likely will NOT need both!

Best

Item	Baby Bargains recommends	Price
Crib	Union crib	$119
Mattress	Moonlight Slumber Little Dreamer	$200
Dresser	DaVinci Jayden 6-Drawer Double	$399
Changing pad	Summer Infant Contoured Changing Pad	$20
Glider Rocker	Dutailier Glider + Ottoman	$550
Bedding	Aiden + Anais sheets (4)	$60
Wearable blanket	Halo SleepSack	$22
Breast pump	Medela Pump in Style with MaxFlow	$199
Bottles	Avent Classic Infant Starter Set	$36
High Chair	Graco Slim Snacker	$60
Bathtub	Fisher-Price 4-in-1 Sling 'n Seat Tub	$38
Potty seat	Nuby My Real Potty Training Toilet	$30
Audio monitor*	VTech Safe & Sound Digital Audio Monitor	$30
Video Monitor	Infant Optics DXR-8	$166
Play Yard/Bassinet	Graco Pack N Play On the Go	$67
Bouncer	4Moms MamaRoo	$220
Humidifier	Crane Adorable Ultrasonic Cool Mist	$40
Swing	Fisher Price Cradle 'n Swing	$121
Safety gate	KidCo Safeway Gates (2)	$86
Thermometer	Vicks Baby Rectal Thermometer	$12
Infant Car Seat	Chicco KeyFit 30	$200
Convertible Seat	Chicco NextFit Zip	$300
Stroller	Baby Jogger City Mini 2	$250
Diaper Bag	Skip Hop Duo	$50
Carrier	Ergo Baby Omni 360°	$130
Clothing	Wait until after showers; see Chapter 4	
	TOTAL	**$3405**

Grandparents

Item	Baby Bargains recommends	Price
Crib	Dream on Me portable crib	$130
Mattress	Safety 1st Heavenly Dreams	$63
Bedding	American Baby Co. sheets (4)	$48
High Chair	Fisher-Price Space Saver	$40
Thermometer	Vicks Baby Rectal Thermometer	$12
Safety gate	KidCo Safeway Gates (2)	$86
Convertible Seat	Cosco Scenera Next	$50
	TOTAL	**$429**

*Audio monitor is optional—you can get either audio or video.

registry cheat sheets

INDEX

index

index

index

BabyBargains.com

What's on our web page?

◆ *Detailed product and brand reviews.*

◆ *Message boards with in-depth reader feedback.*

◆ *More reviews! Cooking, Crafting, Seasonal Fun!*

◆ *Social media feeds with safety recalls & breaking news!*

◆ *Updates and changes since this book went to print.*

BabyBargains.com
Email: authors@babybargains.com
Facebook: facebook.com/babybargains
Twitter: @BabyBargainsBook
Instagram: @RealBabyBargains

More great books!

Expecting 411

Clear Answers & Smart Advice For Your Pregnancy

The Insider's Guide to Pregnancy & Childbirth! $16.95

As seen on Rachael Ray

Go to Expecting 411.com for details!

Baby 411

Clear Answers & Smart Advice For Your Baby

Questions and answers for new parents with detailed advice from an award-winning pediatrician. Sleep, nutrition, growth and more! $17.95

Co-authored by Dr. Ari Brown

Go to Baby411.com for details!

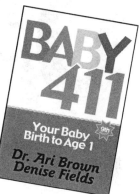

Toddler 411

Clear Answers & Smart Advice For Your Toddler

Temper tantrums? Potty training? Picky eaters? Here's the missing manual for toddlers! $17.95

Co-authored by Dr. Ari Brown

Go to Toddler411.com for details!

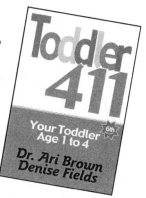

Order online

Baby411.com

or call toll-free to order: **1-800-888-0385**

More info on our books is on WindsorPeak.com

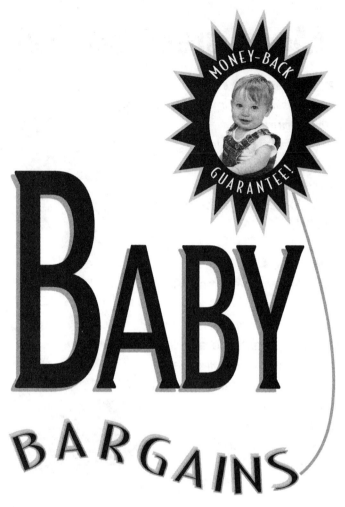

BABY BARGAINS

If this book doesn't save you at least

$250

*off your baby expenses, we'll give you
a complete refund on the cost of this book!*

NO QUESTIONS ASKED!

Just send the book and your mailing address to

**Windsor Peak Press • 436 Pine Street, Suite T
Boulder, CO, 80302.**

If you have any questions, please call
(303) 442-8792